Memory Politics and Transitional Justice

The interdisciplinary fields of Memory Studies and Transitional Justice have largely developed in parallel to one another despite both focusing on efforts of societies to confront and (re-)appropriate their past. While scholars working on memory have come mostly from historical, literary, sociological, or anthropological traditions, transitional justice has attracted primarily scholarship from political science and the law. This series bridges this divide: it promotes work that combines a deep understanding of the contexts that have allowed for injustice to occur with an analysis of how legacies of such injustice in political and historical memory influence contemporary projects of redress, acknowledgment, or new cycles of denial. The titles in the series are of interest not only to academics and students but also practitioners in the related fields. The Memory Politics and Transitional Justice series promotes critical dialogue among different theoretical and methodological approaches and among scholarship on different regions. The editors welcome submissions from a variety of disciplines—including political science, history, sociology, anthropology, and cultural studies—that confront critical questions at the intersection of memory politics and transitional justice in national, comparative, and global perspective.

More information about this series at
http://www.palgrave.com/gp/series/14807

Ivor Sokolić

International Courts and Mass Atrocity

Narratives of War and Justice in Croatia

palgrave
macmillan

Ivor Sokolić
Department of Government
London School of Economics and
Political Science
London, UK

Memory Politics and Transitional Justice
ISBN 978-3-030-08112-6 ISBN 978-3-319-90841-0 (eBook)
https://doi.org/10.1007/978-3-319-90841-0

Cover image: plastique/Alamy Stock Photo
Cover design: Akihiro Nakayama

Printed on acid-free paper

This Palgrave Macmillan imprint is published by the registered company Springer International Publishing AG part of Springer Nature
The registered company address is: Gewerbestrasse 11, 6330 Cham, Switzerland

Acknowledgements

This book was made possible through the support and guidance of many individuals. I am deeply grateful to all of them and hope they continue to provide me with the same encouragement they have so far shown! The book manuscript was the result of my Ph.D. thesis at University College London (UCL), supervised by Eric Gordy. Eric not only had the patience to put up with me during the Ph.D., but also has continued to offer guidance, reassurance, food and jokes since then. Denisa Kostovicova, my supervisor at the London School of Economics and Political Science (LSE), has in many ways continued to carry that torch. Her insightful critiques and ceaseless drive for improvement are an inspiration. My time at the LSE has been a unique learning experience, and this book is hopefully a testament to it.

I am also grateful to the help offered by the editors of this book and series. Jasna Dragovic-Soso has always generously provided me with honest and valuable advice, on much more than just this book. Jelena Subotic, other than providing so much academic inspiration for this work, was always helpful and engaging. Last, but certainly not least, Katelyn Zingg unwearyingly put up with my many emails and questions. She made the process manageable, smooth and, most important of all, fun.

The research for the book was conducted whilst studying at the UCL School of Slavonic and East European Studies (SSEES), where many staff members contributed to my research directly or indirectly. I am grateful to Jan Kubik, Anne White, Allan Sikk, Martyn Rady,

Bojan Aleksov, Richard Mole, Claudia Roland and the elusive Tavi Kladivo-Kosák. In particular, I am grateful to Titus Hjelm, whose comments during my viva examination were one of the most insightful of my university studies and have shaped my work ever since. My colleagues at SSEES, who remain dear friends, also continue to provide helpful advice and support. I am indebted to Philipp Köker, Anna-Cara Keim, Kaneshko Sangar, Licia Cianetti, Costanza Currò, James Dawson, Dario Brentin, Kristen Perrin and Erin Saltman.

I also have to thank my colleagues at the UCL School of Public Policy and the Centre for Multidisciplinary and Intercultural Inquiry (CMII), who helped refine my thinking and who made me into a more open-minded academic, in particular Cathy Elliott and Mark Hewitson, who provided me with support and guidance in those crucial early stages of my career. I am also thankful for working with Daniela Lai, first at UCL and now at LSE, who is a constant source of bright ideas and different perspectives. She is also a great friend. I hope our collaboration continues! My COST exchange at the University of Rijeka remains a fond memory and a continued source of guidance. I cannot thank Vjeran Pavlaković enough for all of his help throughout my career. Thanks must also go to the whole FRAMNAT team for providing insights into my work that few others would have been able to provide.

My fieldwork in Croatia was made possible due to the truly generous amount of help I received from many people. Hrvoje Klasić provided academic and practical help like few others could have. Mate Subašić and Sven Milekić were and remain fountains of knowledge on Croatian politics and society; I would have been lost without them. Maša Tonković Grabovac and the ever-growing Tonković and Grabovac families (Vladimir, Fran, Barbara, Iskra and now Mira) helped organise fieldwork and were always keen to hear about my research, but also provided welcome respite from it! Thank you also to Jessie Hronesova, Nebojša Blanuša, Cody McClain Brown, Tanja Petrović and Eugen Jakovčić; who all may not be aware of how much they helped.

I have been fortunate enough to have a family that has supported my many interests, academic or otherwise. Without them, this book would not have been possible. Hvala mama i tata, bake i dede, for the inspiration, the food, the discussions and all the laughter. Most of all, I must thank my sister Lena, who shares an interest and passion in international criminal law. Although we rarely agreed on an approach or a topic, in academia or otherwise, she could always present that contrarian argument that I could not see.

The day to day of writing this book was not a lonely affair all because of my intelligent, beautiful and supportive best friend in life, my wife Rhiannon. She was there when I was down, she was there when I was frustrated, she was there when it all worked, and she was there when nothing did. She was there for the whole process. Thank you for being you.

Finally, but also most of all, I would like to thank the participants who feature in this book. They wore their hearts out on their sleeves and relived horrible memories, simply because I asked them to. They believed in this project more than anyone else and they believed it could make a difference. I can only hope that it does.

Contents

Abbreviations

CAS	Court of Arbitration for Sport
CPPCG	Convention on the Prevention and Punishment of the Crime of Genocide
EU	European Union
HAZU	Croatian Academy of Sciences and Arts (*Hrvatska akademija znanosti i umjetnosti*)
HDZ	Croatian Democratic Union (*Hrvatska demokratska stranka*)
HNS	Croatian People's Party (*Hrvatska narodna stranka*)
HVO	Croatian Defence Council (*Hrvatsko vijeće obrane*)
ICC	International Criminal Court
ICTY	International Criminal Tribunal for the former Yugoslavia
IHJJ	The Institute for Croatian Language and Linguistics (*Institut za hrvatski jezik i jezikoslovlje*)
IMF	International Monetary Fund
JNA	Yugoslav National Army (*Jugoslavenska narodna armija*)
KOS	Counterintelligence Service (*Kontraobaveštajna služba*)
NATO	North Atlantic Treaty Organization
NDH	Independent State of Croatia (*Nezavisna Država Hrvatska*)
NGO	Non-governmental organisation
OSCE	Organization for Security and Co-operation in Europe
PTSD	Posttraumatic stress disorder
QCA	Qualitative Comparative Analysis
RECOM	The Initiative for RECOM
SDP	Social Democratic Party of Croatia (*Socijaldemokratska partija Hrvatske*)

SDSS	Independent Democratic Serb Party (*Samostalna demokratska srpska stranka*)
SNV	Serb National Council (*Srpsko narodno vijeće*)
UDBA	State Security Administration (*Uprava državne bezbednosti*)
UN	United Nations
UNDP	United Nations Development Programme
UNPROFOR	United Nations Protection Force
UNSC	United Nations Security Council

List of Figures

CHAPTER 1

Introduction

This book engages with a personal and emotional issue: a matter of identity to me, to all participants in this study and to the majority of the Croatian public; a narrative that helps a state, a nation, an ethnicity and many individuals define themselves and make sense of the world around them. It is the narrative of the Homeland War in Croatia.

Even to me, who left Croatia at a young age, it is a facet of my identity. Notions of victimhood and defiance make up who I am and how I respond to life events, since Croats are those who survive, who defy the odds and persevere. I left, but I remember the stories I was told and the images I saw on TV. For many people who were at the front of this war, however, this narrative continues to command a central role in their lives. It defines who they are, and how they see their neighbours, their society, their country and the world around them. They are based on traumatic memories: the smell of decaying bodies from a nearby town; sitting in a bomb shelter during an artillery attack; or watching the Yugoslav National Army (*JNA*) enter Vukovar. This is an emotional narrative. It is everyday. It forms a part of the Croatian social fabric and reverberates in both the public and private spheres.

This book investigates this narrative and how war crimes tribunals, both domestic and international, attempted to influence it. Academics and practitioners, although far from agreeing on the topic, have for some time argued that such courts and related civil society efforts have the potential to instil universal human rights norms in post-conflict,

I. Sokolić, *International Courts and Mass Atrocity*,
Memory Politics and Transitional Justice,
https://doi.org/10.1007/978-3-319-90841-0_1

transitional societies through their expressivist, or extra-legal, effects. This book shows that in Croatia this did not occur; the norms became distorted when they reached local publics. Narratives provide a useful social construction to study expressivist effects of transitional justice, since they are the expression of norms. Given the powerful and emotional nature of the war narrative, this may not come as a surprise. The case study of Croatia highlights the context within which such efforts often operate in, where judicial narratives presented in a top-down fashion by judicial institutions face significant contestation by bottom-up, everyday narratives. If judicial narratives do not conform with everyday narratives, they struggle to take hold in society.

The Homeland War, or *Domovinski Rat*, was the name given to the 1991–1995 conflict in Croatia by the Tuđmanist narrative of the 1990s (Jović 2009). The term can be interpreted as loaded and only representing the Croat side of the conflict, but it has come to be accepted across most of Croatian society since the 1990s. Today, it is commonly used in Croatian politics, culture, education and media. The conflict began with the eruption of violence in 1991, as the dissolution of Yugoslavia gathered momentum, and lasted until 1995. It encompassed much of Croatia and left 13,000–16,000 dead, 500,000 internally or externally displaced, and about 12% of housing structures destroyed or damaged, as well as 30% of industrial infrastructure.[1] As much as 21% of the economy's GDP is estimated to have been wiped out, as well as US $37 billion accrued in damages (London 2003). To this day, 2138 individuals remain missing and many of the over 2 million mines laid in the country are yet to be demined.[2] The conflict in Croatia ended following two Croatian military offensives, Operation Flash and Operation Storm, and the peaceful reintegration of Eastern Slavonia, Baranja and Western Sirmium.

Croats had first-hand experience of the war and a large part of the population witnessed violence of some sort. This contrasts with, for example, the nature of the conflict in Serbia, where much of the conflict was experienced second-hand.[3] Moreover, the conflict had an international nature; International Criminal Tribunal for the former Yugoslavia (ICTY) trials and judgments show that Bosnian Croat forces operating in Bosnia–Herzegovina had continuous and significant military support from the armed forces of Croatia. A chain of command existed, official or unofficial, between Zagreb and armed forces in Bosnia.

The wars in the region were unique in that they were the first to have an international criminal tribunal overseeing their conduct as they took place. They were also the first conflicts that took place in a global environment where human rights had become an important part of international rhetoric (especially so in countries with close ties to Croatia, such as Germany) and in which civil society had a significant international presence. In addition, they were the best recorded conflicts to date, and their day-to-day progress was reported globally. This meant that the situation in which the conflict in Croatia took place, although not completely original and without precedent, contained unique and new elements.

Croatian transition from Yugoslav socialism was not to liberal democracy, but to the competitive authoritarian regime of President Franjo Tuđman and the HDZ (*Hrvatska Demokratska Zajednica* or Croatian Democratic Union). Formal democratic institutions were in place, but they were primarily a means for Tuđman's HDZ of obtaining and exercising political authority, which meant conventional standards of democracy were not met (Levitsky and Way 2002: 52). Media and judicial freedoms were neither fully repressed, nor were they completely free. For example, Tuđman's attempts to revoke the licence of the independent radio station, Radio 101, divided the HDZ and sparked public protest (Levitsky and Way 2002: 58). Likewise, judges did not always limit media freedom, although anti-government outlets often found themselves dealing with the judiciary. Moreover, as later chapters will outline, Tuđman's regime also used language policy as a method of national identity building (Chapter 5) and gave disproportionate power to Croatian war veterans (Chapter 6).

Tuđman died in 1999, and the HDZ lost the parliamentary elections in 2000 to a centre-left coalition that began Croatia's process of transition to liberal democracy in earnest. During the Tuđman regime, Croatian cooperation with the ICTY (at the time the main instrument of transitional justice) was minimal and the process of transitional justice as a whole was scarcely present.[4] Only from the 2000 regime change was the process of transitional justice in the country allowed to gather pace. Not all discussion about the past began at this point, but up until then the HDZ government that ruled the country during and after the war took serious steps to restrict this and hardly encouraged it.[5] To a certain extent, it had prepared the public to resist the temptation to deal with the past according to any narratives other than its own.

The United Nations (UN) Security Council set up the ICTY in May 1993 with the aim of restoring regional security and addressing the serious human rights violations that had occurred during the conflict.

The asserted goal was to restore peace in the midst of the ongoing conflict; it had secondary, broader aims of dispensing justice and achieving reconciliation in the region. These additional aims were gradually added to the Tribunal's long list of goals as time passed, ultimately leaving a range of expectations that no court could be expected to meet. Since inception, the ICTY has at one point or another been expected to create a historical record of events, heal war wounds, reassign collective guilt to individuals, prepare societies for reconciliation and deter future violence (Allcock 2009: 379).

The trial chambers did sometimes state expressivist goals in verdicts, such as to strengthen social solidarity and incubate moral consensus in the public, despite causing a high degree of controversy among lawyers, who often rejected any kinds of goals that were not narrowly legal (see ICTY Prosecutor v. Kordić and Čerkez, IT-95-14/2-A). Trials aimed to draw a line for the future and achieve a sense of legitimacy in the transition (Teitel 2005: 845). A way of doing this was to create a clear division between the past and present.

While the ICTY's success in the region more broadly has been considered imperfect, Croatia's achievements have been relatively impressive in terms of compliance with the Tribunal and handover of indictees. Subotic (2009) and Nettelfield (2010) argue that the particular circumstances that the Croatian state was in since 2000 have allowed for the Tribunal to be more effective there than in other neighbouring states, especially in terms of transfer of accused to the Tribunal. Moreover, these processes were supported by Croatia's own concurrent domestic war crimes tribunals. These struggled with a high number of trials in absentia against ethnic Serbs, especially shortly after the war, as well as issues of bias in favour of ethnic Croats (see, for example, the first instance Lora verdict). State-provided information on trials is out of date, but as of December 2014, 3553 individuals have been tried for war crimes in domestic courts, of which 589 have been sentenced.[6]

Truth-seeking efforts through trials, as well as commissions, face the inherent conceptual problems that "coming to terms with the past" faces. The term is too broad, since it connotes so many different ideas (e.g., remembrance, commemoration, acknowledgement and truth seeking), but it is also too narrow since it expects that the only successful outcome of the process is for a society to come to terms with its past by facing the truth that has been uncovered (Obradović-Wochnik 2013). This can lead projects in this realm to failure, as the connection between knowledge and acknowledgement is not always linear (Obradović-Wochnik 2013). Forcing individuals to accept or reject war crimes, without any middle ground, also simplifies the process of coming to terms with the past to focus on acceptance or rejection of the truth. It ignores the complex process that leads to this, in which a person needs to discuss, interpret, understand and finally come to terms with a past that may be painful or contested (Gibson 2006; Obradović-Wochnik 2013). All of the above examples are a testament to the complicated environment that these efforts have to operate in and how easily they can be appropriated for ethno-national purposes.

The field of transitional justice continues to grapple with the question of why universal human rights norms become distorted or undermined when they trickle down to local publics. This book employs a novel methodological approach to answer this question, using the single case study of Croatia. In Croatia, there exists a dominant war narrative related to the most recent conflict, one of defence against a larger Serbian aggressor. There also exist judicial narratives propagated by transitional justice authorities. At times, these narratives work in concert, but often they also compete. Trials can act as vehicles for such public debate, and they provide an opportunity to produce dialogue about the past with diverse audiences outside of the courtroom (Rangelov 2014). Croatia provides an interesting test case for these effects.

The book explores how international and domestic war crimes trials have led to deliberation over norms and narratives related to the war. It addresses the question: What effect has the transitional justice process in Croatia had on narratives related to the 1991–1995 conflict? Individuals and institutions remember the conflict and the serious human rights breaches that occurred during it through various narratives, or stories that help make sense of the past as well as the present world around them, and in particular, the predominant war narrative. At times, these narratives work in concert and are aligned, but at others, one narrative dominates over another as they are being propagated by various sources with different interests at stake. In some cases, deliberation occurs over narratives as they are contested and reproduced, at the elite level of institutions (top-down) or at the level of the everyday (bottom-up). The book, thereby, also deals with several subquestions: What kind of atmosphere did the transitional justice process in Croatia take place in? How has the process influenced participants' understanding of the world around them (e.g., in terms of understandings of law, trust in institutions, attitudes towards the Serb minority)? And, how have everyday narratives interacted with top-down justice narratives?

The single case study of Croatia captures the complexity and unique nature of the research puzzle (Stake 1995). This is essential in a process as complex as transitional justice or with social constructions such as norms. The study uses and develops concepts key in transitional justice, which make inferences that are relevant outside of this single case (Landman 2008: 28). Such intense examination leads to deeper theoretical analysis and theory development, albeit at the expense of generalisability. That is not to say that single case studies cannot be generalised with at all; a well executed one can address theory and issues that have wider intellectual relevance; it can use concepts which are applicable in other contexts; and it can make inferences that apply to countries or time periods beyond the scope of the original case (Halperin and Heath 2012: 205). The conclusions are, therefore, "contingent generalisations" (George and Bennett 2005: 84).

Single case studies on transitional justice have become more popular in recent times, despite showing ambiguous results thus far (discussed in the following chapter). These have highlighted the expressivist aspects of war crimes trials, but they have also noted the highly complex nature of each case, making comparison difficult. This does not mean that such studies are of no comparative use; rather, it means that cases need to be chosen carefully (Geddes 2003). Croatia provides a critical and exemplifying case study. It is critical, since well-developed theories exist which this thesis tests and provides a better understanding of (Bryman 2016: 62–63). It is exemplifying, since the objective of the analysis is to capture the circumstances of an everyday situation (Bryman 2016: 63; Yin 2009: 48). It is a mixture of the two since many instances of transitional justice exist across the globe, but each is also highly unique. In other words, the case study provides more description of the process in this instance, and it uses established theories to explain a single case, and it also tries to develop theory and identify new variables worth pursuing in future research, although it is far from an outlier case (George and Bennett 2005: 75). Finally, the case study is both internally and externally valid. It makes conclusions about the Croatian case, but it also says something about transitional justice that may be applicable to other cases.

The book makes key contributions to the scholarship on transitional justice more generally by unpacking the interaction between the bottom-up and top-down. This reveals a messier, more nuanced and interactive process of transitional justice than shown in most appraisals. This helps unburden the process of its expectations: international criminal justice is not always delivered from the top-down; the bottom does not only reject or accept messages from the top; it also shapes them; and the process has effects on the level of the everyday in numerous spheres. This analysis presents transitional justice away from the elite actors that form the foundation of the discipline and practice.

Echoing Rooney and Aoláin's (2018) assertion that knowledge in transitional justice has always moved simultaneously between the bottom-up and top-down, this study highlights that the process continues to produce both expected and unexpected results. In situations of societal transition, norms and power structures change, and the process of transitional justice provides opportunities for certain actors to gain power, sometimes at the expense of others. As will be shown in the case of Croatia, war veterans retain a considerable amount of political and economic capital as a part of the process, while the Serb minority suffers, despite the political transition into a liberal democracy in the framework of the European Union. By many measures, Croatia is a success of European integration and judicial reform, but this analysis shows that the legacy of conflict in Croatia has significant effects on the everyday level. The failure of transitional justice to instil human rights norms, therefore, continues to plague Croatian society more broadly. The book makes this contribution to the scholarship by building on established theories of expressivism, but adapting them slightly.

The analysis highlights that expressivist effects of trials are not simply messages communicated by courts to be taken up, or not, in a binary fashion. Instead, expressivist effects are messy and dynamic; they can be negotiated, contested and deliberated. These dynamics, however, become apparent only when the micro, everyday level is analysed. Such an analysis shows that expressivist effects and deliberation are more difficult to achieve than previously thought, but that they also happen in a fragmented fashion. Certain facets of a narrative may be deliberated, others not, but each will have varying levels of effect on society. These are hard to predict and highly context specific.

The context-specific nature of the effects has, thus far, limited the external validity and replicability of the transitional justice scholarship that studies micro-effects. This analysis takes the first steps to show that such work can be comparative, externally valid and replicable. It also shows that analysis of the everyday setting is possible without extensive ethnographic work. That is not to say that such work ought not to be done; on the contrary, it is crucial and the two approaches effectively support each other. The marriage of fieldwork research with ordinary individuals and Qualitative Comparative Analysis (QCA) is novel, since it provides a voice to often disregarded voices in political science, but it does so in a comparative and replicable setting. This paves the way for expansion of these results to other cases and for a more methodologically rigorous approach in a field defined by context specificity.

Methodology and Fieldwork

The empirical data in this book are derived from semi-structured focus groups and dyads conducted in Croatia in 2014 and 2015 across three cities and several non-urban locations.[7] The methodological approach to the topic is one of this book's major contributions to the field of transitional justice. It employs focus groups supported by longitudinal data, follow-up interviews and QCA, to provide an analytically rigorous approach to qualitative research design. This first of its kind approach (combining focus groups with QCA) yields theoretical insights and shows how QCA can be used as a verification method for the validity of focus group and interview data.

The study called for a methodology that allows for research depth, rather than width, since the issues being investigated were both complex and sensitive. Qualitative methods were, therefore, considered more effective than quantitative ones. Finnemore and Sikkink (1998) argue that we can only have indirect evidence of norms, just as we can only have indirect evidence of most other motivations for political action. This poses a methodological problem since norms can be hard to measure (if they can be measured at all); they often only present themselves in interactions between individuals and, consequently, often take a lot of time to observe or study. Norms can benefit from an interactive method of inquiry, such as focus groups, which can help explore narratives that become more apparent through group interaction. They can highlight which narratives are contested, which are reinforced and which are perceived as threatened by others.

Much of the scholarship on narratives has focused on the level of elite political narratives, thereby missing how ordinary people build and negotiate their concept of identity and the nation. These are taken-for-granted and implicit understandings, which can be made explicit using focus groups and in-depth interviews (Fox and Miller-Idriss 2008: 540). Wodak et al. (1999), for example, used focus groups and interviews to explore how ordinary Austrians constructed their national understanding. Söderström (2010) also found the approach useful due to the spontaneous responses it elicits, thereby giving more honest and natural answers to relatively specific questions. The method is particularly well suited to exploring everyday narratives that are reproduced in the micro-setting (Fox and Miller-Idriss 2008: 542).

Surveys could also research this concept by studying attitudes, perceptions and stereotypes, to provide a representative picture of how publics construct the world around them. They are, however, not good at studying the nuanced variation that occurs in everyday speech, which also involves non-verbalised gestures such as shrugs, nods, laughter and silence (Fox and Miller-Idriss 2008: 555). Moreover, exclusive use of survey methodology would not be fit for this purpose, as it can only analyse public perception along one dimension, without investigating the reasons behind these perceptions. Ordinary conversation can, for example, show cynicism where surveys would have merely shown answers that are societally acceptable or appealing to researchers' perceived expectations.

Questions about the Homeland War elicit discussions that refer to the war. Left to their own devices, however, ordinary people may ignore such references in favour of other categories that are more suitable for a given situation (Fox and Miller-Idriss 2008: 556). Here, participant observation could prove to be particularly useful, since the method would not guide participants towards responses. Focus groups compensate for this by, at times, using indirect questioning that can shed light on the interpretive frames that people employ (Fox and Miller-Idriss 2008: 556). In other words, focus groups provide a healthy middle ground: they allow for relatively natural expression of narratives, which can effectively highlight taken-for-granted concepts, while also keeping conversations relatively on-topic. Some degree of structure allows for comparison to nationally representative surveys, while follow-up interviews and indirect questioning provide more open-ended depth to discussions. Finally, focus groups are useful in post-conflict scenarios, where recent history is both a sensitive and emotional topic.

Focus groups elicit the complex interactional dynamics that lead individuals to share some truths, withhold others and build alternate versions of reality in a group (Hollander 2004). They strongly reflect the independence of human opinion by further removing the interviewer from the study (by encouraging the group to discuss among themselves, rather than directly with the moderator, especially compared to individual interviews) and by focusing on social context, where opinion tends to be created, thereby increasing external validity (Albrecht et al. 1993; Söderström 2010: 4). These perspectives may exist independently outside of the group setting, but they are more likely to be revealed through the social gathering and interaction that is inherent to the focus group (Gibbs 1997). They provide sequences of narrative to analyse, rather than only instances.

In terms of the nature of the topic, focus groups are good at tackling abstract concepts and investigating issues that could be illuminated by the display of social norms (Lewis 2003: 60). Moreover, anthropological research has shown that publics that have recently witnessed violence or atrocity (even if from a distance) may hold coping practices that are taken-for-granted in society (Das 2001).[8] Focus groups are adept at exploring taken-for-granted concepts since, more so than any other interview method, they permit spontaneous expression of ideas. They allow individuals to employ familiar language to discuss an issue to an extent that is difficult to replicate in a more structured and formal interview (Bertrand et al. 1992). Essentially, the approach shows not only how individuals feel but also why they feel that way and how they construct narratives.

The social nature of insights gained using focus groups can also become apparent through less direct interactions, such as pauses and laughter. Pauses were often indicative of a lack of knowledge among participants. For example, if a participant struggled to define a war crime:

> *Researcher*: How would you define a war crime?
> (Long pause)
> *Maja*: Interesting.
> (Long pause)
> *Maja*: How do I explain it (dyad with Zagreb teachers)?

The pauses also highlighted awkwardness or an unwillingness to answer questions. For example, Sisak war veterans refused to discuss Croatian involvement in the Bosnian conflict:

Moderator: What is your opinion of the trial of Dario Kordić?[9]
(Long pause)
Ana: I would rather not discuss that.
Lucija agrees
Moderator: Could I maybe then ask you about Tihomir Blaškić?
Ana: I would rather not talk about individuals at all.
Lucija: You asked us about a defensive war, not about individuals.
Moderator: Not a problem, we can skip this (focus group with Sisak war veterans).

Laughter, at the most basic level, showed the poor opinion individuals or whole groups had of certain institutions, for example the ICTY or the Croatian government. These types of responses were common across all groups.

Moderator: What is your opinion of the outcomes of trials at domestic war crimes trials?
All laugh
Eva: We have so many stories.
Ema (pointing at a picture on the wall): Do you see that picture, the one in yellow, read what it says.
Lana: Yes, that is just one of the Croatian soldiers who has been sentenced for war crimes.
Eva: In a Croatian court.
Lana: In a Croatian court. I do not even think we can call the Croatian judiciary the Croatian judiciary (focus group with Zadar war veterans).

Laughter sometimes, much like pauses, also implied unwillingness to answer or a lack of knowledge about a topic. This was striking across a number of groups when discussing the role of the Church:

Moderator: What about the Church as a source of information?
Marko: Oh no (laughs). I think all three religions present in these parts are quite biased in the portrayal of anything. The Islamic community, the Serbian Orthodox Church and the Catholic Church all strongly adhere to…
Andriana (interrupts): Their Church.
Marko: Their flock (laughs). And the infallibility of their own ethnicity. I really think…
(Long pause and researcher moves on to the next question)
(Focus group with Zadar teachers)

Overall, these answers hint at the taboo nature of the topic of Church involvement in the conflicts, which became apparent through these social interactions, rather than direct discussion of it. Focus groups are useful in the case of Croatia and transitional justice since they are effective in gaining trust when interviewing ex-combatants (who also made up a large proportion of the pensioners interviewed in this study), whose trust can be hard to attain and who often attempt to provide narratives that fit with their ideas of what the researcher is looking for (Christensen and Utas 2008; Söderström 2010). When constructed with the appropriate care and run properly, they also become effective in discussing sensitive issues. Moreover, this spontaneity adds to reliability since respondents are not able to coordinate their answers in advance, as they may do in surveys or individual interviews with a similar number of participants (Söderström 2010: 4).

The predominant problem for focus group research is representativeness, especially when compared to surveys. While focus groups do not provide a basis for empirical generalisability, they do allow for conclusions to be drawn about narratives as *types* of collective experience by looking at sequences rather than merely instances of speech (Stanley 2016: 244). Additionally, the social context in which focus groups are held is inextricably linked to the group process, and it is a dynamic that warrants specific attention. The social contexts of focus groups, in other words the relationships among the participants and between the participants and the researcher, as well as the more comprehensive social structures within which the discussion takes place, all influence the way the data are generated and the nature of what is produced (Albrecht et al. 1993; Hollander 2004; Morgan 1997; Stewart and Shamdasani 1990). Follow-up interviews were used to alleviate the risk of the social context of the focus groups from affecting the data, and they were a means to further explore the most interesting opinions expressed.

There was a notable difference between focus groups, dyads and interviews, especially follow-up interviews. As the following chapters will show, data from focus groups proved to be far richer and more useful in the analysis. In some ways, follow-up interviews were unnecessary other than to confirm that social context did not contaminate focus group data in any way (and narratives did not change in the individual setting). Their main use was to cover areas that were not discussed in focus group discussions, especially with particularly talkative groups, such as war veterans and pensioners. Individual interviews or dyads were often used with teachers since focus groups proved hard to organise. The lack of group dynamic did affect the nature of the data, but focus groups with teachers were relatively well structured compared to other target segments (they were the least verbose). Dyads and interviews, therefore, did not differ as much from focus groups as they may have with other target segments.

The transcripts were analysed using narrative analysis. This approach was suited to the qualitative, single case and constructivist nature of the study, since it focuses on identifying the key narrative (or story) that is being told by participants, and it looks at how this narrative is constructed, what the intention of the participant is, what the nature of the audience is, and what the meaning of the narrative is (Riessman 1993). It also suits the open-ended nature of the focus group discussions, which allow for narrative segments and follow-up questions. Other approaches in discourse analysis are instead based on segmenting data, which can at times lead to an incomplete analysis or to a "culture of fragmentation" that decontextualises the data (Atkinson 1992).

Interpretation of data in a constructivist approach is a reflexive endeavour in which meanings are constructed, rather than discovered (Mauthner et al. 1998). The researcher, the method and the data are reflexively interdependent and interconnected (Mauthner and Doucet 2003: 414). This book is, therefore, infused with my epistemological and ontological assumptions. Moreover, the story present cannot be decontextualised from my own personal background (a Croatian citizen of Croat ethnicity who has lived abroad for sometime) and institutional surroundings (studying for a Ph.D. and then working at British universities, but also the broader academic environment such a project takes place in). It was, therefore, important to ask how participants' accounts were meaningful in this research context and how data were constructed. Different researchers, especially those with differing backgrounds or those looking at the data during later time periods, may interpret these categories differently. Conclusions were, therefore, connected to the existing literature, and a more systematic research design (using mixed methods and QCA) was employed to increase validity, reliability and replicability.

The most significant shortcoming of focus groups, however, is their lack of representativeness. The study employed survey methodology to alleviate this in two ways, by referring to previous nationally representative surveys conducted in Croatia and by handing out a survey to all participants prior to the focus groups, dyads or individual interviews. The representative studies helped inspire both the survey and focus group questions in this study. They allowed for a representative comparison to be made with the collected data. Generally, these results were similar to nationally representative studies, other than for teachers who stood out from the representative results, as well as from the two other target segments. For the sake of brevity, only the most relevant results are summarised below.

During the fieldwork, it became apparent that there were problems associated with the study of norms in post-conflict societies that were not well covered in the methodological or transitional justice literatures. The topics being discussed in the focus groups were not sensitive, but they did touch upon sensitive issues and in the group setting had the potential to cause significant upset to participants. General suspicions regarding the researcher and the research aim frequently made it difficult to recruit participants.

This was often alleviated through my own status as both an insider and an outsider. As a Croatian citizen who has lived abroad for the majority of his life, I was able to gain access to certain situations due to an understanding of Croatian cultural specificities that an outsider would not be able to easily, or at least quickly, attain. This made it easier to establish trust and rapport with participants (Van Ginkel 1998: 256). This very insider status and intimacy can also be a curse, especially when discussing norms that have a certain taken-for-granted status, which I may also take for granted (Kempny 2012: 43). Moreover, it necessitated me to take on a position of naïveté in front of participants, always being careful not to become manipulative in the process.

The most concerning issue throughout the fieldwork, and one that at times caught the researcher by surprise, was the prevalence of PTSD among participants. This manifested itself exclusively in the focus groups and highlighted the powerful and potentially harmful effects of the group dynamic. A large proportion of the participants in the war veterans' groups and some of the pensioners' groups discussions had suffered extreme trauma and loss during the war (some groups had a dual role as victim support groups). Many were diagnosed with severe PTSD; in extreme cases, this had led to suicide attempts (which the group openly acknowledged during sessions) and recurring health problems. This, however, only showed itself in focus group discussions rather than prior to them, further exemplifying the unpredictable but also truthful nature of the group dynamic. Regardless of the precautions taken, PTSD did present a serious problem in the fieldwork and a significant peril to participants' health. There was, therefore, a constant need to be aware of how such sensitive topics can affect individuals.[10]

QCA was used as a control in this study to alleviate the problem of validity, reliability and replicability in qualitative research. The basic premise of QCA is that combinations of necessary and sufficient conditions can causally explain outcomes in qualitative research (Ragin 1989). Initially, a truth table is used to list all possible combinations of conditions and outcomes, which shows how often they appear in the set of cases that is being considered (Ragin 1989). Boolean algebra is then employed to derive implicants, which are used to conclude what combinations of conditions are necessary or sufficient for the outcome to occur or not (Ragin 1989). The method has been commonly used in political science (Avdagić 2010; Krook 2010; Pennings 2003; Vis 2009; Werner 2009) and international relations (Chan 2003; Koenig-Archibugi 2004; Maat 2011; Thiem 2011). It has also been applied to a lesser degree in law (Arvind and Stirton 2010; Miethe and Drass 1999; Musheno et al. 1991; Williams and Farrell 1990) and anthropology (Moritz et al. 2011).

QCA is based on dichotomisation, which can introduce problematic measurement biases in fundamentally non-dichotomous phenomena (Rihoux 2006). Two pitfalls need to be kept in mind when using QCA. Firstly, few authors using the various types of QCA consider possible measurement error in enough detail; as with any research tool, it cannot be applied blindly. Secondly, contrary to the original design of QCA as a tool for testing propositions of deterministic necessary and sufficient conditions, many scholars implicitly or explicitly employ it as a tool for inductive theory generation (Hug 2013). In this study, however, the purpose of QCA is to illustrate and to validate. QCA helps illustrate patterns that occurred across the interviewed target segments and helps ascertain why they occurred. The QCA was completed using R and the QCA package for R developed by Dusa and Thiem (2012).

The participants in this study were ordinary, inasmuch as they did not form a part of any elites. They were also targeted, since the study spoke to only middle and high school history teachers, members of smaller war veterans' associations and pensioners in Zagreb, Sisak, Zadar and a non-urban location for each segment.[11] When it was not possible to organise focus groups, then a dyad or an individual interview was organised. Follow-up interviews were held with a number of these individuals.

In total, 52 individual took part in 13 "groups" (Fig. 1.1). 30 were male, and 22 were female. Pensioners were predominantly male (only two females), and teachers were roughly evenly split, while three of the five war veterans' groups were wholly female.

Middle and high school history teachers were targeted because they are central to the process of teaching young people about norms, values and narratives. Holding the groups across four locations allowed for a comparison across communities that had different levels of exposure to the war and to the transitional justice process. The target segment was small enough to reach a good portion of the population in each location, somewhat alleviating the lack of representativeness in focus group research.

Pensioners, the second target segment, are a highly politicised and large grouping in Croatian society. They are interesting since they lived through Yugoslavia, the Homeland War, the Tuđman regime and the post-Tuđman period. They were educated under a different system than the one currently in place. Finally, pensioners were evenly spread between the urban and non-urban settings, especially compared to the other target segments.

Location	Target segment	People per interview
Zagreb	Pensioners	4
Zagreb	War Veterans	4
Zagreb	Teachers	2; 1; 1
Zadar	Pensioners	4
Zadar	War Veterans	6
Zadar	Teachers	3
Sisak	Pensioners	5
Sisak	War Veterans	3
Sisak	Teachers	3
Non-urban	Pensioners	5
Non-urban (Banovina)	War Veterans	5
Non-urban (Slavonia)	War Veterans	2
Non-urban	Teachers	2; 1; 1

Fig. 1.1 Overview of focus groups (If a dyad was held with, for example, two additional individual interviews, then this is denoted as "2; 1; 1")

The third target segment was composed of members of war veterans' associations. As an influential and vocal grouping, they allowed for an exploration of attitudes about transitional justice in this influential part of Croatian civil society. The aim was to target veterans' groups that are not consistently being quoted in the newspapers, since their opinions are readily available.

The focus groups were held in and drawn from the cities of Zagreb, Sisak and Zadar, as well as one non-urban location for each segment other than for war veterans. Zagreb was used as it is the largest city in Croatia, and it remains the political and cultural centre of the country. It also provides an example of a large metropolis that was not on the frontline of the war. Sisak was selected because it was directly affected by the war, a domestic war crimes trial dealt with crimes committed in the city and, as an industrial hub, it has a larger working class population than most cities. Zadar was used since it is in a different region of Croatia than Sisak and was also directly affected by the war. Moreover, the region is known as a hotbed for Croatian right-wing, often nationalist, politics. The non-urban locations were determined based on where it was possible to find participants, although an attempt was made (relatively successfully) to keep the locations within a close distance to the three chosen cities, rather than in completely different parts of Croatia.

The Research Environment

The fieldwork took place from September 2014 until March 2015, during which time a number of events relevant to the research were ongoing in society. These in great part featured in discussions and are listed below in descending order of relevance.

Cyrillic Signs in Vukovar

The 2011 Croatian census found that ethnic Serbs comprise over one-third of the population in Vukovar, thereby requiring bilingual signs in the city. This resulted in a series of demonstrations in Vukovar in late 2013, as well as some other Croatian cities, to protest this move. The initial rally involved over 20,000 individuals, featured slogans such as "*VUKOVAR, NE ВУКОВАР*"[12] and was likened to previous public shows of support for the Croatian generals in Split. The proposed bilingualism frustrated war veterans and many ordinary citizens due to the wartime experience of the city. Signatures were also collected across the country for a referendum to change the law on minority rights and bilingualism.

War Veterans' Protest on Savska Road

The demonstrations on *Savska Road*, in front of the Croatian Ministry of Veterans' Affairs, lasted from October 2014 until April 2016. They involved a number of war veterans' associations asking for the resignation of the Minister of Veterans' Affairs. They continued despite a change in government and, therefore, minister. They were not in the interview guide, but were frequently brought up as an example of the plight of war veterans in Croatia, of their connection to Croatian right-wing parties or of their privileged position in society.

Provisional Release of Vojislav Šešelj

Vojislav Šešelj was provisionally released from the ICTY on medical grounds in November 2014. Not only did this lead to a marked increase in criticism of the Tribunal in focus groups, it even led to a participant cancelling a follow-up interview as they found the event too upsetting. From that point on the release was often used by participants as an example of ICTY inefficiency.

Arrest of Milan Bandić and the Sale of INA

Corruption and the generally poor economic situation in Croatia featured heavily in all discussions. This was exacerbated in October 2014 by the arrest on corruption charges of the long-standing Mayor of Zagreb, former Presidential candidate and current Member of Parliament, Milan Bandić. In addition to this, during December 2014, there were several large demonstrations in Sisak to protest against the selling off and subsequent redundancies at the largest Croatian oil company, INA, whose refinery is based in the city. All discussions in Sisak, as well as in some of the other locations, featured much discussion on this topic. This is relevant to the study because, as Chapter 6 will show, participants did not make a semantic distinction between the processes of transitional justice and neoliberal transition. Instead, they saw them as inherently connected.

2015 Parliamentary Elections

The 2015 parliamentary elections were announced in September and held in December of that same year. Informal campaigning had begun far in advance, so the topic of an upcoming election was common throughout discussions. Moreover, the centre-right "Patriotic Coalition" led by the opposition HDZ frequently employed war veterans, nationalist symbols and war memories in their rhetoric.

Other than current events around them, participants had already been primed on transitional justice issues through the media. From 2000 until 2015, transitional justice was defined predominantly and, at times, exclusively by reporting on the Ante Gotovina trial (Fig. 1.2).[13] This trial has come to define much of the Croatian state's and society's relationship with the transitional justice process more broadly. This media frame influences how the public view the process of transitional justice, but the media frame itself is also indicative of the environment that journalists work in.

Participants in the study generally distrusted all sources of information on the transitional justice process, including the ICTY, domestic courts and the government (Sokolić 2017). On the other hand, individuals who took part in the conflict and television images (e.g., of the shelling of Vukovar or Dubrovnik) were highly trusted. This atmosphere of general distrust and cynicism, coupled with the perceived reliability of former combatants and victims, paved the way for everyday narratives to have more influence than top-down narratives imposed by institutions.

Trial	Total Thematic Reports
Gotovina	1996
Glavaš	468
Blaškić	338
Norac	302
Merčep	280
Kordić	185
Lora	119
Total	3,688

Fig. 1.2 Total number of thematic articles per case from 2000 until 2015 (This table analyses only printed media. Arguably, printed media mirror television coverage (Funkhouser 1973: 64). Peruško (2011: 12) has also shown that media concentration (measured by audience and advertising share of the top three sources in each medium) is high for both television and daily newspapers)

Plan of the Book

The second chapter provides a theoretical overview of transitional justice globally, in the former Yugoslavia and in Croatia. It also looks at the literature on human rights norms. In doing so, it highlights how little consensus there is on what transitional justice is and what effect the process has had on societies. The chapter argues that much remains to be understood in how the process works and how Croatia provides an understudied case in comparison with other Balkan states. This allows the book to further the understanding of promoting transitional justice in the region. The theoretical framework and contribution of the book is outlined in some detail in this chapter, with a focus on the deliberative understanding of transitional justice developed by Rangelov (2014). The discussion also engages with the theoretical literature on international criminal law and expressivist aspects of war crimes trials, developed by Teitel (2000), Osiel (1998) and Drumbl (2007).

The subsequent four chapters focus wholly on the empirical data. Chapter 3 outlines the Croatian war narrative in some detail, by bringing together previous studies and results from the focus groups, dyads and interviews. It outlines the pervasive, nearly universal among ethnic Croats, notion that Croatia was a victim of Serbian aggression. Croatia's role in the conflict was purely self-defensive. This narrative forms the basis of the nation-building and state-building projects in the state. The chapter outlines the key facets of the war narrative, how they are reproduced in Croatian legislation (through the Declaration on the Homeland War and the Declaration on Operation Storm), Croatian society and among participants in this study. The chapter provides more detail on the defining features of it, which have previously been identified in the scholarship, but it also expands on them and adds a further facet, the notion that the war is not yet over. The justice narrative competes and interacts with the war narrative, but the war narrative's strength makes it difficult for the justice narrative to take hold in Croatia and, consequently, for the trickle-down effects of human rights norms to occur. Emotional notions of defence and victimhood, as well as the local and personal discussion of the conflict, make it difficult for other narratives to undermine the predominant understanding of the conflict.

Chapter 4 examines the justice narrative in some depth by outlining the stymied development of understandings of law in Croatia. This has been stymied due to the strength of the war narrative and the distrust of the ICTY and domestic judiciary. This has allowed for a tolerance for certain crimes to exist, such as revenge crimes, crimes of passion or killings of Serb civilians. This chapter outlines the nature of such attitudes and attempts to answer why this is. Transitional justice institutions had to operate in the context of localised complexities and normative expectations in attempting to instil a rule of law norm in the public. Despite the ICTY and, especially recently, domestic courts providing legally sound judgments and strongly adhering to legal justice over political justice, this has not led to concurrent understandings of law.

Chapter 5 investigates how Croats view the minority Serb population in Croatia, a view that has also been affected by the war narrative. Serbs constitute the "Other" to Croatian identity, which is defined primarily (although not exclusively) through language and religion. The analysis finds that the predominant war narrative influences both notions of identity and perceptions of the Serb minority in the state. The Orthodox Church was, therefore, seen as aggressive, as opposed to the forgiving Catholic Church. Not only were Croats attacked during the war, but also so was the Catholic Church, and general notions of reconciliation were highly based on religion. Moreover, the general impression was that Serbs were not seen as deserving more rights, despite respondents expressing openness towards minorities in general. This relationship was starkly highlighted by the events surrounding the introduction of Cyrillic signs in the city of Vukovar.

Chapter 6 then examines the role of war veterans and their associations, which have been staunchly opposed to the transitional justice process and continue to be the most influential part of Croatian civil society. This chapter looks at their position in society, how they are viewed by others and how they view themselves. The narrative surrounding war veterans, their sacrifice and the problems they face is unifying. They embody the spirit of the war narrative since they are regarded as the truest victims of the Homeland War, the ones who made the greatest sacrifices.

War veterans themselves remain preoccupied with the war narrative and continue to see a need to defend Croatia, the values of the Homeland War and their own rights in society. This makes it easy for political actors to manipulate them, especially right-wing parties, like the HDZ (Croatian Democratic Union or *Hrvatska demokratska zajednica*), who have in the past given war veterans special benefits due to their shared priorities regarding the Homeland War. While war veterans remain respected by the Croatian public, war veterans' associations are on the whole distrusted and viewed as fragmented, politically manipulated and too numerous. The position of war veterans highlights the need for social justice, alongside restorative and transitional justice, in the aftermath of conflict.

Chapter 7 presents the results of the QCA. This brief chapter uses QCA to illustrate and validate the focus group results. It identifies patterns that occurred across the interviewed target segments and helps ascertain why they occurred. For example, how did teachers express different attitudes towards transitional justice and specifically where did their views differ from other target segments? Moreover, the method more clearly illustrates where the war narrative is particularly strong and where there is some debate. QCA also helps validate results by systematically showing how certain discussions recurred across groups and how debate over certain topics may have led to a different understanding of transitional justice. The chapter argues that groups that delibertated on transitional justice issues also thought the ICTY was necessary. Those who felt it was necessary also questioned or debated over recent history and dominant narratives. Levels of distrust proved to be a further key differentiator across groups. For example, is the Croatian government simply distrusted or is it also infiltrated and looking to split the public? Are Serbs inherently aggressive? Are all returnees accomplices to war crimes? The QCA highlighted that those with lower degrees of distrust and pessimism with these institutions also deliberated on transitional justice issues.

Chapter 8 validates the results of previous chapters by examining how Croatian involvement in the conflict in Bosnia and Herzegovina is interpreted by the public, elites and media. It looks at how this fits into the war narrative and then analyses elite and media responses to the verdict and in-court suicide of Slobodan Praljak to examine if these events, which had the potential to undermine the war narrative, had any effect on it. The chapter points to a framework of nesting orientalism, through which all levels of Croatia society see Bosnia as the inferior "Other". Croatia is seen as Bosnia's saviour, rather than an aggressor in the conflict, and the various verdicts eliciting Croatia's involvement in the conflict have had little to no effect on the war narrative. Praljak's death presented a key expressivist moment in the transitional justice process that did not show any signs of the trickle-down effects of norms, but left much of the public unhappy with the ICTY. This highlights the importance of extra-legal messages of international war crimes trials, which can be positive or negative, as well as difficult to control.

The conclusion of the book, in Chapter 9, points to the ambiguous effects of the transitional justice process in Croatia. It highlights how constraints at the level of the everyday, such as the atmosphere of cynicism and distrust of institutions, greatly affect how individuals regard transitional justice authorities and the narratives they present. Justice narratives struggle to connect with personal and local everyday narratives, unless they are in line with everyday expectations. This greatly affected how participants came to understand the world around them. A thorough and society-wide reckoning with past wrongdoings committed by Croatian forces or state authorities has not occurred, despite rulings at the ICTY and in domestic war crimes trials showing that they did happen. In so many facets, the war narrative enjoyed universal agreement among study participants and nearly universal agreement with the Croatian public, meaning the trickle-down effects of norms and justice cascades did not occur. In other instances, however, with some groups and target segments, the complex interaction between two, or more, narratives produced a deliberation on topics relevant to transitional justice. This does not mean that norms associated with the process will take hold in society, but it does at the very least lead to a discursive space marked by numerous narrative options, rather than a monopoly.

In the case of Croatia, as with many other case studies around the world, norm advocates are present and influential in society. These norm advocates, however, do not promote human rights but instead primarily promote the war narrative and, often, the more extreme elements of it. The conclusion argues that this analysis provides a further case study for how pressure for norm change comes from a variety of sources and that this pressure can be for or against human rights norms. The case of Croatia shows how pressure from below can hamper the spread of human rights norms, especially when combined with dominant and emotional everyday narratives.

Notes

1. Estimates for the number of dead vary from 13,583 (Ivo Goldstein 1999) to 15,790 (Živić 2003). Cruvellier and Valinas (2006) estimate that roughly 500,000, of both Serbs and Croats, were displaced due to the

conflict in Croatia alone. The figures for damaged structures are taken from Tanner (2001: 278).

2. For figures on missing persons, see the Croatian Red Cross database of missing persons (familylinks.icrc.org/croatia/en). For figures on landmines in Croatia, see Soldo et al. (1999).
3. The 1999 NATO bombing campaign was, however, experienced directly in Serbia and is also the strongest memory associated with the conflict there.
4. Some initiatives did exist for post-communist transitional justice, such as the restoration of property that was taken following 1945, but this was not aimed at the 1991–1995 conflict.
5. It should be noted, however, that the post-2003 HDZ government did not do this.
6. The Croatian State Attorney's Office provides these figures. See www.dorh.hr/fgs.axd?id=1841.
7. All collected data have been anonymised, and the names used in this book are fictional.
8. It is questionable how "recent" the conflicts in the former Yugoslavia are, as nearly 20 years has passed since they ended. Obradović-Wochnik (2013) has shown that the public in Serbia similarly continues to speak as if past is continuing, as if the wars are not over.
9. Dario Kordić and Tihomir Blaškić were initially indicted in 1995 together with a number of other individuals for the events that occurred in the Lašva Valley part of Bosnia, but their cases were later separated. Blaškić was sentenced to 45 years' imprisonment in 2000 after being found guilty of committing, ordering, planning or otherwise aiding in crimes against the Bosnian Muslim population in the region. In 2001, Kordić was sentenced to 25 years' imprisonment for many of the same or similar crimes, committed in the same localities, as Blaškić. In 2004, Blaškić had his sentence reduced on appeal after his legal team successfully showed that, due to the Kordić judgment, it was clear that Blaškić did not have effective control of troops in the area. The appeal was based on evidence that had been withheld until President Stjepan Mesić provided documents from the intelligence services, showing the presence of a parallel chain of command. In other words, Kordić's conviction allowed for Blaškić's release; moreover, the good outcome for Blaškić was a bad outcome for the Croatian state. The trials raise the issue of the involvement of the Croatian state in the conflict in Bosnia, which changes the nature of the conflict there to an international one. Combined, the two trials show that the conflict in Bosnia was politically driven and that Croatian state intelligence services operated an unofficial chain of command with Bosnian Croat forces.

10. For a more extensive overview of these problems, see Sokolić (2016).
11. There was an additional non-urban group of members of war veterans' associations, since the two were simultaneously organised.
12. This translates to "Vukovar (in the Latin alphabet), not Vukovar (in Cyrillic)".
13. Ante Gotovina was the Croatian general in charge of the controversial Operation Storm. After a 2001 indictment by the ICTY, he spent four years in hiding, before being captured. In 2011, he was convicted of committing crimes against humanity and sentenced to 24 years' imprisonment, but in 2012, he was acquitted on appeal and immediately released. The former general has inspired the strongest public reactions in Croatia and also led to the most serious tensions with the ICTY (Cruvellier and Valinas 2006: 9). More than any other case or individual, this one has been emblematic of the nexus of politics, symbols, rituals and collective memory in Croatia (Pavlaković 2010).

References

Albrecht, T. L., Johnson, G. M., & Walther, J. B. (1993). Understanding communication processes in focus groups. In D. L. Morgan (Ed.), *Successful focus groups: Advancing the state of the art* (pp. 51–64). Newbury Park: Sage.

Allcock, J. B. (2009). The international criminal tribunal for the former Yugoslavia. In C. Ingrao & T. A. Emmert (Eds.), *Confronting the Yugoslav controversies: A scholars' initiative* (pp. 346–389). West Lafayette: Purdue University Press.

Arvind, T., & Stirton, L. (2010). Explaining the reception of the code Napoleon in Germany: A fuzzy-set qualitative comparative analysis. *Legal Studies, 30*, 1–29.

Atkinson, P. (1992). *Understanding ethnographic texts*. Newbury Park: Sage.

Avdagić, S. (2010). When are concerted reforms feasible? Explaining the emergence of social pacts in Western Europe. *Comparative Political Studies, 43*, 628–657.

Bertrand, J. T., Brown, J. E., & Ward, V. M. (1992). Techniques for analyzing focus group data. *Evaluation Review, 16*, 198–209.

Bryman, A. (2016). *Social research methods*. Oxford: Oxford University Press.

Chan, S. (2003). Explaining war termination: A Boolean analysis of causes. *Journal of Peace Research, 40*, 49–66.

Christensen, M., & Utas, M. (2008). Mercenaries of democracy: The 'politricks' of remobilized combatants in the 2007 general elections, Sierra Leone. *African Affairs, 107*, 515–539.

Cruvellier, T., & Valinas, M. (2006). *Croatia: Selected developments in transitional justice*. New York: International Center for Transitional Justice.

Das, V. (2001). *Remaking a world: Violence, social suffering, and recovery.* Berkeley: University of California Press.

Drumbl, M. A. (2007). *Atrocity, punishment and international law.* Cambridge: Cambridge University Press.

Dusa, A., & Thiem, A. (2012). *QCA: Qualitative comparative analysis.* R package version 3.2.2.

Finnemore, M., & Sikkink, K. (1998). International norm dynamics and political change. *International Organization, 52,* 887–917.

Fox, J. E., & Miller-Idriss, C. (2008). Everyday nationhood. *Ethnicities, 8,* 536–563.

Geddes, B. (2003). *Paradigms and sand castles: Theory building and research design in comparative politics.* Ann Arbor: University of Michigan Press.

George, A. L., & Bennett, A. (2005). *Case studies and theory development in the social sciences.* London: MIT Press.

Gibbs, A. (1997). Focus groups. *Social Research Update, 19.* Available at http://sru.soc.surrey.ac.uk/SRU19.html. Accessed 02 Jun 2018.

Gibson, J. L. (2006). Can truth reconcile divided nations? In J. D. Meernik & T. David Mason (Eds.), *Conflict prevention and peacebuilding in post-war societies: Sustaining the peace* (pp. 176–195). Abingdon: Routledge.

Goldstein, I. (1999). *Croatia: A history.* London: Hurst.

Halperin, S., & Heath, O. (2012). *Political research: Methods and practical skills.* Oxford: Oxford University Press.

Hollander, J. A. (2004). The social contexts of focus groups. *Journal of Contemporary Ethnography, 33,* 602–637.

Hug, S. (2013). Qualitative comparative analysis: How inductive use and measurement error lead to problematic inference. *Political Analysis, 21,* 252–265.

ICTY Appeals Chamber. (2004). Prosecutor v. Kordić and Čerkez, IT-95-14/2-A.

Jović, D. (2009). Croatia after Tudjman: The ICTY and issues of transitional justice. *Chaillot Paper, 116,* 13–27.

Kempny, M. (2012). Rethinking native anthropology: Migration and auto-ethnography in the post-accession Europe. *International Review of Social Research, 2,* 39–52.

Koenig-Archibugi, M. (2004). Explaining government preferences for institutional change in EU foreign and security policy. *International Organization, 58,* 137–174.

Krook, M. L. (2010). Women's representation in parliament: A qualitative comparative analysis. *Political Studies, 58,* 886–908.

Landman, T. (2008). *Issues and methods in comparative politics.* London: Routledge.

Levitsky, S., & Way, L. (2002). The rise of competitive authoritarianism. *Journal of Democracy, 13,* 51–65.

Lewis, J. (2003). Design issues. In J. Ritchie & J. Lewis (Eds.), *Qualitative research practice: A guide for social science students and researchers* (pp. 47–76). London: Sage.

London, A. (2003). Croatia. In D. Brett (Ed.), *Europe review 2003/04: The economic and business report* (pp. 70–78). Saffron Walden: Walden Publishing.

Maat, E. D. (2011). Sleeping hegemons: Third-party intervention following territorial integrity transgressions. *Journal of Peace Research, 48*, 201–215.

Mauthner, N. S., & Doucet, A. (2003). Reflexive accounts and accounts of reflexivity in qualitative data analysis. *Sociology, 37*, 413–431.

Mauthner, N. S., Parry, O., & Backett-Milburn, K. (1998). "The data are out there, or are they?" Implications for archiving and revisiting qualitative data. *Sociology, 32*, 733–745.

Miethe, T., & Drass, K. (1999). Exploring the social context of instrumental and expressive homicides: An application of qualitative comparative analysis. *Journal of Quantitative Criminology, 15*, 1–21.

Morgan, D. L. (1997). *Focus groups as qualitative research.* London: Sage.

Moritz, M., Giblin, J., Ciccone, M., Davis, A., Fuhrman, J., et al. (2011). Social risk-management strategies in pastoral systems: A qualitative comparative analysis. *Cross-Cultural Research, 45*, 286–317.

Musheno, M. C., Gregware, P. R., & Drass, K. A. (1991). Court management of AIDS disputes: A sociolegal analysis. *Law & Social Inquiry, 16*, 737–774.

Nettelfield, L. J. (2010). *Courting democracy in Bosnia and Herzegovina: The Hague tribunal's impact in a postwar state.* Cambridge: Cambridge University Press.

Obradović-Wochnik, J. (2013). *Ethnic conflict and war crimes in the Balkans: The narratives of denial in post-conflict Serbia.* London: I.B. Tauris.

Osiel, M. (1998). *Mass atrocity, collective memory and the law.* New Brunswick: Transaction Publishers.

Pavlaković, V. (2010). Croatia, the international criminal tribunal for the former Yugoslavia, and general Gotovina as a political symbol. *Europe-Asia Studies, 62*, 1707–1740.

Pennings, P. (2003). Beyond dichotomous explanations: Explaining constitutional control of the executive with fuzzy-sets. *European Journal of Political Research, 42*, 541–567.

Ragin, C. C. (1989). *The comparative method: Moving beyond qualitative and quantitative strategies.* Berkeley: University of California Press.

Rangelov, I. (2014). *Nationalism and the rule of law: Lessons from the Balkans and beyond.* Cambridge: Cambridge University Press.

Riessman, C. (1993). *Narrative analysis.* Newbury Park: Sage.

Rihoux, B. (2006). Qualitative comparative analysis (QCA) and related systematic comparative methods: Recent advances and remaining challenges for social science research. *International Sociology, 21*, 679–706.

Rooney, E., & Aoláin, F. Ní. (2018). Transitional justice from the margins: Intersections of identities, power and human rights. *International Journal of Human Rights, 12*, 1–8. https://doi.org/10.1093/ijtj/ijy001.
Söderström, J. (2010). Ex-combatants at the polls: Exploring focus groups and electoral meaning. *Anthropology Matters Journal, 12*, 1–16.
Soldo, S., Puntarić, D., Petrovićki, Ž., & Prgomet, D. (1999). Injuries caused by antipersonnel mines in Croatian army soldiers on the east Slavonia front during the 1991–1992 war in Croatia. *Military Medicine, 164*, 141–144.
Sokolić, I. (2016). Researching norms, narratives and transitional justice: Focus group methodology in post-conflict Croatia. *Nationalities Papers, 44*, 932–949.
Sokolić, I. (2017). Sources of information on transitional justice in Croatia. *Croatian Political Science Review, 53*, 77–104.
Stake, R. E. (1995). *The art of case study research*. Thousand Oaks: Sage.
Stanley, L. (2016). Using focus groups in political science and international relations. *Politics, 36*, 236–249.
Stewart, D. W., & Shamdasani, P. N. (1990). *Focus groups: Theory and practice*. Newbury Park: Sage.
Subotic, J. (2009). *Hijacked justice: Dealing with the past in the Balkans*. Ithaca: Cornell University Press.
Tanner, M. (2001). *Croatia: A nation forged in war*. New Haven: Yale Nota Bene.
Teitel, R. G. (2000). *Transitional justice*. New York: Oxford University Press.
Teitel, R. G. (2005). The law and politics of contemporary transitional justice. *Cornell International Law Journal, 38*, 837–862.
Thiem, A. (2011). Conditions of intergovernmental armaments cooperation in western Europe, 1996–2006. *European Political Science Review, 3*, 1–33.
Van Ginkel, R. (1998). The repatriation of anthropology: Some observations on endo-ethnography. *Anthropology & Medicine, 5*, 251–267.
Vis, B. (2009). Governments and unpopular social policy reform: Biting the bullet or steering clear? *European Journal of Political Research, 48*, 31–57.
Werner, T. (2009). Congressmen of the silent south: The persistence of southern racial liberals, 1949–1964. *The Journal of Politics, 71*, 70–81.
Williams, L., & Farrell, R. (1990). Legal response to child sexual abuse in day care. *Criminal Justice and Behavior, 17*, 284–302.
Wodak, R., de Cilia, R., Reisigl, M., & Liebhart, K. (1999). *The discursive construction of national identity*. Edinburgh: Edinburgh University Press.
Yin, R. K. (2009). *Case study research: Design and methods*. Los Angeles: Sage.
Živić, D. (2003). Demografske odrednice i posljedice starenja stanovništva Hrvatske [Demographic determinants and consequences of the ageing of Croatia's population]. *Revija za socijalnu politiku, 10*, 307–319.

CHAPTER 2

Transitional Justice as a Means of Deliberating the Past

This book employs a deliberative understanding of the transitional justice process, as proposed by Rangelov (2014), which is suited to the study of normative contestation in the process. This approach, inspired by previous works of Osiel (1998) and Teitel (2000), focuses on the capability of trials to bring about the discursive engagement of actors through public deliberation, which involves multiple representations and perspectives of the past (Rangelov 2014: 48). While trials are quite rigid instruments for societal change, they can act as a mechanism for public debate that can change narratives of nationalism (Rangelov 2014: 46). Trials can encourage multiple interpretations of the past and contestation in the public domain (Rangelov 2014: 48). This study, drawing on the theory of deliberative transitional justice, views trials as vehicles for public debate that provide an opportunity to produce dialogue about the past with diverse audiences outside of the courtroom (Rangelov 2014: 48). Public discourse does not guarantee what interpretation of the past will be discussed in public, but it is this uncertainty that is filled with opportunity (Rangelov 2014: 48). The process is not without its pitfalls: trials can help a state or nation distance itself from committed crimes by framing them as exceptional or by drawing a line with the past and not analysing the present. But given the diverse and often ambiguous goals of transitional justice institutions, such as "reconciliation" or "coming to terms with the past", the less ambitious goal of fostering deliberation may at the very least provide an opportunity for marginalised or

I. Sokolić, *International Courts and Mass Atrocity*,
Memory Politics and Transitional Justice,
https://doi.org/10.1007/978-3-319-90841-0_2

castigated parties to engage in narratives and to contest them (Rangelov 2014: 49). As this work will show, "Deliberative justice starts with the stories and interpretations offered by the participants in the courtroom drama; it is sparked by the trial, but takes on a life of its own" (Rangelov 2014: 51). It is possible that the removal of justice from the Balkans to The Hague forced publics in the region to have a discussion about war crimes. The opposite is, however, also possible: that a distant court has less contact with its target public and is, therefore, open to challenges to its legitimacy.

The book takes a constructivist view of norms and, therefore, views them as historical and social constructions. Actors respond to cultural factors in their environment and the world around them is "talked into existence" through narratives (Carlsnaes et al. 2012). Norms in the study are defined as collective expectations for the proper behaviour, values and perceptions of actors with a given identity (Katzenstein 1996). Under this theory, norms can either define identities or prescribe behaviour, or they can do both. In some situations, norms can operate as rules that define the identity of an actor, therefore, having certain constitutive effects that specify what actions will cause relevant others to recognise a particular identity. In other types of situations, norms can function as standards that guide the proper enactment of a previously defined identity. At such times, norms have regulative effects that specify standards of proper behaviour. Finally, norms can serve these purposes but also coexist and come into conflict with one another.

According to this definition, norms not only influence actors' goals and how they go about achieving them, but they also affect other related normative concepts. Broad, underlying norms can reverberate throughout a society and shape the identities and behaviour of actors at different levels. Models, such as the spiral or boomerangs ones, show how norms at one level can cascade to others (Risse et al. 1999; Finnemore and Sikkink 1998; Lutz and Sikkink 2001). Such models assume the presence of norm advocates who promote certain normative ideals to stimulate normative shifts. These actors were present in Croatia, but it is debatable how much influence they ever had. As such, the country provides a useful case study for how the spiral model of norm change, developed by Risse, Ropp and Sikkink (1999), may not work in all situations and may need to be tweaked. This model assumes that pressure on human rights norm-violating governments will come from below, through domestic norm believers and transnational human rights networks, following a trickle-down of norms from above. In this sense, it does not investigate pressure against such movements by any actors other than the government (e.g. war veterans in Croatia) and it views norm change as a one-directional movement in favour of human rights norms. Subotic (2009) finds that the spiral model underestimates the strength of elite resistance and overestimates the power of norm supporters, since norm believers can be absent in these situations or lack the power to influence social change. She revises the model by adding more actors to it, who can all either promote or resist human rights norm change. This book provides a further case study for this theory and will show how pressure for norm change (for or against human rights) comes from a variety of sources. It argues that norm advocates from below were strong in the case of Croatia, but that they were not advocates of human rights. This is in line with recent scholarship on trickle-down processes more broadly, which are now being questioned (e.g. see Cianetti 2017).

Finnemore and Sikkink (1998) have expanded on the work of Katzenstein with a purpose to relate this to processes of transitional justice. They show that we can only have indirect evidence of norms, just as we can only have indirect evidence of most other motivations for political action. Norms, by the above-mentioned definition, embody a quality of "oughtness" and shared moral assessment. They prompt justifications for action and leave a trail of communication among actors that researchers can search for and analyse. Norms as shared assessments also raise the question of how many actors must share the assessment before it is called a norm. Furthermore, the norm may be regional, but not global, or even only exist within a small community. Norms are "continuous, rather than dichotomous, entities... [They] come in varying strengths" (Finnemore and Sikkink 1998: 892). Agreement has to be reached among a critical mass of actors on an emergent norm in order to create a tipping point, after which agreement becomes widespread in numerous empirical cases and only then can evidence be found about common features of critical mass. This theory goes a long way to help in the identification of norms but it also shows the danger that ambiguity poses to a study, which requires certain steps to facilitate analysis. This study attempts to achieve this by tracing deliberation of narratives associated with norms, rather than by trying to establish the dominance of a norm. The theoretical framework also draws inspiration from the "norm localisation" concept, first introduced by Acharya (2004, 2009) and furthered by Tholens (2012). This model of norm diffusion differs from previous ones in that it focuses on domestic, rather than international norms and it places these in a dynamic process. Moreover, it engages a broader range of local actors in the matchmaking process, rather than only institutions. The analysis adapts this theoretical framework slightly: it assumes that the process is even more dynamic and that norms are not simply matched, but that they are negotiated, contested and deliberated. This also echoes the work of Zimmermann, who argues that the precision of international norms is the critical variable in an "interactive translation loop" (Zimmermann 2017: 774).

Norms of behaviour are also intrinsically connected to identity narratives, which form the basis for actors' behavioural choices (Wendt 1999: 366). Norms are not isolated variables, instead they are connected to narratives that individuals or communities use to relate to the world around them (Meyer 2005). They also constitute actions, since action only "becomes meaningful in the process of narrating a constitute story of the self" (Browning 2008: 11). Narratives, therefore, are norms and by studying societal narratives this study simultaneously delves into societal norms. It is, however, difficult to present evidence that is directly applicable to norms; the book instead traces the contestation of narratives. Narratives are also better to analyse than concrete outcomes such as official apologies and criminal convictions, since these can far too easily be used for political purposes. The fact that they occur is not necessarily indicative of a change in beliefs or attitudes in society, although such acts may themselves have an effect on populations. Focusing on criminal convictions would be to judge the transitional justice process along legal criteria alone (e.g. in terms of precedents set, number of successful prosecutions, indicted individuals brought to trial, cases completed), instead the focus here is on how the political and cultural environments in Croatia have been affected.

Narratives are essentially stories that make the past real and shape understanding of both the past and the present (Subotic 2015: 179; White 1984). Individuals use narratives to understand the world and to create their own identities, both at the individual and at the state level (Sommers 1994). Because of these characteristics, they spread through interaction, often with counter-narratives based on "opposing" stories (Subotic 2015: 180). What may have been institutionally produced can spread and become stronger in culture, art, education or any other corner of society. While homogenous narratives may be desirable in normative terms, they may not actually be possible in practice (Obradović-Wochnik 2013a: 139). This interactive understanding of narratives is based on the notion of a "self" and an "other" that helps define the "self" (Neumann 1999; Subotic 2009). Narratives, therefore, gain meaning through interaction with other narratives (Subotic 2015).

There is a difference in how elite narratives, produced from above, and everyday narratives, from below, are reproduced and how individuals accept them. Elite narratives (top-down) are often imposed, from either domestic or international institutions (political, judicial, economic, military, media, etc.), and can be ignorant of cultural specificities that may hamper their work. They are often, therefore, fragmented and not fully implemented. Everyday narratives (bottom-up) on the other hand are reproduced through networks of families, friends and smaller scale social groups, which are quite powerful in the region. Moreover, the nation as a discursive construct is shaped through everyday conversation, choice, performance and consumption (Fox and Miller-Idriss 2008: 538).

All of the above amount to memory being a process and "dealing with the past" in a constructive fashion involves multiple memories interacting with each other (Smith 2004: 263). It involves fact-finding, self-criticism and facing off to denial. Silence and agreement are intrinsic to this process, although not necessarily in a constructive way. Dialogue has to occur, both at the micro- and macro-levels. Halbwachs (1992) and Nora (1992) argue that memory only has meaning in the larger system of group meaning and that there are as many memories as there are groups. Less obvious social divisions also need to be borne in mind, such as those that are not only divided by different memories of war but also by historical structural inequalities (Ströhle 2013: 264). Institutions seeking to influence memory need to take this into account in their work and address narratives at multiple levels in order to be successful.

Transitional Justice in Theory

The literature on transitional justice is both broad and varied. Transitional justice was first used to describe societies in transition from undemocratic to democratic regimes (Kritz 1995). The term has since then taken on a variety of broad and specific meanings, encapsulating both political and legal transformations (Nagy 2008; Sriram 2007). There is little consensus over what the term means, it can apply to different types of transitions and there is no consensus as to what criteria to measure the process by (Nettelfield 2010). Concepts it is frequently linked to, such as "coming to terms with the past" and "reconciliation", have been plagued with an equal degree of ambiguity. For example, Dragovic-Soso and Gordy (2010) have attempted to define "coming to terms with the past" as "genuine transformation in popular consciousness", but as Dragovic-Soso admits, the use of the term remains limited by the inconsistent use of the phrase (Dragovic-Soso 2014). Obradović-Wochnik (2013b) argued that this ambiguity has prevented Serbian civil society initiatives working on "coming to terms with the past" to connect with the public, due to the narrow and binary definition of the term they used. Teitel (2000) coined the specifically legal definition, most relevant to this study, which focuses on legal responses to deal with the repercussions of human rights abuses committed by repressive regimes. Since then numerous studies have looked at the process through this narrow view, often focusing on the dynamic between deterrence, retribution and expressivism (Mani 2002; Roht-Arriaza 2006; Teitel 2000).

Many studies, based on both broad and narrow definitions of the term, have been relatively critical of the transitional justice process and its application (Baines 2007; McEvoy and McGregor 2008; Millar 2012; Miller 2008; Shaw 2007). Early analyses of the ICTY were equally pessimistic. Bass captured the general sentiment of these studies when he stated that war crimes trials represent "the least awful alternative" (Bass 2000: 304), a view that remains prevalent in more recent studies (Dembour and Kelly 2007; Haslam 2007). Comparative and quantitative large-N analyses have shown ambiguous results: predominantly that they have no effect or little effect on societies (Hafner-Burton and Ron 2007; Hafner-Burton and Tsutsui 2007; Horne 2015; Lynch and Marchesi 2015) but at times that they do have an effect (Sikkink and Walling 2007). Thoms et al. (2010) provide a contemporary review of the efficacy of transitional justice efforts globally by focusing on state level policies and institutions. They find that empirical evidence remains insufficient, that second-generation systematic approaches have only just started and that, as discussed above, current conclusions tend to be highly varied (Thoms et al. 2010). They believe this is because most studies focus on short-term outcomes and often use narrow criteria for success. Their general conclusion is that most studies find transitional justice to have either positive or no effects, rather than negative ones, but they stress that even that observation has to be treated with caution, given the lack of comparative analyses (Thoms et al. 2010). Bass (2000) does, however, point at the expressivist legacy of documentation that these trials often create, which have been noticed in single case qualitative research. These produce more fruitful analyses of the microcosms that these processes take place in.

Rangelov and Teitel (2011) argue that today transitional justice is different in a variety of ways. It has moved from exceptional transitional responses in times of crisis to normalised or entrenched justice-seeking; increasingly disassociated from the politics of transition and less frequently linked to periods of conflict, whether past or current. It has also started to involve a growing variety of actors beyond the realm of the state, who are often agents in the globalisation of transitional justice. These actors have diverse interests and aims at stake in the process, but they nevertheless largely adopt a judicialised discourse. The process has changed so much that it is debatable how "transitional" it actually is and if the terminology and concept are still relevant.

Rangelov (2014) proposes a different interpretation of transitional justice, one of deliberation, by drawing on the earlier works of Osiel (1998) and Teitel (2000). He focuses on the capability of trials to bring about the discursive engagement of actors through public deliberation, which involves multiple representations and perspectives of the past (Rangelov 2014: 48). This deliberation has the potential to question the role of nationalism and the complicity of the nation in past events (Rangelov 2014: 49). More generally, he identifies a shift from legalisation to judicialisation and from state to private actors. Law, therefore, currently has multiple politics and purposes. The key effect of this is the normalisation of justice-seeking across a range of social conditions, such as conflict, peace and transition. Similarly, Kent (2011) argues that transitional justice is about the past and working through it.

This book, as well as a number of recent studies focusing on former Yugoslav states (Gordy 2014; Nettelfield 2010; Obradović-Wochnik 2013a; Ostojić 2014; Pavlaković 2014; Subotic 2009), analyses the expressivist aims and effects of war crimes trials. Osiel (1998) argues that law's key goals of deterrence and retribution should not receive the same amount of attention in transitional situations, when prosecutions should be evaluated on their pedagogical potential. When such trials are effective as public shows, they can lead to a shift towards more liberal values. These aims also have to be proven to work effectively in unison with the more traditional aims of deterrence and retribution. Domestic and conventional criminal courts also have expressivist aims in their work (Anderson and Pildes 2000; Feinberg 1970) and court decisions hold a greater significance than most other occurrences (Brooks and Gewirtz

1996). Even retribution has been argued to be a form of expressivism (Hampton 1984).

The discord between retribution, deterrence and expressivism arises from the application of traditional criminal law, developed to address conventional deviance, to mass atrocity, which is a unique phenomenon. Despite the acknowledgement of this by most scholars and practitioners, Drumbl (2007) points out that the methods of punishment and sentencing for such crimes remain surprisingly ordinary when compared to Western legal systems. Courts often prove to be insensitive to the nuances of affected societies, especially with regard to reconciliation (Osiel 2009). For example, Ostojić (2014) shows how a disregard of local political nuances in Serbia alienated transitional authorities and threatened the legitimacy and stability of domestic institutions.[1] Transitional justice efforts are, therefore, most likely to succeed if they act in accordance with the domestic political situation.

Drumbl (2007) concludes that domestic or international tribunals designed for the purpose of punishment for war crimes struggle to achieve the aims of retribution and deterrence, while greater success (although still limited) is achieved in pursuing expressivist goals. Expressivist goals are not held in the same high regard by courts and practitioners as retribution or deterrence, but such aspects of trials can have a strong messaging effect and can help affirm the value of law in society (ICTY Prosecutor v. Kordić and Čerkez, IT-95-14/2-A). This can lead to a level of pedagogical performativity that can be hard to reproduce via any other legal mechanism.

Trickle-Down Effects of Norms

The premise that expressivist messages of courts may lead to norm change in societies is based on the belief that norms "cascade" or "spillover" from one level of society to another. Finnemore and Sikkink (1998: 895) outline the process of normative change as a three-stage "cascade". During the initial stage of norm emergence, norm entrepreneurs use their organisational platforms to call attention to issues by naming, interpreting and dramatising them. They attempt to persuade a critical mass of norm leaders to embrace these new ideas. Once these entrepreneurs achieve widespread success, the second stage begins, as a tipping process pushes the norm towards universal acceptance and other actors join in.

The second stage is characterised more by a dynamic of imitation, as norm leaders attempt to socialise other actors to become norm followers. The reasoning for this second stage, where the "cascade" through the rest of the population begins in proper, can vary. It can range from a combination of pressure for conformity; desire to enhance legitimation (both domestic and international); processes of socialisation or institutionalisation; and, demonstration effects. During the third stage, norm internalisation occurs and norms acquire a taken-for-granted quality. They are no longer debated, but instead, they are widely accepted. In other words, the logic of appropriateness (discussed below) is so heavily integrated in law, bureaucracy and expectations of behaviour that people and states conform to them naturally, out of conviction and habit.

Finnemore and Sikkink (1998: 897) additionally outline three logics that guide norms: the logics of appropriateness, consequences and emotion. Of these, the logic of appropriateness is the most relevant to this study and leads to several conclusions in the realm of international criminal justice. First, as norms of criminal accountability for war crimes and other violations of international humanitarian and human rights law begin to cascade, the notion of individual responsibility should also gain international momentum. Local actors in affected states, not only advocates in advanced liberal democracies, should increasingly blame atrocities on individuals (i.e. specific leaders), rather than collectives (i.e. whole communities or ethnicities).

The logic of appropriateness, coupled with the theory of norm cascades, captures the mentality and tactics of advocates of international criminal accountability. It remains, however, debatable how norms gain social force in a situation when the institutional and social requirements for the rule of law are absent. The difficulty in accounting for this scenario arises from the potential absence of norm leaders or a lack of willingness in the population to accept a norm. Justice cascades have since been identified in comparative regional studies, most notably of Latin America. Lutz and Sikkink (2001) offer such a study, in which they also go on to identify a larger human rights norm cascade in the region that the justice cascade was a part of. They argue that the success of these processes is inextricably linked to the wider progress of human rights and democracy norms in the region.

Risse, Ropp and Sikkink (1999) provide an analysis that looks at human rights norm change specifically in a transitional situation at state level. They identify a "spiral model" that they claim is universally applicable in such circumstances. The model's first phase involves state repression that is serious enough to disallow any significant opposition to challenge the state's violations of international human rights norms. A state may never move past this phase. If a state does move past this, then the next two phases involve the gathering of information on the norm-violating state by human rights networks and the government making concessions to domestic opposition. This allows for the opposition to gain strength, which can lead to pressure from above and below. Finally, the fourth phase involves human rights norms attaining prescriptive status in the state, which can eventually lead to the full acceptance and implementation of them. This means that even actors opposed to the norm change may start using the language of human rights norms. This may be only for show or for strategic purposes, such as to avoid punishment, but it does lead to a spillover effect.

The authors claim that the model is universally applicable, despite the exclusion of the former Yugoslavia from their study. They reach this conclusion by treating collective understandings embedded in domestic institutions and political cultures as fixed, rather than dependent on politics. This questions if the model is actually universally applicable and if it has been over-applied. After all, it is debatable if any model could accurately capture transition in all situations. Despite this, the authors make some useful points. Firstly, they identify socialisation and institutionalisation of norms as important. Second, they show that international organisations, both governmental and not, can act as "teachers" of norms. Third, they confirm that human rights norms are more likely to be implemented and complied with, if they resonate or fit with existing collective understandings. This last point is particularly relevant to a society such as Croatia, where a long tradition of human rights norms already existed and was present in the law but eroded during the conflict.

Subotic (2009) and Lamont (2010) have questioned the universal validity of these models by focusing on the former Yugoslav states. In her analysis of Croatia, Serbia and Bosnia, Subotic argues the "spiral model" is incorrect as it assumes that domestic norm believers are required to take the lead in norm change. In many states, these are absent or lack the authority to influence social change, while states may still display institutional markers of compliance. Lamont (2010) agrees with this and points out that most Latin American analyses studied NGOs that were initially composed of direct relatives of victims. The Krajina Serb community, for example, was almost completely ejected from Croatia in 1995, which may help to explain the relative absence of local NGO pressure since the victims of human rights abuses were no longer members of the domestic political community. Subotic (2009) identifies three types of international pressure that lead to normative change. Coercion ties compliance with material rewards; symbolic pressure appeals to a state's desire to be perceived as a legitimate international actor; and, bureaucratic pressure works under conditions of uncertainty when states comply because they think it will resolve internal problems.

International pressure on states does not enter a domestic political vacuum; rather, it always interacts with domestic political conditions to guide strategies of compliance. Relevant factors for this are domestic demand from below, veto players (also known as spoilers) and competing coalitions (Subotic 2009). Subotic identifies three major coalitions that can act as agents of normative and institutional compliance, other than the ones mentioned by Finnemore and Sikkink. Norm resistors are political elites that are opposed to policy change and who will use international norms to further consolidate their rule. Instrumental adopters use norms to distinguish themselves from other groups and to position themselves as international reformers in society. Compliance in this case is still driven by external incentives, such as appeals to legitimacy. Finally, true believers fully accept international norm models and often spearhead norm adoption, but are frequently internally divided and weak. Subotic's work, as well as this genre of research in general, provides some common sense observations on transitional justice and norm change that are useful for guiding future research. Moreover, recent trends in the scholarship point to the role of emotion in transitional, post-conflict contexts. Emotion, politics and ideology are deeply intertwined in such societies, especially for ex-combatants (Lawther 2017).

Transitional Justice in the Former Yugoslavia

Initial studies of the ICTY were generally critical of the Tribunal's work and concluded that it has negative effects, if any. Bass (2000) saw the ICTY as a gesture by Western powers to give the appearance of moral concern for the Yugoslav states. Snyder and Vinjamuri (2003) argue that the prosecution of perpetrators of atrocities according to universal standards risks causing more atrocities than it could ever prevent, because it does not pay sufficient attention to political realities. They argue that improvements in Serbian, Croatian and Bosnian democracy and human rights preceded and facilitated improved relations with the ICTY, and were not caused by it. More broadly, they argue that neither the Yugoslav nor the Rwandan tribunals had a significant impact on reducing atrocities globally or on changing the reasoning of actors in East Timor, Chechnya, Sierra Leone and any other conflicts.

Stover and Weinstein (2004) contend that a primary weakness of writings on justice after war and mass atrocity is the lack of objective evidence to substantiate claims about how well criminal trials achieve the goals ascribed to them. They believe insufficient attention has been paid to the effects, both positive and negative, that tribunals have had on post-war societies. They claim that any goals of attempting to broaden the ICTY mandate to include extra-legal goals in order to promote reconciliation among opposing parties was unrealistic. Trials alone could not establish an incontrovertible historical record since each group could reinterpret the facts according to their own views. They do raise two important implications on public pedagogy of trials: that the relationship between a tribunal and the local populace is a critical dimension of its success; and, that the domestic legal system in a state must be influenced by the international one for effective war crimes trials to take place in the country where the crimes were committed. They argue that there is no direct link between criminal trials (international, national and local/traditional) and reconciliation, although this could change over time. Social reconstruction after ethnic conflict is a slow and fragmented process, occurring at multiple levels (individual, community and state) that are influenced by a range of different factors, including social identity, fear, collective memory, governmental policies, security and protection, and past experience with the international community.

Single case studies of ICTY effects on specific states have yielded ambiguous, although generally more optimistic, results. McMahon and Forsythe (2008) find that the ICTY had little progressive effect on Serb political leaders, parties, institutional change or society, primarily due to the strength of traditional Serb nationalism. The ICTY did, however, play an important role in maintaining the concentration of the international community focused on Serbia by building a network of governments, regional organisations and NGOs committed to peace building in the region. The authors also highlighted such networked pressures at play in neighbouring states. In Croatia, this often came in the form of demands from the EU, NATO and the US government, who even went as far as threatening to block IMF and World Bank loans. Although they find no evidence for the Tribunal influencing actors when acting in isolation, they do ask the important question of whether similar transnational pressures could have been achieved in Serbia in the absence of the ICTY?

Ostojić (2014) is also pessimistic and attributes Serbia's lack of cooperation with the ICTY to the international community's disregard of the domestic political situation (as opposed to the prevalence of "norm resistors"), which ultimately alienated domestic authorities. Dragovic-Soso and Gordy (2010), on the other hand, adjudge the record of transitional justice in the region and country to be mixed with regard to a range of transitional efforts. They find that judicial institutions have lacked consistency, efforts at truth commissions have consistently failed and that civil society has been divided with regard to reconciliation. Despite the plethora of negative views in the literature, Gordy (2014) warns that the progress of transitional justice should be put into context and that disenchantment with particular incidents can all too easily be allowed to taint the whole process. The fact that these painful memories are being discussed and confronted at all is exceptional, while the speed at which it has happened is unprecedented. Gordy (2014) admits the international community had a key role in bringing about this confrontation, at times even forcing it, but he also points to the participation of civil society in the region, which often spearheaded efforts in documentation, research and debate. These initiatives operated on the cultural level, as much as on the political and legal ones. The studies discussed above show, once again, that time is needed to see the full effects of the ICTY and that transitional justice in a region can be affected by multiple causes with many domestic and international variables at play. This is made all the more complex by the emphasis on dangerously ambiguous terms, such as "reconciliation" and "coming to terms with the past".

Subotic (2009) also stresses the importance of complexity in this environment. She regards the Tribunal as one instrument in a range of options that can pressure states to comply with international human rights norms. She finds that in the cases of Croatia, Serbia and Bosnia compliance with such norms becomes a political strategy that allows states to go through the motion of fulfilling international demands while actually rejecting the profound social transformation that norms require. This challenges accounts that predict increasing social support for international models of transitional justice through the creation of lasting coalitions with domestic allies and application of pressure on domestic governments to change their politics. In Serbia, this led to the transitional justice process being hijacked by domestic political actors who used it as an international and domestic strategy to achieve specific local goals. In Bosnia, on the other hand, the process was politicised by the internal structure of the Bosnian state, which was restricted due to the Dayton Peace Agreement. Her analysis of Croatia is discussed in a later section.

Nettelfield (2010) provides a more optimistic view of the ICTY. She argues that, contrary to much contemporary analysis, Bosnia would have been much worse off without the ICTY. She claims that the most effective way to address the question of effectiveness, without any agreed-upon criteria, is to be explicit about the methods utilised and about the basis for findings in the course of evaluation. She shows how the ICTY has contributed to expanding the norm of accountability for war crimes; increased civil society's support of the criminal justice process; built a fact-based historical record to remove any myth-based narrative of the war; raised the military's trust in judicial investigations of war crimes; and, developed domestic capabilities for prosecutions. Nettelfield clearly shows that international criminal law has its rightful place in transitional circumstances, but it can only be a small part of the process of post-conflict social repair. Bosnia is a unique state, which limits the number of comparisons that can be drawn with it. Nevertheless, the powers the courts have to facilitate political participation from below and to create judicial capacity are useful in the former Yugoslavia and beyond.

Most studies of the transitional justice process in Croatia have focused on political elites. Many authors argue that politicians proved to be more effective at preventing the spread of transitional justice norms than trials were at enabling their spread. Peskin and Boduszynski (2003) found that ultimately politicians had more influence over how the Tribunal was accepted by the population than anything that the Tribunal or the Outreach programme had to say. They also point out that there was effectively no domestic pressure from civil society in Croatia to investigate war crimes committed by the Croatian government and impetus for this was almost completely external (Peskin and Boduszynski 2003: 1123).[2] Lamont (2010) frames this in the larger strategy of successive Croatian governments to accept the normative and legal framework of the Tribunal system, while also occasionally mounting legal challenges to specific indictments and investigations. This meant that the state was propagating countervailing norms that often limited its ability to cooperate with Tribunal requests. Despite prosecution and conviction of

Croatian generals, Croats continued to believe that its own citizens did not perpetrate war crimes (Lamont 2004). Prime Minister Ivo Sanader and his government regarded compliance as an unavoidable legal obligation, while at the same time attempting to challenge the Gotovina indictment before a domestic audience. Strategic compliance with the Tribunal was designed to fit within a broader legalistic strategy of defiance that allowed HDZ-led governments to present their formal compliance with international obligations, while also contesting ICTY indictments.

Lamont (2010) identifies this as particularly evident in Croatian civil society, which served to harden non-compliance attitudes. While elites continued to advocate human rights norm affirming rhetoric, as per ICTY requests, civil society pushed more aggressively for a complete rejection of the court's jurisdiction. This came for the most part from war veterans' and victims' organisations, which were driven by recent war memories and access to state funding. Domestic and foreign human rights NGOs were comparably weaker and faced opposition from other groups and the media. Subotic (2009) also found that in Croatia the overriding goal of integrating the state into the EU was so strongly shared by most political actors that it superseded all other ideological differences. This was due to a "European" self-identity, defined in many ways in opposition to Serbia, which overpowered existing nationalist narratives. Instrumental adoption served the Croatian state well and allowed for governments to present transitional justice as a necessary step to Europe. This meant that Croatia was proactive internationally and reactive domestically to the needs of the process. The strategy allowed the state to prove to the international community that they respected international rules while preserving almost intact the national understanding of the character of the war and Croatia's role in it.

Zambelli (2010) frames this within Croatia's attempt to distance itself from the Balkans through a process of "othering". This meant that Croatia's situation shifted from the identity of a post-war victim of aggression that viewed the outside world with suspicion and fear, towards an active advocate of change in the region and a supporter of international institutions such as the ICTY. In order to achieve this, the state had to redefine the nature of its cooperation with the ICTY and rearticulate the definition of sovereignty it was employing in its official discourse. Croatia's identity as a law-abiding and law-governed state began to depend heavily on its cooperation with the ICTY. Being capable of trying criminals in domestic tribunals, as well as allowing their trials abroad, demonstrated the state's maturity and its belonging together with Western European countries. An important question that arose in the early stages of this discourse was concerned with whether collaboration with the Tribunal would erode state sovereignty. Croatia had to comply with EU conditions, among many reasons, in order to conform to its identity as a Western and democratic country. Non-compliance would have meant staying at the "Balkan" level of closed-minded nationalism and pursuing of antiquated interpretations of sovereignty and state interests. In other words, it would have brought it closer to the feared "other". Moreover, Zambelli stresses the importance of the potential criminalisation of the Homeland War as a significant obstacle to the new coalition government that followed the Tuđman era. After all, the war was and still is considered one of the foundations of the modern Croatian state and a cornerstone of Croatian national identity. This also extended to the ICTY, which was and is seen as potentially criminalising the Homeland War.

The other common theme of the transitional justice analyses on Croatia is that of interpretations and understandings of the past in Croatian society and politics. Pavlaković (2010) analyses the process of constructing the past in the country and argues that association of memory with one's own ethnicity is in turn a potentially significant barrier to reconciliation. If people view the past through the prism of ethnicity, they are likely to view the present and future in the same way, thereby further reinforcing ethnic divisions. The presence of ethnic narratives critically influences an individual's response to the ICTY and the truths that it establishes. Pavlaković presents this issue as a juxtaposition between the Croatian politicians' version of the truth, constructed through public commemorations to create a purely victorious narrative, and the counter-narrative that the ICTY has created, which casts the country as a victim and a perpetrator of crimes.

The above issue is further exacerbated by selective truth acceptance in Vukovar (Pavlaković 2010). Serbs and Croats typically accept only those truths that support and corroborate their own ethnic narratives, while at the same time discarding or denying those that do not. Because both the Serb and Croat meta-narratives are firmly based around the notion of a defensive war, they are often not willing to accept that their own side may have committed war crimes. When they somewhat begrudgingly do concede that crimes were carried out, it is usually attributed to individual excesses, while crimes committed by the other group were premeditated and sanctioned. Clark (2012) provides an insight into this and the interplay between war facts and war myths. She adopts a micro-level approach to the Tribunal's legacy, looking at its impact on the ground and, specifically, at whether and to what extent it has aided inter-ethnic reconciliation in Vukovar. The fact that the Tribunal has held so few trials in relation to Vukovar has impacted on inter-ethnic relations in two crucial ways. First, as guilt has not been individualised to any significant extent, this has created the space for individuals to decide for themselves who is culpable, and all too frequently they fall back on notions of collective guilt. Second, because neither side believes that it has received justice from the Tribunal, this has encouraged people to focus and draw attention to the suffering and pain that members of their own ethnic group endured during the war. Clark concludes that it is simplistic to assume that trials contribute to reconciliation by documenting the truth and that we cannot assume the existence of one "truth" that everyone can agree upon. She identifies the prevalence of competing truths in Vukovar and that the ICTY, therefore, operates in an environment of opposing and competing truths. Truth is a highly contested concept in the former Yugoslavia and there are few shared truths about the events of 1991. For example, Serb interviewees consistently referred to the war as a civil war, while Croat interviewees highlighted that it was a war of Serbian aggression. Clark's work concludes that the ICTY has had little positive impact on reconciliation between Serbs and Croats in the city. In doing so, it has effectively problematised two commonly used claims: that criminal trials aid reconciliation through the dispensing of justice and through the establishment of truth.

Closely related to this is the interplay between legitimate defenders and war criminals. Clark frames this around Operation Storm, the case of General Gotovina and what she calls rejected truths. In Vukovar, and in Croatia more generally, there exists a strong identity based upon defence. This is particularly so among former combatants and it is one of the principal reasons why the "truths" that the ICTY uncovers may fail to gain local acceptance. The Tribunal's original judgment against General Gotovina fundamentally challenged the accepted wisdom that the Homeland War was a purely defensive war. In order for the population to accept the Tribunal's judgment, they would have had to radically review their views and perceptions of the war. In other words, they would have been forced to go against the national meta-narrative.

The biggest obstacle to this, according to Clark, is that Croatia's politicians and media have continued to promote the national meta-narrative and have cultivated a deep sense of Croatian victimhood. Moreover, the majority of the media has only sporadically and often in a biased manner reported about decisions in favour of Croatian Generals. By doing so, they have contributed to the escalation of an obviously deeply imbued attitude in a major part of Croatian society, that of denying or justifying that crimes were committed by their own side. There appears to be little will to settle and reconcile these competing versions of the truth in Croatia. There were, however, some notable exceptions, such as *Feral Tribune*, *Novosti*, *Novi List*, as well as a range of newer online portals that reported on these issues in a more objective and critical manner. These have, however, all come under attack recently and many have been forced to change, if they still exist at all.

Pavlaković (2010) delves into the issue of General Gotovina in more detail and finds the case emblematic of the nexus of politics, symbols, rituals and collective memory in Croatia, as well as more broadly in Yugoslavia. He points out that history is constructed not only through facts, but also through myths that are often more influential than statistics. In another study, Pavlaković (2007) highlights that commemorations and trials have significantly affected the way history is being constructed in Croatia, for the most part without the participation of historians. As discussed above, Croatian politicians used public commemorations to create a purely victorious narrative of the founding of the state, while the ICTY has attempted to construct a counter-narrative.

Today, the rhetoric at the anniversary of Operation Storm has changed a number of times, due to the initial judgments and later acquittals in the cases of Gotovina and Markač. Croatian politicians now acknowledge that war crimes did occur and that there were Serbian victims as well as Croatian ones, something that would not have realistically been possible during the Tuđman era. Even if the ICTY can be discredited as a "historian", Pavlaković reminds readers that the archives collected by the Tribunal and the transcripts from the trials have become invaluable resources to researchers working on this time period. He concludes by identifying two key trends with regard to the dynamic between legitimate defenders and war criminals. That Croatian leaders are now willing to cooperate with the ICTY and in doing so, admitting that war crimes have taken place. On the other hand, that no systematic effort has ever existed and may never exist to demystify the Homeland War or challenge the glorification of General Gotovina and others like him. The most recent acquittals of Croatian Generals show that the construction of history and a national meta-narrative in Croatia remains an actively ongoing process.

The most recent relevant work by Rangelov (2014) argues that Croatia provides an opportunity to analyse how judicial processes can promote public deliberation about nationalist narratives and representations of the past (through the lens of deliberative justice). The predominant war narrative, however, continues to affect judicial outcomes: most cases are conducted in the lower courts (which remain biased) and participation of the accused in the war (if they were a member of the Croatian police or armed forces) is often used as a mitigating circumstance in sentencing (Rangelov 2014: 150).

Overall, although works on Croatia are few, they do highlight the most relevant themes to the transitional justice process in the country. First, they focus on the importance of identity in elites' strategies of compliance with the ICTY. Second, they investigate the concept of competing narratives within the state, both among elites and the public. Together they point to an ambiguity in messages and actions from an elite level that translates into competing "truths" at the everyday level.

Conclusion

Transitional justice has been assessed from a vast range of perspectives, leading to an equally broad range of conclusions, with no consensus over whether the process helps societies recover from past human rights abuses or not. Both positive and negative studies, however, stress that local and collective understandings of law and the past are the key to such rehabilitation. Transitional justice and associated processes occur not only at the level of politics or law, but also on the levels of culture and emotion. The interplay between these is highly dependent on the relationships that exist between individuals, institutions and societal groupings.

An analysis of these can help shed further light on the effects of transitional justice and can ascertain if norm spillover does occur in the mechanistic fashion some models describe. The little literature that exists on Croatia focuses on themes that can help with this, such as the mythology surrounding the Homeland War and competing narratives among elites and the public. Broad concepts, such as identity and reconciliation, have been studied at the micro-level in specific locations, such as Vukovar. Specific concepts that are arguably better suited to analysis, such as norm compliance, have also been studied, but only at the level of elites. These studies do not take enough steps to avoid the methodological trap of interpreting state compliance as indicators of norm entrenchment or diffusion. Norms and narratives as constituent parts of identity could provide a more easily analysed concept in this sense. Moreover, analysis of everyday norms and narratives is missing in Croatia, other than in Vukovar. This means that there is a lack of research on how top-down and bottom-up narratives interact in Croatia.

Notes

1. Ostojić is not the only person to reach this conclusion; Fatogoma (2017) argues that transitional justice efforts in Côte d'Ivoire were ineffective because they did not reflect local political conditions and tensions.
2. This is no longer wholly true and since the 2003 study there have been a greater number of efforts.

References

Acharya, A. (2004). How ideas spread: Whose norms matter? Norm localization and institutional change in Asian regionalism. *International Organization, 58,* 239–275.

Acharya, A. (2009). *Whose ideas matter? Agency and power in Asian regionalism.* Ithaca: Cornell University Press.

Anderson, E., & Pildes, R. H. (2000). Expressive theories of law: A general restatement. *University of Pennsylvania Law Review, 148,* 1503–1575.

Baines, E. K. (2007). The haunting of Alice: Local approaches to justice and reconciliation in northern Uganda. *International Journal of Transitional Justice, 1,* 91–114.

Bass, G. J. (2000). *Stay the hand of vengeance: The politics of war crimes tribunals.* Princeton: Princeton University Press.

Brooks, P., & Gewirtz, P. (1996). *Law's stories: Narrative and rhetoric in the law.* New Haven: Yale University Press.

Browning, C. S. (2008). *Constructivism, narrative and foreign policy analysis: A case study of Finland.* Oxford: Peter Lang.

Carlsnaes, W., Simmons, B. A., & Risse, T. (2012). *Handbook of international relations.* London: Sage.

Cianetti, L. (2017). Tricke-down social inclusion: The EU minorities agenda in times of crisis. *Journal of Common Market Studies.* https://doi.org/10.1111/jcms.12618.

Clark, J. N. (2012). The ICTY and reconciliation in Croatia: A case study of Vukovar. *Journal of International Criminal Justice, 10*, 397–417.

Dembour, M. B., & Kelly, T. (2007). *Paths to international justice: Social and legal perspectives*. Cambridge: Cambridge University Press.

Dragovic-Soso, J. (2014). The parting of ways: Public reckoning with the recent past in post-Milošević Serbia. In T. Waters (Ed.), *The Milošević trial—An autopsy* (pp. 389–408). Oxford: Oxford University Press.

Dragovic-Soso, J., & Gordy, E. (2010). Coming to terms with the past: Transitional justice and reconciliation in the post-Yugoslav lands. In D. Djokić & J. Ker-Lindsay (Eds.), *New perspectives on Yugoslavia: Key issues and controversies* (pp. 193–212). London: Routledge.

Drumbl, M. A. (2007). *Atrocity, punishment and international law*. Cambridge: Cambridge University Press.

Fatogoma, A. D. D. (2017). Resistance to transitional justice in the contact of political violence in Côte d'Ivoire. In B. Jones & J. Bernath (Eds.), *Resistance and transitional justice* (pp. 17–34). London: Routledge.

Feinberg, J. (1970). *Doing and deserving: Essays in the theory of responsibility*. Princeton: Princeton University Press.

Finnemore, M., & Sikkink, K. (1998). International norm dynamics and political change. *International Organization, 52*, 887–917.

Fox, J. E., & Miller-Idriss, C. (2008). Everyday nationhood. *Ethnicities, 8*, 536–563.

Gordy, E. (2014). *Guilt, responsibility, and denial: The past at stake in post-Milošević Serbia*. Philadelphia: University of Pennsylvania Press.

Hafner-Burton, E., & Ron, J. (2007). Human rights institutions: Rhetoric and efficacy. *Journal of Peace Research, 44*, 379–384.

Hafner-Burton, E., & Tsutsui, K. (2007). Justice lost! The failure of international human rights law to matter where needed most. *Journal of Peace Research, 44*, 407–425.

Halbwachs, M. (1992). *On collective memory* (L. Coser, Trans.). Chicago: University of Chicago Press.

Hampton, J. (1984). Moral education theory of punishment. *Philosophy and Public Affairs, 13*, 208–238.

Haslam, E. (2007). Law, civil society and contested justice at the international criminal tribunal for Rwanda. In M. B. Dembour & T. Kelly (Eds.), *Paths to international justice: Social and legal perspectives* (pp. 57–82). Cambridge: Cambridge University Press.

Horne, C. M. (2015). The timing of transitional justice measures. In N. Nedelsky & L. Stan (Eds.), *Post-communist transitional justice: Lessons from twenty-five years of experience* (pp. 123–147). New York: Cambridge University Press.

ICTY Appeals Chamber. (2004). Prosecutor v. Kordić and Čerkez, IT-95-14/2-A.

Katzenstein, P. J. (1996). *The culture of national security: Norms and identity in world politics*. New York: Columbia University Press.

Kent, L. (2011). Local memory practices in East Timor: Disrupting transitional justice narratives. *The International Journal of Transitional Justice, 5*, 434–455.

Kritz, N. J. (1995). *Transitional justice: How emerging democracies reckon with former regimes*. Washington, DC: United States Institute of Peace Press.

Lamont, C. K. (2004). A new Croatian right: Nationalist political parties and contemporary Croatian politics. *Balkanistica, 17*, 45–66.

Lamont, C. K. (2010). *International criminal justice and the politics of compliance*. Farnham: Ashgate.

Lawther, C. (2017). The truth about loyalty: Emotions, ex-Combatants and transitioning from the past. *International Journal of Transitional Justice, 11*, 484–504. https://doi.org/10.1093/ijtj/ijx019.

Lutz, E., & Sikkink, S. (2001). The justice cascade: The evolution and impact of foreign human rights trails in Latin America. *Chicago Journal of International Law, 2*, 1–33.

Lynch, M., & Marchesi, B. (2015). The adoption and impact of transitional justice. In N. Nedelsky & L. Stan (Eds.), *Post-communist transitional justice: Lessons from twenty-five years of experience* (pp. 73–98). New York: Cambridge University Press.

Mani, R. (2002). *Beyond retribution: Seeking justice in the shadows of war*. Cambridge: Polity Press.

McEvoy, K., & McGregor, L. (2008). *Transitional justice from below: Grassroots activism and the struggle for change*. Oxford: Hart.

McMahon, P. C., & Forsythe, D. P. (2008). The ICTY's impact on Serbia: Judicial romanticism meets network politics. *Human Rights Quarterly, 30*, 412–435.

Meyer, C. O. (2005). Convergence towards a European strategies culture? A constructivist framework for explaining changing norms. *European Journal of International Relations, 11*, 523–549.

Millar, G. (2012). Between western theory and local practice: Cultural impediments to truth-telling in Sierra Leone. *Conflict Resolution Quarterly, 29*, 177–199.

Miller, Z. (2008). Effects of invisibility: In search of the 'economic' in transitional justice. *The International Journal of Transitional Justice, 2*, 266–291.

Nagy, R. (2008). Transitional justice as global project: Critical reflections. *Third World Quarterly, 29*, 275–289.

Nettelfield, L. J. (2010). *Courting democracy in Bosnia and Herzegovina: The Hague tribunal's impact in a postwar state*. Cambridge: Cambridge University Press.

Neumann, I. B. (1999). *Uses of the other: "The East" in European identity formation*. Minneapolis: University of Minnesota Press.

Nora, P. (1992). *Les lieux de mémoire*. Paris: Gallimard.

Obradović-Wochnik, J. (2013a). *Ethnic conflict and war crimes in the Balkans: The narratives of denial in post-conflict Serbia*. London: I.B. Tauris.

Obradović-Wochnik, J. (2013b). Serbian civil society as an exclusionary space: NGOs, the public and "coming to terms with the past". In V. Bojičić-Dželilović, J. Ker-Lindsay, & D. Kostovicova (Eds.), *Civil society and transitions in the western Balkans* (pp. 210–229). Basingstoke: Palgrave Macmillan.

Osiel, M. (1998). *Mass atrocity, collective memory and the law*. New Brunswick: Transaction Publishers.

Osiel, M. (2009). *Making sense of mass atrocity*. Cambridge: Cambridge University Press.

Ostojić, M. (2014). *Between justice and stability: The politics of war crimes prosecutions in post-Milošević Serbia*. Farnham: Ashgate.

Pavlaković, V. (2007). Eye of the storm: The ICTY, commemorations and contested histories of Croatia's Homeland War. *Wilson Center*. Available at https://wilsoncenter.org/publication/347-eye-the-storm-the-icty-commemorations-and-contested-histories-croatias-homeland-war. Accessed 23 Nov 2012.

Pavlaković, V. (2010). Croatia, the international criminal tribunal for the former Yugoslavia, and general Gotovina as a political symbol. *Europe-Asia Studies, 62,* 1707–1740.

Pavlaković, V. (2014). Fulfilling the thousand-year-old dream: Strategies of symbolic nation-building in Croatia. In P. Kolstø (Ed.), *Strategies of symbolic nation-building in south eastern Europe* (pp. 19–50). Farnham: Ashgate.

Peskin, V., & Boduszynski, M. (2003). International justice and domestic politics: Post-Tudjman Croatia and the international criminal tribunal for the former Yugoslavia. *Europe-Asia Studies, 55,* 1117–1142.

Rangelov, I. (2014). *Nationalism and the rule of law: Lessons from the Balkans and beyond*. Cambridge: Cambridge University Press.

Rangelov, I., & Teitel, R. G. (2011). Global civil society and transitional justice. In M. Albrow, H. Seckinelgin, H. Anheier, et al. (Eds.), *Global civil society 2011: Globality and the absence of justice* (pp. 162–177). New York: Palgrave Macmillan.

Risse, T., Ropp, S. C., & Sikkink, K. (1999). *The power of human rights: International norms and domestic change*. Cambridge: Cambridge University Press.

Roht-Arriaza, N. (2006). The new landscape of transitional justice. In N. Roht-Arriaza & J. Mariezcurrena (Eds.), *Transitional justice in the twenty-first century: Beyond truth versus justice* (pp. 1–16). Cambridge: Cambridge University Press.

Shaw, R. (2007). Memory frictions: Localizing the truth and reconciliation commission in Sierra Leone. *The International Journal of Transitional Justice, 1,* 183–207.

Sikkink, K., & Walling, C. B. (2007). The impact of human rights trials in Latin America. *Journal of Peace Research, 44,* 427–445.

Smith, A. L. (2004). Heteroglossia, "common sense," and social memory. *American Ethnologist, 31,* 251–269.

Snyder, J. L., & Vinjamuri, L. (2003). Trials and errors: Principle and pragmatism in strategies of international justice. *International Security, 28,* 5–44.

Sommers, M. R. (1994). The narrative constitution of identity: A relational and network approach. *Theory and Society, 23,* 605–649.

Sriram, C. L. (2007). Justice as peace? Liberal peacebuilding and strategies of transitional justice. *Global Society, 21,* 579–591.

Stover, E., & Weinsten, H. M. (2004). *My neighbor, my enemy: Justice and community in the aftermath of mass atrocity.* Cambridge: Cambridge University Press.

Ströhle, I. (2013). Kosovo Liberation Army veterans' politics and contentious citizenship in post-war Kosovo. In S. Pavlović & M. Živković (Eds.), *Transcending fratricide: Political mythologies, reconciliations, and the uncertain future in the former Yugoslavia* (pp. 243–264). Nomos: Baden-Baden.

Subotic, J. (2009). *Hijacked justice: Dealing with the past in the Balkans.* Ithaca: Cornell University Press.

Subotic, J. (2015). Genocide narratives as narratives-in-dialogue. *Journal of Regional Security, 10,* 177–198.

Teitel, R. G. (2000). *Transitional justice.* New York: Oxford University Press.

Tholens, S. (2012) *International norms and local agents in peacebuilding: Small arms control in post-war Kosovo and Cambodia.* PhD thesis, European University Institute.

Thoms, O., Ron, J., & Paris, R. (2010). State-level effects of transitional justice: What do we know? *The International Journal of Transitional Justice, 4,* 329–354.

Wendt, A. (1999). *Social theory of international politics.* Cambridge: Cambridge University Press.

White, H. (1984). The question of narrative in contemporary historical theory. *History and Theory, 23,* 1–33.

Zambelli, N. (2010). A journey westward: A poststructuralist analysis of Croatia's identity and the problem of cooperation with the international criminal tribunal for the former Yugoslavia. *Europe-Asia Studies, 62,* 1661–1682.

Zimmermann, L. (2017). More for less: The interactive translation of global norms in postconflict Guatemala. *International Studies Quarterly, 61,* 774–785.

CHAPTER 3

The Narrative of the Homeland War in Croatia

In Croatia, there is a pervasive, nearly universal among ethnic Croats, notion that Croatia was a victim of Serbian aggression. According to this narrative, Croatia led a war of self-defence, with the aim of not only saving the Croatian state, but preventing the destruction of the Croatian nation (Pavlaković 2014: 19). This narrative was also central to the nation-building process in the state, together with other strategies such as severing all ties with the multinational Yugoslav state and providing a history of continuity of the Croatian state into history (Pavlaković 2014: 31). At the same time, a justice narrative is also present in Croatia, one based on the norms of transitional justice. Actors who wish to promote one or the other have similar expressivist goals, those of building a narrative, authenticating it as the truth and passing it on to the society in question (Drumbl 2007). The official war narrative and the justice narrative exist in the same space and interact with each other—at times coming into conflict and undermining each other, and at other times affirming each other and becoming aligned.

The war narrative has previously been extensively outlined by the literature on Croatia and transitional justice, especially Banjeglav (2012), Jović (2009, 2017), Koren (2011) and Pavlaković (2014). This has included detailed breakdowns of its various facets, many of which are also reproduced in the Declarations on the Homeland War and Operation Storm. This study uses those categorisations and builds on them. The justice narrative is, however, less well defined. In this study, the justice narrative is defined as the stories that transitional justice institutions

I. Sokolić, *International Courts and Mass Atrocity*, Memory Politics and Transitional Justice, https://doi.org/10.1007/978-3-319-90841-0_3

in Croatia and in The Hague try to impart on the Croatian public. These include specific versions of events as presented by courts through, for example, trial transcripts and sentences, as well as broader norms concerning the primacy of rule of law, regardless of circumstances. The justice narrative comes into conflict with the war narrative over the notion of a defensive war. ICTY convictions, such as those of Dario Kordić and Mario Čerkez, form a large part of the justice narrative and show that the Croatian state supported armed forces outside of its own territory for purposes other than the defence of the Republic of Croatia. Such convictions have the potential to undermine a narrative of defence. The notion of a joint criminal enterprise by the Croatian wartime political and military leadership held similar potential, while domestic and international trials relating to war crimes by Croatian military personnel undermine the notion that crimes could not be committed in a defensive war.

At the same time, the justice narrative at times supports the war narrative or sees judgements that are aligned with it. For example, the justice narrative asserts that all war crimes must be investigated and processed, which Croatian authorities have been more than happy to do with regard to Serbian perpetrators. Both narratives stress the importance of fact-finding, although one in a more universal sense than the other. Most significantly, ICTY decisions can be in conflict with or in line with the war narrative. The final verdicts in the Operation Storm case reaffirmed the war narrative (and the creation of the Croatian state): that the operation was legitimate and that no joint criminal enterprise was present.[1] The dominant national narrative is thus constantly contested by both external and internal sources (Ashplant et al. 2000: 16). At times, this led to fierce rejection of war crimes processes, when they ran counter to the official war narrative, at other times the processes fit into or were modelled to fit into official narratives about the past (Ristić 2014: 96).

The war narrative is important since it forms a kind of founding, or refounding, myth in Croatia. Much like in other societies, this helps the society explain its origins and define what it stands for (Eliade 1963). Foundational myths help societies reach a consensus about the foundational values of their political community by building solidarity, societal integration and even democracy (Ciper 2012: 8). Such myths are often marked by "monumental didactics" (Osiel 1998: 4), in other words, public recounting of the heroic deeds as a national narrative. A myth of refounding marks a clear period of change from the recent past and celebrates the achievements of the main protagonists of this separation. Myths of founding and refounding frequently centre on legal proceedings or the drafting of legal documents, for example the Magna Carta for Great Britain and the Declaration of Independence for the USA (Osiel 1998: 5). War narratives, in particular, are composed of emotional symbols and images related to struggle, survival and sacrifice, unlike more pacifistically minded narratives, such as the justice narrative (Pavlaković 2014: 22). Wars and ethnic conflict provide particularly strong inspiration for the creation of national narratives of the past and many modern nations have built national sentiment on these foundations (Ristić 2014; Zertal 2005).

The following section of this chapter outlines the key characteristics of the war narrative and the two parliamentary documents that quasi-legally enshrine it. The section draws on existing scholarship to describe these elements, which are then elaborated on in the rest of the chapter through focus group, interview and survey data. In the final section, a new facet of the war narrative is analysed, the notion that the war is not over and that it remains central to many participants' lives. The conclusion presents the results of the QCA, which shows which facets of the war narrative are deliberated over and which are not.

Key Facets of the War Narrative

The Croatian war narrative is concerned with the notion that the war was defensive; that it was an attempt to create a democratic Croatian state, which the Croatian people expressed a desire for through a referendum; that a distinction must be made between the Greater Serbian aggressor and the victim; that the most recent war memory must be kept alive; and that war heroes must be protected. It is inscribed by parliament in institutionalised form in the Declaration on the Homeland War (*Deklaracija o Domovinskom Ratu*) and the Declaration on Operation Storm (*Deklaracija o Oluji*). Croatia's first post-Tuđman government was initially willing to actively cooperate with the ICTY but, due to a public backlash and the threat of certain facets of the war being criminalised, they issued the Declaration on the Homeland War in 2000, the same year they came to power. The Declaration enshrined, in official writing, several key concepts (Narodne Novine 2000):

- That the "basic values of the Homeland War are unequivocally accepted by the whole Croatian *narod* and all citizens of the Republic of Croatia". In other words, the declaration is considered to be binding to all citizens.
- That "the armed aggression against the Republic of Croatia was conducted by Serbia, Montenegro and the *JNA* with an armed rebellion from a part of the Serb population in the Republic of Croatia".
- That "The Republic of Croatia led a just and legitimate, defensive and liberating, not an aggressive and conquering war against anyone in which it defended its territories from Greater Serbian aggression within its internationally recognised borders".
- That "the Croatian judiciary is obliged to process all possible cases of individual war crimes, serious transgressions of human rights and all other crimes committed in the aggression against the Republic of Croatia".
- That the Croatian parliament "calls for all citizens, state and civil institutions, trade unions, associations and media, obliges all state officials and all state bodies of the Republic of Croatia" to protect these principles and values.
- Finally, the stated reason for issuing the declaration was "to stop the radical politicisation of the Homeland War and the worrying polarisation of Croatian society".

The Declaration puts in official state writing a single interpretation of the past, regardless of whether or not it is correct, which paints Croatia as exclusively a victim of international "Greater Serbian" aggression; it puts the whole blame for the start of the conflict on Serbia (and none on the Tuđman regime); it ignores that there were elements of civil war (despite this still being an academically debated issue); and it denies any official Croatian involvement in Bosnia, despite ICTY rulings contradicting this (Pavlaković 2014). Moreover, it binds all citizens, media and public bodies to follow these points and elevates them to the status of core values of the Croatian state and *narod*.[2] It also includes contradictions that were reflected in focus group discussions. For example, it refers specifically to *individual* war crimes (Narodne Novine 2000: Article 6), a common manner of describing alleged Croatian war crimes, while also referring to crimes committed in *aggression*, which are seen as planned and committed by Serbia, Serbs and the *JNA* as a group. In comparison with the memory and narrative surrounding the Second World War, the Homeland War provides a much stronger foundation on which to build consensus and, subsequently, a nation state (Pavlaković 2014: 37). Certain topics on the Homeland War continue to be debated, both publicly and academically; however, there exists a general consensus that the Declaration and most of the themes outlined represent the truth. For example, the very term "Homeland War" is loaded, but is now used across nearly all of Croatian society, media and politics to refer to the conflict (Jović 2009: 23; Pavlaković 2014: 39).[3] This chapter will outline these various themes in greater detail and attempt to show how pervasive they are in Croatian society.

Operation Storm had the potential to undermine the notion of Croatian defence since it was an aggressive military occupation to retake lands (at times, this is also how it is justified as being defensive, because its aim was to *re*take *lost* lands). The Declaration on Operation Storm was issued in 2006 in order to pre-empt an ICTY verdict that might criminalise the military operation. Unlike its earlier counterpart, it does not focus on the core values of the Croatian state, but instead it attempts to define the nature and events of the operation. It cites key facts, actors, dates and goals, much like a historical document, although it is not academic in nature since it does not use sources or define terms (Koren 2011). It was less influential than the Declaration on the Homeland War, although it also aimed to create an official version of events during the 1990s (Koren 2011). It does, however, nevertheless include large elements of the war narrative:

- One of the justifications for the operation was that "from the occupied territories of the Republic of Croatia, Serb forces organised and conducted systematic aggression against the free and liberated parts of our country and neighbouring Bosnia and Herzegovina" (Narodne Novine 2006: Article 1).
- Article 2 focuses on the legally legitimate nature of the operation, but also on the cooperation with the government of Bosnia and Herzegovina and the Tuđman-Izetbegović agreement specifically (Narodne Novine 2006: Article 2).
- Article 5 states that "Operation Storm was, by all accounts, organised and executed in the last moment, because the defeat of the Serb forces prevented a repeat 'scenario' of Srebrenica in other parts of Bosnia and Herzegovina, especially in Goražde, Bihać, Sarajevo, Tuzla, Cazinska Krajina and Posavina" (Narodne Novine 2006: Article 5).

This last point of the Declaration is particularly interesting, since it was often reproduced (word by word with regard to Bihać) in focus groups. Overall, the Declaration presented a change of tact from its earlier counterpart, since it no longer focused so much on defence (it is more focused on response to aggression), but instead it focuses on cooperation with Bosnia, as well as allies in the West, thereby countering any arguments over Croatian aggression in the neighbouring state. Despite being the less influential of the two declarations, it still enshrined facets of the war narrative in writing, thereby quasi-legally undermining the justice narrative, and elements of it were reflected in focus group discussions. The declarations reflect a general desire among certain political segments to prohibit any questioning of the war narrative. For example, the leader of the HDZ in 2014, Tomislav Karamarko, called for any questioning of the Homeland War to be "restricted to their own room, courtyard or house – certainly not in the public arena" (Blanuša 2017: 174). Others have called for changes to Croatia's criminal code, in order to sanction those who deny the defensive character of the Homeland War and Operation Storm (for more details, see Blanuša 2017: 175).

The core components of the dominant war narrative are summarised in the literature, and apparent in transcripts, as those of:

Defence: The conflict is seen as an act of self-defence against an aggressor (Jović 2009). As Pavlaković (2014) notes, even the Croatian word for war veterans of the Homeland War is *branitelji*, or "defenders", reinforcing this image of defence. Respondents consistently returned to notions of self-defence in the focus groups, dyads and interviews, when asked about the war but also when discussing other topics, such as the role of the Serb minority in Croatian society. It was often used to justify other views or to excuse actions (e.g. Croat war crimes).

Survival and struggle: As already discussed above, war narratives draw on emotional reactions based on symbols of struggle. In Croatia, this is presented as the fledgling state being unprepared and unarmed for the coming conflict (Banjeglav 2012: 26; Peskin and Boduszynski 2003: 1129). In the transcripts, this was often referred to in terms of the "barefooted" or "bare-armed" Croatian soldiers who, without any preparation (as opposed to Serbs, who did prepare), fought off and survived the aggression.

Aggressors: Since Croatia is seen as having acted in self-defence, there must exist aggressors. These are frequently referred to as "Serbs/Serbia", "Greater Serbs/Serbia", "*JNA*", "Chetniks", "communists" or any combination of these words (e.g. "Serbo-chetniks"). Yugoslavia is often paired with communism, whereas Serbs are often collectively referred to as Chetniks (Banjeglav 2012: 10–11; Jović 2009; Pavlaković 2014). In the group discussions, aggression was referred to overtly, but it was also often implied by participants stressing how Croatia did not attack anyone, how the Croatian army never left the territory of the Republic of Croatia, and how the situation would have been different had Croatia been "gone to someone else's home".

Yugoslavia as broken: This part of the narrative, less present than the others, is more central to the nation-building narrative than the war narrative. The two, however, often overlap and appear together. In the war narrative, this is represented as betrayal by Yugoslav institutions, especially the *JNA*. The public is also split on the issue; some see the cause of this as Milošević and were not directly opposed to the idea of Yugoslavia. Others, however, see Yugoslavia as destructive for Croatia. Moreover, Pavlaković (2014: 32) points out that many facets of Yugoslavia's breakup, including all of the above, as well as the hundreds of refugees, the appearance of extremist groups (such as Chetniks) and wartime media reporting, are all today associated with the Yugoslav state itself, rather than simply the violent dissolution of it. This part of the narrative was also used by participants to highlight how the current Croatian state had been infiltrated by unwanted elements or had not changed much from Yugoslavia, since they saw a continuity in Yugoslavia not functioning and the modern Croatian state not functioning. War veterans, for example, interpreted this as a problem of lustration, since they believed the same people to be in power in both regimes.

Victimisation: The Croatian victimisation narrative is built around several focal points, such as Vukovar[4] and Dubrovnik, whose destruction (in the case of Dubrovnik more symbolic) is expressed across all of Croatian society (Banjeglav 2012: 14; Jović 2009). This facet of the war narrative is frozen, sanctified and cannot be questioned (Blanuša 2017). Further symbols are war crimes committed by the Yugoslav People's Army (and associated paramilitary groups) and destruction in other localities, which are more locally pronounced (e.g. the attacks on Sisak and Zadar, murders in Petrinja, Glina, Škabrnja and so on). This component was reflected in the importance attributed to the Croatia–Serbia ICJ genocide case by Croatian elites. Their unhappiness with the final ruling (the case was dismissed) focused on the lack of recognition given to the amount of suffering and the level of victimhood experienced by Croatia.[5] Participants not only referred to the key focal points, but they also created a distinction between "us, Croats, the victims" and "them, Serbs, the aggressors". Much like with the notion of defence, victimisation was often used in passages to excuse and relativise certain Croatian actions.

War is not over: Finally, there is a perception among certain groups of society that the Homeland War, or at the very least the struggle for Croatian independence, is not over. Elite-level perpetuation of this notion is outlined extensively by Jović (2017). The war was still central to some individuals' lives, and they saw issues from it as unresolved. This is sometimes attributed to Greater Serbian forces still being alive and present (inside or outside of Croatia); at other times, it is seen as an attempt by the international community to take away Croatian independence (e.g. through international tribunals or the EU). This also includes the notion that the Croatian government "works against Croatia" and that it has been infiltrated by unwanted elements. This is connected to the notion that the "other" to Croats, namely Serbs, have throughout history been oppressors of the Croat people and that history is repeating itself, so Croatia has to once again defend itself (MacDonald 2002). This particular facet of the war narrative has not been outlined in the literature before, but it became obvious in the transcripts as participants consistently referred to an ongoing or constant defence, as if the war or struggle had not ended yet for them. Participants in this study, but war veterans in particular, consistently talked of the centrality of the war in their lives. It is, however, important to note that it is possible that this narrative is specific to the data-gathering methods. In other words, that this centrality was brought about by the moderator asking questions about the Homeland War, which elicited narratives that may have otherwise been marginalised.

This is important to the process of transitional justice because trickle-down effects of human rights norms (Lutz and Sikkink 2001; Osiel 2009) compete with these narratives. If they are to take hold in society, they have to somehow exist alongside these competing narratives or overcome them. These narratives evolve as they are reproduced, but this reproduction is marked by repetition rather than innovation, which makes them particularly hard to change (Bernhard and Kubik 2014: 286). The broader implications of this for transition are that political actors who try to change such narratives often have a polarising, and therefore destabilising, effect on democratic establishments (Bernhard and Kubik 2014; Linz 1978; Sartori 1976). By challenging the legitimacy of the narrative, they also challenge the legitimacy of political elites (Banjeglav 2012: 26). Consequently, what is contested, reinforced and threatened (or not) in the narrative becomes important for analysing the trickle-down effect of norms.

The War Narrative

The sheer pervasiveness of the belief that Croatia was a victim of Serbian aggression and was, therefore, acting in self-defence is apparent in survey results. For example, Fig. 3.1 highlights the percentage of the public that believes Serbia needs to admit it committed aggression against Croatia for relations to improve (Kolstø 2011).

The group discussions and individual interviews reflected this since not a single participant expressed a different opinion in either setting. Even groups that did not agree on many topics agreed wholly on this one. That Croatia was attacked was seen as fact across all groups:

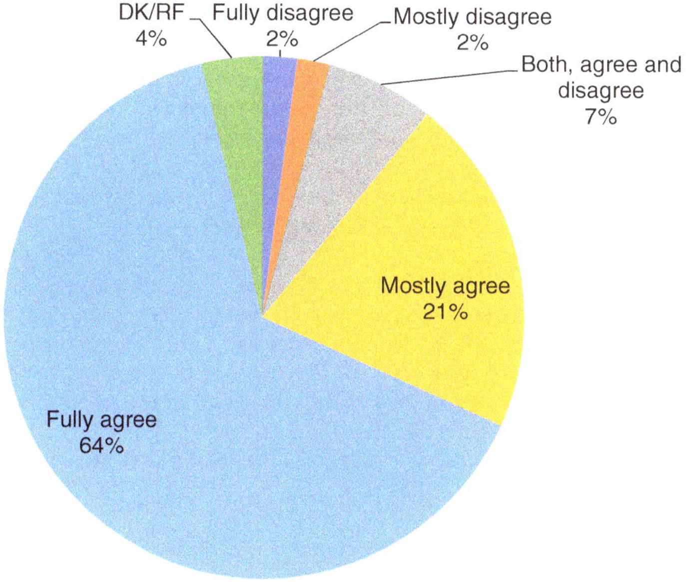

Fig. 3.1 Serbia needs to admit that it committed aggression against Croatia in order for relations to improve (Kolstø 2011)

Dinko: I think that Croatia led a defensive war and that there was no need to try some of our [generals]. Although it is possible to commit a war crime as a country in defence, again, I think the guilt should not have been equalised so much.

Marko: Given the number of killed Serb and Croat civilians, where we know that many more Croat civilians died and much more property was destroyed and cultural monuments and everything on the Croat side because this all took place on the territory of the Republic of Croatia. I think that, although more Serbs were tried, maybe many more should have been. Or at least this ratio should have been different. Maybe they should have focused on the worst or those most responsible, and here I mean mainly the leadership of the previous state, the leadership of Serbia, the leadership of the RSK, and of course then also some of our Croatian generals who were responsible. In this way they instead started a great number of cases that created a sense of suspicion in the *narod* that maybe they were trying to equalise the aggressor and the victim.

Dinko agrees.

Andriana: Yes.

Dinko: Especially after the first judgment to Gotovina, of 24 years, because of that and because of this joint criminal enterprise and such things.

Marko: And let us look the excessive artillery shelling of Knin, which firstly was not shelled, it was attacked with rockets, and secondly, it was damaged far less and attacked less than any other Croatian city that was close to the front line (focus group with Zadar teachers).

-

Blanka: It was not [a civil war], it was a war, an aggression against Croatia and Croatia defended itself. If someone is killing me then I will not accept that it was a civil war. No one from Croatia went to Serbia.

Jasna: Vučić held fiery speeches with Šešelj about how the Croats should be destroyed, and today he is the Prime Minister of the Serbian government.

Blanka: I am too emotional, it is better if I do not speak (focus group with non-urban war veterans Banovina).

-

Silvio: For Croatia it was a true defensive war against the neighbouring *narod* who was not allowing us our freedom and who wanted to conquer us militarily, subdue us and force us to stay in the failed state of Yugoslavia (interview with non-urban teacher).

These passages highlight the complex narratives interwoven in the theme of self-defence. The Zadar teachers begin with the admission that crimes were possible in the context of a defensive war, but then throughout the passage go on to compare numbers of victims and damage between the Serb and Croat sides (without mentioning actual figures), thereby accusing transitional justice authorities of attempting to equalise guilt. They end the sequence by stating that Knin was not attacked by artillery, but by rockets. The cumulative effect is that by comparing levels of suffering and citing possible technicalities over how the destruction of Knin came to happen, they minimise notions of Serb victimhood and suffering, which was proven by investigators and trials. The non-urban war veterans group, on the other hand, highlights how this narrative of suffering (on both sides) is always followed by the caveat of "the other" as the aggressor or initiator of violence holding a larger share of the blame. Moreover, the passage also highlights how this narrative is laced with emotion.

The concept is intrinsically attached to related themes, such as Serbian aggression, Croatia never attacking Serbia and no one wanting the war. The self-defence argument is also related to more abstract topics and worries, such as the fear of an equalisation of guilt, to war crimes trials, to the failing Yugoslav state and even to a war of the *narods*. There was, however, no agreement over whether the conflict was seen as ethnic or political, since there was no consensus over if the *narod* or the state was attacked. Teachers, who disagreed with other target segments on topics, were equally vociferous in their agreement that Croatia was attacked. Great importance was attributed to the label "defensive" in describing the war. In Zadar, war veterans lamented that the Homeland War is not a good name for the conflict, "because it has to be called defensive" (focus group with Zadar war veterans). An equal amount of importance was attached to the conflict not being labelled a civil war or an armed conflict. Highly emotional narratives regarding this theme did not follow legal logic, but rather a folk theory of law (discussed in more detail in the following chapter) that helped justify the foundation of the Croatian state. Croatia is also seen, in accordance with the Declaration on the Homeland War, as not wanting a war and therefore having no part in starting it.

The notion of defence in the eyes of the Croatian public has implications for transitional justice since it makes it hard for any narratives, other than the war narrative, to exist in the discursive space. The everyday narrative of defence poses a barrier to understandings of justice imposed from above, and attributes blame wholly to one side of the conflict, further endangering any prospects for reconciliation in society. The fact that Croatia did not start the war is supported by the widely held belief that Croatia was unarmed, unprepared and unorganised in the lead-up and early phases of the conflict. Imagery of struggle and survival related to these themes creates the backbone of the narrative of Croatian defence and victimhood, on the one hand, and Greater Serbian aggression, on the other. Again, this was expressed strongly across all target segments and locations. References to being "barehanded" and "barefoot" were common with war veterans' groups in particular. This was often juxtaposed with the Serb or *JNA* side, which was considered far more prepared:

> *Ana*: The war was forced on us, we met it unprepared, barefoot, without weapons. I went to war in sneakers (focus group with Sisak war veterans).
>
> -
>
> *Eva*: We had nothing to defend ourselves with at the beginning.
> *Lara*: We had to buy our own weapons. I bought myself a pistol and a rifle, all by myself.
> *Eva*: That is because the Yugo-army took all of the munitions, weapons, down to the smallest bullet and to airplanes, with them (focus group with Zadar war veterans).

Serbs here are seen as scheming and conniving, as opposed to the innocent and unprepared Croats. The Zadar war veterans also highlighted that this unpreparedness was starker in the case of women, who "had not finished regular army training, who did not know how to hold a rifle" (follow-up interview with Zadar war veteran). Teachers displayed this narrative, but often analysed it through the arms embargo placed on Croatia at the time. For example, the Sisak teachers agreed in their belief that it was not possible that Knin was destroyed during Operation Storm as much as had been claimed, since "as the professors say, no one knows where they could have found so much ammunition and artillery to fire, because there was none at [the Croatian army's] disposal. In order to even begin a counter-attack, they had to first conquer weapons depots. For the army to even function properly, given an embargo was placed on the sale of weapons to the Republic of Croatia" (focus group with Sisak teachers). Unpreparedness was attributed to the unforeseen start of the conflict, which surprised Croats but which Serbs were prepared for.

This feeling of the unorganised and unprepared defence was frequently brought up as a mitigating circumstance in discussions, but it is also present in court rulings and arguments, such as the Mirko Norac ruling and in the Tihomir Blaškić defence closing arguments. In more extreme instances, it is used to explain the reasoning behind crimes committed against civilians, sometimes even partially excusing them. The image of barehanded defence also frequently involved references to how young the Croatian soldiers were, creating an image of a young, baby-like Croatian army pitted against the well-armed, professional *JNA*, "You know that we did not really have our own army in 1991. These young boys went there naked and barefoot. In sneakers and jeans. We had to cloth them, knit gloves for them. I have this information first-hand" (focus group with Zagreb pensioners). These points of view also help explain (together with many others) why most Croats do not feel there was an organised effort by Croatian authorities to expel Serbs from Croatia, since the war was led in such an unorganised fashion. Indicative of this are the results of the Belgrade Centre for Human Rights (2011) survey, which found that 63% of the Croatian public did not think there was such an effort, as opposed to 26% who think there was.

There was consensus across groups that Croatia could not have committed any aggression, since Croatia did not go to Serbia, but rather that "they came here". It was not enough to state that Croatia was attacked, but a comparison was made that Croatia did not attack at all:

Stjepan: Did we destroy their state? We were not there. We did not even burn a house there, nor did we kill anyone. But they destroyed everything here.
Goran: We killed them here when they came.
Stjepan: They are guilty for everything that was destroyed. The factories and everything (focus group with non-urban pensioners).

-

Marijan: I do know this: that our Croatian armed forces did not go into Serbia (interview with Zagreb pensioner).

For the most part, the *JNA* or "Serbs" are referred to as the aggressors, meaning a certain type of military formation. Across all groups, there was, however, also mention of Serb civilian involvement in the fighting, which was not considered to be the case for Croats. This built an image of honest defence versus conniving aggression. The image of honest defence was further based on the premise that Croats only attacked individuals who had weapons in their hands or posed a direct threat to Croatian soldiers. These arguments often excused alleged war crimes:

> *Josip*: If the circumstances and facts from the time were realistically evaluated, I think there would not have been cause to prosecute Mirko Norac for war crimes. Norac, as one of the people in charge of Croatian formations in Lika, where he is also from, did not lead any actions against people who did not have weapons in their hands. They had weapons in their hands.
>
> *Dalibor*: That is right.
>
> *Josip*: He led operations against Serbs who took weapons in their hands and fought against their own homeland, against her government and her citizens, Croats (dyad with non-urban war veterans Slavonia).

Key to this was the notion, prevalent across all groups interviewed, that Serb civilians frequently and historically carried arms, which they used against the Croatian army in the Homeland War. In other words, the Serbs as a group are seen as aggressive and armed for the purposes of attacking Croats or achieving Greater Serbian goals:

> *Silvio*: War is a very unfortunate situation. I have never been, but from what I know, it is hard to stay sane in such a situation, especially since it has historically been proven that among the Serb population it is often hard to tell who is a soldier and who is a civilian. Civilians often armed themselves, even women, even older women. If a scout passes by, a certain military unit, through a village where there is no fighting, and a civilian, even an old lady, there were such stories, takes out a bomb or a pistol and starts to act militarily—what can you as a soldier, surrounded by gunpowder, blood and smoke, do except to eliminate the threat? But then, when a reporter, some agency or the UNPROFOR arrives and sees the situation and sees the dead old lady on the ground, not being aware of what happened, of course their conclusion can be that a war crime occurred (interview with non-urban teacher).

The above passage employs a particularly common and powerful image of armed Serb civilians, often used to justify alleged war crimes during Operation Storm, the *baka* (grandmother) with a rifle:

Mario: Of course we know what a war crime is, but as you can imagine yourself, maybe you heard some stories, of what actually happened in the field, what kind of unbelievable situations.
Maja: Yes. You have certainly had the opportunity to hear these.
Mario: Yes. On some battlefields you had the case—a *baka* shoots at you and kills your friend, your fellow fighter.
Maja: Yes. These are the most common examples.
Mario: And now, of course someone shot the *baka*. Now people come and see—the dead *baka*. This is just a trivial example.
Maja: But one of many (dyad with Zagreb teachers).

Given the general belief that Serb civilians bore arms against the Croatian army, it is not surprising to see certain (often based on legal verdicts) war crimes being questioned by the general public, but especially by more extreme elements, including war veterans. In group discussions with all war veterans and some pensioners, this led to a questioning of well-known cases such as those of Norac, Glavaš, Gotovina and Merčep, among others. It comes as no surprise then that numerous respondents, and much of the Croatian public, see military operations such as Operation Storm (an organised military action) as legitimate retaking of Croatian land and that collateral damage (civilian or otherwise) was natural, given the nature of the aggressor. Moreover, some individuals even saw the case of the Zec family (an incident involving paramilitaries, unrelated to any military goal) as justified or at the very least unexplained. The consequences for transitional justice are profound since the rule of law was not given much priority in these situations in relation to the aims of the war.

Victimisation (Croatia as a victim of aggressive Serbian politics) was primarily centred around several national symbols, such as Vukovar and Dubrovnik, as well as a range of smaller ones particular to regions. Vukovar, however, is the nationally dominant symbol; central to the war narrative; and one that has the single greatest capability to raise tensions between the states of Croatia and Serbia, between these two ethnicities in Croatia and between various political parties and actors.[6] Proof of this was the crisis with Cyrillic that was ongoing at the time and which was frequently used to discuss how and why Vukovar is special in Croatia. In many ways, the concept of Croatian victimhood is defined by the image of Vukovar as the "heroic, victim city". It was discussed as such across all of the groups and was frequently used as a reference point in related narratives:

Vlasta: Has anyone from the Serbian side apologised?

Mladen and Marijan: Tadić apologised.

Vlasta: Please, this is not an apology. He said "I am sorry" if I remember correctly, he said "I am sorry that Vukovar suffered". He did not say what it suffered from.

Marijan: No, he apologised.

Vlasta: No! This is not an apology! He said he was sorry for the victims of Vukovar, but he did not admit the mistake. He did not say which victims. Vukovar was not hit by an earthquake. Or a flood. This is not an apology.

Ante: And what was Tadić doing during the war?

Vlasta: I do not know what he was doing.

Ante: So how can he apologise for something that he did not do?

Mladen: He represented Serbia.

Vlasta: He was in Vukovar as the President of Serbia, but he did not admit their fault.

Ante: How did he not?

Vlasta: He did not say "we attacked Croatia, I am sorry, Vukovar suffered due to Serbian politics". Croatian victims today want an apology.

Mladen: I look at it this way. This is my personal impression. That Tadić is honest and that he would like to apologise. But he has Serbian politics he needs to lobby with and the electorate there and so on. So he cannot do what we want him to do.

Marijan: I understood him to have apologised. To have said he was sorry.

Vlasta: Do you know how many people died in Croatia? And it is difficult for him.

Mladen: Of course.

Vlasta: 20,000 people died in the Homeland War.

Mladen: It is horrific. And in Vukovar they watch criminals walk down the street.

Vlasta: Could he not have said that it was their mistake and to apologise. He did not have to say that it was his fault, but that it was the fault of Milošević's aggressive politics. He could have said that.

Ante: Who sent [Milošević] to The Hauge?

Mladen: That is what I wanted to say, that ultimately the Serbs sent him to The Hague.

Vlasta: Well alright, they sent him. They had to.

Ante: What more do you want!

Marijan: Do not argue, we are just talking.

Vlasta: You are defending Milošević and Serbian aggression (focus group with Zagreb pensioners)!

In this long exchange, Vukovar is used as the example of Croatian suffering, but the passage highlights many more dynamics at play in the narrative. Serbian politics is seen as continuous from the Milošević regime to the current one, and Vlasta condemned the others for defending this new regime, since they therefore also defended the old one. How they viewed politics today was judged based on how they viewed the past. Moreover, as the discussion became more heated, Vlasta used Croatian victimhood and suffering, expressed using casualty figures, to highlight the legacy of Serb aggression, thereby also preventing any further debate, although only momentarily. It briefly stopped the discussion as participants individually acknowledged the suffering, highlighting the powerful impact of such a symbol in exchanges.

For teachers, Vukovar was over and over again used as an example of how difficult it is to teach the Homeland War in class, due to the complicated nature of the Homeland War narrative and, in particular, Vukovar. The Zagreb teachers quoted above prior to the start of the formal discussion lamented how they could not teach about Vukovar since they found it hard to be objective, since the subject was too emotional for them, despite students asking for more material on it. Another Zagreb teacher claimed it was too politically fraught and that she feared how parents would react. Teachers across all groups agreed that ultimately children seem to be gaining this knowledge from their close family, more than school, which generally focused more on the Second World War. This shows a highly emotional and personal connection with the war narrative, which can be hard to undermine by competing narratives.

The War Is Not Over

The final element of the war narrative is a perception that the Homeland War somehow continues. This was most common among war veterans, but it was expressed in different ways among all of the groups. At the most basic level, this is the feeling that tensions remain present, while on the more extreme end it is the idea that what the Serbs "did not manage to do with weapons and the task the *JNA* did not complete, will be won at the negotiating table" (dyad with non-urban war veterans Slavonia). This sentiment is also reproduced at the elite level, most famously by prominent HDZ politician Vladimir Šeks, who stated that the Homeland War continues with the battle for the interpretation of the war (Jović 2017: 28). The development in this part of the war narrative is linked to the militarisation of Croatian society since 2013 and the concurrent glorification of the war (ibid.: 333). Calls for compulsory military service and the introduction of military parades are examples of this. It is also expressed in how war veterans perceive Croatian international relations: in an ongoing border dispute with Slovenia, war veterans called for the "defence of our borders" (Vučković 2018) and threatened to organise their own fleet of boats to protect the Croatian border (Index.hr 2018). In focus groups, participants referred to notions that Serbs would still readily kill Croats; that calls for hatred remained prevalent; that Croatia is somehow still being disadvantaged economically; that the war had not stopped (especially in Vukovar); or that the war had turned into a phase of attrition:

Lucija: Listen, I am not a historian. I have not completed any great schools, but I tell you, what has started in Vukovar will spread to all of Croatia.
Sara: If they start to rape.
Lucija: Let me ask you, in what state is there another state? And our government has allowed the Republic of Serbia. In a state you have another state. In which state? In England would they allow another state (focus group with Sisak war veterans)?

-

Dinko: What is happening now is that Croatia is attacking Serbia over Šešelj, and Serbia is attacking Croatia over Cyrillic, because it cannot keep ten signs safe. Tensions are being kept high (focus group with Zadar teachers).

-

Alen: I, as a journalist, call this a permanent ideological civil war. There is no shooting, there are no bombs being put in theatres. It is not like Dublin in Ireland, or like Belfast or Spain. However, here this kind of war continues for 40 years. And in certain phases it becomes very intense. And this is a fact in Croatia. Everyone knows this (focus group with Zagreb war veterans).

The Sisak war veterans use graphic terminology, such as "rape", to liken Cyrillic signs in Vukovar to the cities secession from Croatia and to conquest by Serbia. Especially with war veterans and pensioners, just like in discussions about Croatian government institutions and the media, much of this is attributed to a kind of infiltration of the system by unwanted elements (teachers did not express this attitude). The Zadar pensioners below saw the Croatian state as failing them to the extent that they saw it as an affront against Croatian independence. This led to an impression among the two older target segments that war will come again and could do so at any time:

> *Ilija*: It is important for us to say what we think of our neighbours, the Serbs, how we now view them. In no way and never will we once again look at each other the same. Even if we lived another 100 years. They will come again. They said that even our great-grandchildren will fall victim to the Serbs.
>
> *Vladimir*: They teach that. But we do not. Our future generations will not hate. They are vengeful. If there is a war, they will attack.
>
> *Goran*: They are vengeful. If there is a war, they will attack. If they cannot fight with anyone, they will fight between themselves.
>
> *Stjepan*: People take this hatred and animosity from generation to generation. From old Yugoslavia, to the Second World War to now (focus group with non-urban pensioners).

The last passage is quite striking, considering the community where the group took place was not on the frontline (although it was slightly hit by the war) and was not ethnically mixed. It did, however, see Serbs as intrinsically aggressive due to historical interpretations of the Second World War. It is possible that homogenous communities have more extreme views since they have so little interaction with the other ethnicity, but the strength of the stance is nevertheless surprising. It is also possible that older generations fear the Croatian state may disappear, since their lived experience is one of the states disappearing. Those who lived through the Second World War would have witnessed the dissolution of three states.

The fears present among pensioners and war veterans are best described by a Zadar war veteran, "Greater Serbia is an idea that lives and will continue to live in many Serbs and generations after us" (focus group with Zadar war veterans). The idea of "Greater Serbia" is considered a key element of Serbian aggression as much as it is seen as proof of future aggression or the conflict not being over, but instead continuing in a different sphere. In many Croatian eyes, the concept is one of a Serbian state continuously looking to aggressively expand across its borders; this perceived continuity in Serbian foreign policy helps explain both previous acts of aggression and contemporary actions. Additionally, the distinction made between the savage and aggressive Serbs and the victimised Croats helps perpetuate the difference between the two states. This is also used to justify the separation of the states, and thereby the war, as well as the fact that it was not a civil war. This makes the war narrative particularly detrimental to certain aspects of reconciliation since so many events are interpreted as attacks on Croatia.

How the War Narrative Is Reproduced

The reproduction of the war narrative involves two distinct features, other than the categories described above: the first is a preoccupation with numbers, and the second is a personal and local manner of speaking about events. This is important for expressivist efforts in transitional justice because such efforts need to be able to connect with already present narratives. If they fail to do so, they may be ignored or misunderstood completely. This means that it is important to consider where to speak to people (everyday narratives versus top-down narratives) and how to speak to people (in this case, to use numbers or not).

Various sets of figures or statistics were frequently used in group discussions and interviews to prove points to the moderator or to other participants. For instance, during a heated discussion about the number of Croatians indicted for war crimes in the Zagreb pensioners groups, one participant shouted at the other, "Do not speak off the top of your head! You have to use data" (focus group with Zagreb pensioners). The same participant then later frequently repeated that 600 *branitelji* are being tried in Croatia, using it as proof of their superior knowledge. Numbers were often seen as important in many of the other groups and were used as definitive proof of one point or another. A Zagreb war veteran, for example, claimed, "Up until 1995, 10,000 Croatian soldiers have been convicted in military courts of the Croatian Army for minor or major offences. I will not go into the details of whether these convictions included war crimes, and how many if so, but they did happen" (focus group with Zagreb war veterans). The main numbers cited during discussions were the number of dead (Croatian military personnel or civilians) and the number of war veterans, although there was no consensus over numbers, which many participants felt was the crux of the problem:

> *Lana*: Today in Croatia we do not have, after all this time, the exact number of dead Croatian *branitelji*. We have some partial figures. [The Ministry of War Veterans' Affairs] use some number of 7000 dead *branitelji*. There is a great epidemic among the *branitelji*, 29,000 people have already died. We ask ourselves, we really ask ourselves, I will say it out loud, what was this ammunition irradiated with (focus group with Zadar war veterans)?

The above passage was typical of the narrative found in the war veterans' groups since it used figures to justify conspiracy theories (over which there was no consensus across groups) and it saw a general disagreement with officially provided figures. There is no official number of dead that has ever been published or agreed on, which helps feed this narrative, but also leads to the general notion that if anything is known, it is that the number of dead is unknown. Generally, there was a worry that numbers were being manipulated, for any range of reasons, especially among war veterans. All of the war veterans' discussions involved a large deal of citing numbers and data to support arguments:

> *Blanka*: In the region of Petrinja 128 Croatian *branitelji* from Petrinja died, 134 from other parts of Croatia. More than 350 civilians were killed, and there are 21 Croatian *branitelji* listed as missing and 74 civilian victims (focus group with non-urban war veterans Banovina).

This last passage is a good example of how numbers are often used to compare Croatian suffering to Serbian suffering. Despite the disagreement over total figures and the acknowledgement that numbers are being manipulated by various sources, figures of Serbian casualties were rarely mentioned. Comparisons were, therefore, made between the number of Croatian victims and anecdotal stories of Serbian victims. Numbers can be problematic on a different level as well; if a more precise figure can be found, it can be used to verify one side's narrative over another, triggering defensive reactions in the counterpart.

During the course of the focus group discussions and interviews, it also became apparent that participants across all of the groups discussed the Homeland War in a personal and local way. This was particularly common among the war veterans' groups, which often also contained numerous direct victims of the war. Respondents in these groups, therefore, frequently jumped to personal stories. Survey data also show that the public seem to identify quite strongly with their city, village and county, slightly more so than they do with Croatia (Kolstø 2011). Schäuble (2014: 167), in her anthropological fieldwork in Sinj, found that people there connected more to local traditions, grounded in everyday experience, than to nation state efforts to represent particular versions of history.

A personal and local way of speaking about the war became particularly evident when groups discussed their understanding of the war, war crimes trials and the conflict in Bosnia. It was common for war veterans to claim they had a good understanding of the war since they had "felt the war on their own skin" and had "seen it first-hand". This sentiment, however, was present across most of the other groups as well. One teacher proclaimed that they did "live through that time after all" (dyad with Zagreb teachers). The question "Do you think you have a good understanding of the Homeland War?" led to similarly personal responses with teachers and with pensioners. This was sometimes referred to in terms of personal experience, whereas others referred to it in terms of the personal experience of others they had spoken to. For example:

> *Mario*: I personally think I do. Not only from written sources, but also from my conversations with people. When I put all of that together then I think I have a fairly complete picture (dyad with Zagreb teachers).

-

> *Davor*: About its general characteristics, from people who experience it as such. I can only say what I saw and what I experienced (dyad with Sisak pensioners).

Interestingly, respondents were often aware that their own understanding could be subjective since they were "participants". Responses were often also accompanied by references to local events or locations, especially in locations on or close to the frontline. In Sisak in particular, such responses were commonplace:

> *Mario*: It depends on the segment. For example, concerning the beginning of the Homeland War in the Sisak area. The constructions, the armament, here I am on my stomping ground. With regard to reported facts, I do not know anything (focus group with Sisak teachers).

Respondents in Zagreb discussed the war on a personal level as much as those in other locations, despite this being the location that saw the smallest amount of violence. The excerpt below is a typical example of this:

[Discussing sources of information on the war]

> *Mario*: I think, as I said at the start, that those sources that are available together with the experience, since we lived through those days.
>
> Maja agrees.

Mario: I just started high school.
Maja: As did I.
Mario: So you remember it all. And with later chats with people, participants. So a written source is not even necessary (dyad with Zagreb teachers).

In Sisak on the other hand, discussions frequently referred to how INA and the local refinery fared during the war. The personal and local understanding of the war is also transposed to interpretations of war crimes trials, be they international or domestic, and the view of crimes during the conflict in general. Among war veterans and victims, as well as the rest of the public, there is a distinct disappointment with the ICTY and war crimes trials in general (which has been shown in survey research. See: Pavlaković 2014), but little is said about how such disappointment is always related to local incidents.

Moderator: Have there been enough judicial processes for the breaking of humanitarian laws during the war?
Lucija: I don't know how much you know about Sunja, about these parts here. There was also massive artillery fire here, all kinds of stuff happened, every day at least 1000 artillery shells fell, how many people died. No one has been punished for that. Everyone talks about Dubrovnik etc. All these cities experienced the same as us (focus group with Sisak war veterans).

Such a local narrative makes the potential educational effects of transitional justice questionable. All of the above results, however, do not account for the fact that opinions and attitudes could be influenced from a variety of sources. More importantly, what it does show is the difficult and complex environment such efforts have to work in. Overall, the consequence of this is that narratives (re)produced close to home become more powerful than narratives produced further afield and references to everyday life give them additional credibility. Top-down narratives, such as the justice one, struggle to compete with such bottom-up narratives since the everyday worldview is so strongly associated with what respondents' viewed as the truth.

Conclusion

The 1991–1995 conflict is seen as one of self-defence against an aggressor. This opinion is nearly universally accepted (85% agree to a lesser or greater extent, while only 4% disagree; Kolstø 2011). No single participant disagreed with this notion in group discussions and interviews. Moreover, the idea of defence was expressed in every other mention of the war and was constantly brought up in discussions. This part of the narrative was built on personal and local experiences (e.g. participants frequently referred to local, rather than national events, as proof), and consequently, Croatia is seen by nearly all of the public as not having any part in starting the war and, therefore, bearing no guilt. This theme provides a basis for all other parts of the war narrative.

Survival and struggle form another cornerstone of the war narrative, as Croatia is seen as being unarmed, unprepared and unorganised for the required defence. Each target segment highlighted this in their own manner; for example, teachers discussed the arms embargo placed on Croatia, pensioners discussed their own experiences of having no weapons, and women's war veterans' groups discussed the lack of training women had for war. Again, this was discussed in personal and local terms. The surprising nature of the conflict for Croatia was also seen as explaining why Croatia could not have planned any crimes, since they did not have the time or the means to do so. This is further supported by (and may help explain) survey evidence that Croats do not feel there was an organised effort to expel Serbs from the country. Unpreparedness was used as a mitigating circumstance in many discussions of potential war crimes, which has direct implications on how verdicts in trials are accepted in the country.

It was common to hear, across all groups, that Croatia did not go to Serbia; rather, that "they" (Serbia, *JNA*, the Serbs, the Chetniks and so on) came "here". Aggression was, in some cases, seen as a war crime in and of itself. This is relevant to transitional justice because aggressors are seen as composing a whole, or a large part, of the Serb minority in Croatia. This involved the powerful image of the *baka* with a rifle, representing the notion of armed Serb civilians attacking Croatian soldiers, thereby justifying potential Croatian crimes against Serb civilians.

This apologetic attitude towards war crimes is also present in the narrative of victimisation, another central part of the war narrative. Croatian victimhood is built around several focal points, chief among which is Vukovar. It is seen as representing the whole Croatian struggle, both during the war and today (in terms of ethnic tensions and political manipulation). Vukovar was discussed across all groups as what could have happened anywhere in Croatia, had the aggressor won. It was also seen as exemplifying ICTY ineptness and was frequently cited as the biggest war crime in Croatia. Teachers cited Vukovar as an example of how difficult it was to teach the Homeland War to students, and all target segments saw this notion of victimhood as a further mitigating circumstance in committed crimes, since they were often committed as revenge by victims of Serbian aggression.

Finally, there was a feeling among many participants that the war is not over, that it is continuing and that the Greater Serbian plan still exists. This notion was present in different ways with different groups, but it was always somehow highlighted. War veterans saw a continuation of the war "on the negotiating table"; pensioners (and war veterans) saw an infiltration of the system and a generally aggressive standing by Serbs and Serbia; and teachers highlighted general tensions present between neighbouring ethnicities and states (they did not, however, see this as an overt continuation of the war). More generally, there are unresolved issues that all participants attached an immense amount of importance to: missing persons, criminals walking freely close to victims, leftover mines and so on. There is also a clear generational difference here, since the two older segments (pensioners and war veterans) held more extreme views in this regard compared to teachers. This has the potential to continue perpetuating the war narrative by calling for a continuous defence against aggression, be it overt or covert.

All aspects of the war narrative are reproduced through the frequent use of numbers, as well as personal and local experiences. This means that any efforts to influence the overall narrative would have to engage with these. In other words, this could involve producing some kind of generally accepted figures (e.g. the number of dead) and dealing with narratives on a local, not just a national, level. Such attempts are not only highly complex but also hampered by local resistance to change.

One of the most striking aspects of the war narrative during focus group discussions was its sheer universality.[7] All groups and respondents wholly agreed on its interpretations of defence and Croatian struggle for survival. All groups discussed the conflict in exactly the same manner. War veterans, in particular, expressed total unanimity of opinions across all interviewed groups. They all followed a script that argued, in addition to the above, that Serbian aggression could not be questioned, that Yugoslavia was criminal, that Vukovar was the symbol of Croatian suffering, that the war was not over, and that Croatian involvement in Bosnia was positive. Teachers and pensioners generally agreed with war veterans on most of these points, but did feature debate on these topics. Teachers questioned continued tensions, generally felt these were not a continuation of aggression and debated Croatia's role in Bosnia. Pensioners also deliberated, but what the comparison highlights is how much the Zagreb pensioners and the Sisak teachers stand out from their counterparts in the rest of Croatia. The Sisak teachers, a small city that was on the frontline during the war, expressed the war narrative in similar terms to the war veterans. This may be because the strength of everyday narratives, such as the war narrative, is particularly strong in smaller localities. This may also explain why the Zagreb pensioners show such different opinions, since the influence of everyday narratives is weaker in a larger city, although it is not possible to generalise with such data (Fig. 3.2).

The justice narrative competes and interacts with the war narrative, but the war narrative's strength makes it difficult for the justice narrative

		Unanimity across groups			Some debate among groups (up to 4 groups)		Debate across many groups (over 4 groups)		
	Aspect of war narrative	*Self-defence*	*Survival and struggle*	*Local and personal (yes/no)*	*Vukovar (are elements questioned? Yes/no)*	*Aggression (any debate over if it was only Serbian or if it is a war crime)*	*Yugoslavia criminal; Milosevic criminal; or both views present*	*War not over (yes/no)*	*Croatian involvement in Bosnia had negative elements (yes/no)*
Teachers	Zagreb	Agree	Agree	Yes	**Yes**	**Some debate**	**Both**	**No**	**Yes**
	Zadar	Agree	Agree	Yes	No	**Some debate**	Milosevic criminal	**No**	**Yes**
	Sisak	Agree	Agree	Yes	No	No debate	Yugoslavia criminal	**No**	No
	Non-urban	Agree	Agree	Yes	**Yes**	**Some debate**	**Both**	**No**	**Yes**
War veterans	Zagreb	Agree	Agree	Yes	No	No debate	Yugoslavia criminal	Yes	No
	Zadar	Agree	Agree	Yes	No	No debate	Yugoslavia criminal	Yes	No
	Sisak	Agree	Agree	Yes	No	No debate	Yugoslavia criminal	Yes	No
	Non-urban Banovina	Agree	Agree	Yes	No	No debate	Yugoslavia criminal	Yes	No
	Non-urban Slavonia	Agree	Agree	Yes	No	No debate	Yugoslavia criminal	Yes	No
Pensioners	Zagreb	Agree	Agree	Yes	**Yes**	**Some debate**	**Both**	**No**	Yes
	Zadar	Agree	Agree	Yes	No	No debate	Yugoslavia criminal	Yes	**No**
	Sisak	Agree	Agree	Yes	No	No debate	Milosevic criminal	**No**	**Yes**
	Non-urban	Agree	Agree	Yes	No	No debate	**Both**	Yes	No

Fig. 3.2 Overview of debates surrounding the war narrative (bold text denotes debated counter to war narrative)

to take hold in Croatia and, consequently, for the trickle-down effects of human rights norms to occur. Emotional notions of defence and victimhood, as well as the local and personal discussion of the conflict, make it difficult for other narratives to undermine the predominant understanding of the conflict. Perceptions of Serbian aggression and the subsequent struggle for Croatian survival affect interpretations of the rule of law, thereby preventing the spread of rule of law norms (discussed in the following chapter). The feeling that the war is not over means that the present-day events are seen as a continuation of the aggression. Moreover, for some this is seen as an attempt to return to Yugoslavia, which is seen as a criminal entity. In other words, current and past events are being interpreted through the prism of the Homeland War. The issue of Bosnia encapsulates much of this debate, since even this conflict outside of the territory of the Republic of Croatia is being interpreted based on the understanding of the conflict in Croatia.

Even a small degree of deliberation, especially among the youngest of the target segments, points to how the justice narrative and the war narrative are interacting. They also point to some degree of success of the justice narrative to initiate debate within society. Respondents construct a context for understanding the past from a variety of perspectives, and the war narrative has an advantage over others being propagated from outside sources due to its everyday nature, which makes it much more trusted. In comparison, the justice narrative is far removed from the everyday since it is seen as coming from institutions based in The Hague or Zagreb. The effect is that transitional justice contestation of the war narrative can potentially discredit the process, rather than change narratives, because it can be interpreted as a continued attack on Croatia. The war narrative's dominance in the discursive space means that the Croatian public interpret a range of phenomena through the perspective of the Homeland War, the most significant of which are discussed in the subsequent chapters.

Notes

1. This concerns only the individuals on trial in this case (Ante Gotovina, Ivan Čermak and Mladen Markač). Other individuals implicated in the joint criminal enterprise died before any potential processes were held.
2. *Narod* can be taken to mean people or nation, defined in an ethnic sense. The word is composed of the root *rod*, from the verb *roditi*, to give birth (Hayden 1996: 791). By definition, this view of the people or the nation only encompasses those of a specific ethnicity. *Narod* was left in the original Croatian form in excerpts to highlight this.

3. Exceptions are certain NGOs, members of the ethnic Serb community (although the ones interviewed in this study did use it) and certain political parties.
4. The Croatian city of Vukovar, on the Serbian border in the northeast of the country, was the scene of an 87-day siege by the Yugoslav People's Army (*JNA*) and Serbian paramilitary forces in 1991. It was the most badly damaged Croatian city during the war and following its fall, a number of war crimes took place in and around it. Prior to the war, it was one of the most ethnically diverse parts of Croatia.
5. This ruling potentially undermined the Croatian interpretation of events, since it belittled Croatian victimhood; on the other hand, the dismissal of the Serbian claim to genocide reinforced the interpretation that Operation Storm was a legitimate military operation.
6. The study involved several individuals who were from Vukovar and had lost numerous family members and friends during the conflict.
7. The conflict in Bosnia and Herzegovina features in this table because it forms a part of the war narrative, but it is discussed in more detail in Chapter 8.

References

Ashplant, T. G., Dawson, G. L., & Roper, M. (2000). *The politics of war memory and commemoration*. London: Routledge.

Banjeglav, T. (2012). Conflicting memories, competing narratives and contested histories in Croatia's post-war commemorative practices. *Politička Misao, 49,* 7–31.

Bernhard, M. H., & Kubik, J. (2014). *Twenty years after communism: The politics of memory and commemoration*. Oxford: Oxford University Press.

Blanuša, B. (2017). Trauma and taboo: Forbidden political questions in Croatia. *Politička Misao, 54,* 170–196.

Ciper, T. (2012). Funkcija političkog mita. O koristi mitskog za demokraciju [The function of political myths. About the uses of myth for democracy]. *Anali hrvatskog politološkog društva*, *9*(1), 7–19.

Drumbl, M. A. (2007). *Atrocity, punishment and international law*. Cambridge: Cambridge University Press.

Eliade, M. (1963). *Myth and reality*. London: Allen & Unwin.

Hayden, R. M. (1996). Imagined communities and real victims: Self-determination and ethnic cleansing in Yugoslavia. *American Ethnologist, 23,* 783–801.

Index.hr. (2018). Veterani prijete: Dajemo Plenkoviću 72 sata da riješi problem sa Slovenijom ili ćemo mi [The veterans threaten: We give Plenković 72 hours to fix the problem with Slovenia of we will do it]. *Index.hr*. Available at http://www.index.hr/vijesti/clanak/veterani-prijete-dajemo-plenkovicu-72-sata-da-rijesi-problem-sa-slovenijom-ili-cemo-mi/1017251.aspx.

Jović, D. (2009). Croatia after Tudjman: The ICTY and issues of transitional justice. *Chaillot Paper, 116*, 13–27.

Jović, D. (2017) *Rat i mit: Politika identiteta u suvremenoj Hrvatskoj* [War and myth: The politics of identity in contemporary Croatia]. Zagreb: Fraktura.

Koren, S. (2011). "Korisna prošlost"? Ratovi devetesetih u deklaracijama hrvatskog sabora ["Useful past"? The wars of the ninites in the declarations of the Croatian Sabor]. In T. Cipek (Ed.), *Kultura sjećanja: 1991. Povijesni lomovi i svladanje prošlosti* [Culture of memory: 1991. Historical breaks and overcoming the past] (pp. 123–156). Zagreb: Disput.

Kolstø, P. l. (2011). *Strategies of symbolic nation-building in west Balkan states: Intents and results.* University of Oslo. Available at http://www.hf.uio.no/ilos/english/research/projects/nation-w-balkan/.

Linz, J. J. (1978). Crisis, breakdown, and reequalibration. In J. J. Linz & A. C. Stepan (Eds.), *The breakdown of democratic regimes* (pp. 1–97). Baltimore: The Johns Hopkins University Press.

Lutz, E., & Sikkink, S. (2001). The justice cascade: The evolution and impact of foreign human rights trails in Latin America. *Chicago Journal of International Law, 2*, 1–33.

MacDonald, D. B. (2002). *Balkan holocausts? Serbian and Croatian victim-centred propaganda and the war in Yugoslavia.* Manchester: Manchester University Press.

Narodne Novine. (2000). *Deklaracija o Domovinskom Ratu* [Declaration on the Homeland War]. Available at http://narodne-novine.nn.hr/clanci/sluzbeni/265079.html.

Narodne Novine. (2006). *Deklaracija o Oluji NN* [Declaration on Operation Storm]. Available at http://narodne-novine.nn.hr/clanci/sluzbeni/127530.html.

Osiel, M. (1998). *Mass atrocity, collective memory and the law.* New Brunswick: Transaction Publishers.

Osiel, M. (2009). *Making sense of mass atrocity.* Cambridge: Cambridge University Press.

Pavlaković, V. (2014). Fulfilling the thousand-year-old dream: Strategies of symbolic nation-building in Croatia. In P. Kolstø (Ed.), *Strategies of symbolic nation-building in south eastern Europe* (pp. 19–50). Farnham: Ashgate.

Peskin, V., & Boduszynski, M. (2003). International justice and domestic politics: Post-Tudjman Croatia and the international criminal tribunal for the former Yugoslavia. *Europe-Asia Studies, 55*, 1117–1142.

Ristić, K. (2014). *Imaginary trials: War crime trials and memory in former Yugoslavia.* Leipzig: Leipziger Universitätsverlag.

Sartori, G. (1976). *Parties and party systems: A framework for analysis*. Cambridge: Cambridge University Press.
Schäuble, M. (2014). *Narrating victimhood: Gender, religion and the making of place in post-war Croatia*. Oxford: Barghahn.
Vučković, S. (2018). Dišu kao jedan [They are breathing as one]. *Dnevno.hr*. Available at http://www.dnevno.hr/domovina/disu-kao-jedan-branitelji-slazemo-se-moramo-zastititi-nase-ribare-1113758/.
Zertal, I. (2005). *Israel's holocaust and the politics of nationhood*. Cambridge: Cambridge University Press.

CHAPTER 4

Understandings of Law in Croatia

The UN Secretary General's report on transitional justice in 2004 reflected its intrinsic connection to the rule of law by stating, "Justice, peace and democracy are not mutually exclusive objectives, but rather mutually reinforcing imperatives". The UN Security Council, when setting up the ICTY, was "Determined to put an end to such crimes and to take effective measures to bring to justice the persons who are responsible for them" and was "convinced that in the particular circumstances of the former Yugoslavia the establishment as an ad hoc measure by the Council of an international tribunal and the prosecution of persons responsible for serious violations of international humanitarian law would enable this aim to be achieved and would contribute to the restoration and maintenance of peace" (UNSC Report 827 1993). Broader aims of dispensing justice and achieving reconciliation in the region were secondary. Some scholarship also assumes that transitional justice is a necessary requirement for the establishment of the rule of law and that they reinforce each other (McAuliffe 2010; Teitel 2005), although the reality of the dynamic is far more complex. For example, if post-Second World War justice is considered to be transitional justice (it did deal with transition), then it did successfully consolidate regimes and democracy, but it did not necessarily establish the rule of law or implement it. Karsai (2000b) has argued that in the aftermath of the Second World War, when Hungarian leaders were faced with the inherent conflict between legal security and injustice, which forms the rule of law, they chose

I. Sokolić, *International Courts and Mass Atrocity*,
Memory Politics and Transitional Justice,
https://doi.org/10.1007/978-3-319-90841-0_4

unjust and inexpedient law, unless its conflict with justice was intolerably great (Karsai 2000a: 1). Drawing on the works of Gustav Radbruch (1946), they viewed the fundamental purpose of law as the creation of order and justice (Karsai 2000a: 2).

Crimes against humanity express the core rule of law norm and its inescapable protective reach (Teitel 2005: 853). Such offences may be committed anywhere and under any circumstances; they may, therefore, be subject to international adjudications and prosecution by any state as a matter of universal concern (Luban 2004). This concept has, however, been challenged. Controversies surrounding Article 98 of the ICC and Belgium's efforts at testing universal jurisdiction are both representative of this. Article 98 of the ICC has been challenged by the USA entering a number of bilateral agreements with the purpose of bypassing ICC jurisdiction over US nationals. It has also been challenged by Malawi and Chad in the arrest and surrender of Sudan's President Omar Al Bashir (Tladi 2012). Belgium passed a universal jurisdiction law in 1993 (expanded in 1999) that allowed it to hear cases concerning violations of humanitarian law, including genocide and other crimes against humanity, which happened anywhere, without any connection to Belgium. Again, this was challenged by the USA and Belgium had to give in to political pressure, which ended in the relinquishment of all elements of universality in the law (Panakova 2011).

Transitional justice aims to move society from instability towards stability, which includes adherence to human rights and general democratic principles, and this move involves the establishment of the rule of law (Sarkin 2015: 127). Both transitional justice and the rule of law aim to achieve peace and stability in the long-term and share similar short-term goals, consequently both deal with the establishment and strengthening of institutions (Sarkin 2015). This applies more to domestic initiatives than the ICTY, which has generally avoided claims that it is doing anything more than providing trials. Despite the numerous synergies between the two, the transitional justice process in many countries has often impeded what many would classify as the establishment of the rule of law (McAuliffe 2010: 129). It remains different to legal justice (especially when taking the form of show trials or political justice) because it is primarily symbolic (McAuliffe 2010: 135). Legal justice, on the other hand, has four distinct characteristics: the law applied must be clear and unambiguous; the independent judiciary must not be influenced by government; judges should be consistently unbiased in their interpretation of the law; and due process must be adhered to strictly (Elster 2004:

86; McAuliffe 2010: 129; Shklar 1964). Not adhering to one or more of these facets does not turn legal justice in political justice, but these facets are often ignored due to the necessities of transition (Elster 2004: 91). For example, adversarial trials can limit pedagogical effects and the potential for reconciliation (Stover 2005: 23). Such trials can also constrain domestic understandings of legality and lower credibility in judicial institutions (McAuliffe 2010: 154).

In Serbia, this has had two distinct outcomes. First, the rule of law developed via ICTY conditionality has led to limited development of a culture of law (Brodersen 2014). Second, the negative perception of the ICTY and domestic judiciaries has hampered diffuse support for these institutions (Hagan and Ivković 2006).[1] Using conditionality to establish the rule of law is problematic since, other than domestic and EU factors, it also depends on the performance of the ICTY (Brodersen 2014). Moreover, this process of subordinating justice to political institutions also empties law of its meaning, thereby eroding potential for reconciliation and stability (Subotic 2009). Unfortunately, the difficulties the institution experienced with victim interaction, lenient sentences, ambiguous decisions and contact with the region's publics meant that it struggled to spread a culture of law (Brodersen 2014: 27). Conditionality, among a range of factors, meant that it was seen as a tool of the international community to control the region and the ICTY never came to represent justice, limiting its potential to establish a rule of law norm (Brodersen 2014; Spoerri and Freyberg-Inan 2008). Despite administering fair trials, the ICTY therefore never managed to develop a significant culture of law, at least in Serbia (Brodersen 2014: 248).

The lack of diffuse support is based on the institution's poor image and inconsistencies interacting with the processes of localisation, where norms are contested (Hagan and Ivković 2006: 131). This is based on the notion that in situations where individuals feel they have an inability to influence structures of power around them, there is a greater risk of legal cynicism arising (Sampson and Bartusch 1998: 783). The great pessimism and distrust associated with the image of the ICTY in the former Yugoslavia meant that it was always going to struggle with its broader goals of democratisation and the establishment of the rule of law, as long as confidence in judicial independence was lacking (Hagan and Ivković 2006: 135). More broadly, legal prosecutions also came into conflict with political goals of the former Yugoslav states. Croatian leaders felt compelled to comply with EU conditionality, partly due to their own vision of Croatian identity as a Western and democratic state (Zambelli 2010: 1673). Its identity as a law-governed state depended on ICTY cooperation and the ability to try criminals domestically (Zambelli 2010).

The justice narrative in Croatia contained this inherent dynamic between the rule of law and transitional justice. As previously discussed, it also simultaneously interacts with everyday narratives and understandings of the war and the rule of law. The local dimensions of international justice, therefore, cannot be ignored (Slaughter 2004). The amount of atrocities committed in the former Yugoslavia, and the relatively short mandate of the ICTY (although it can be argued this is no longer so short) also required it to collaborate with local judicial institutions to properly address the crimes committed (Hagan and Ivković 2006: 51). The ICTY had to be aware of local norms, understandings and attitudes, since its legitimacy was dependent on working in synchronisation with them and thereby creating a balance between local, national and international preferences (Arendt 2006; Hagan and Ivković 2006: 81). Respondents in focus groups reflected this as they constructed a context for their understanding of crimes and trials out of a variety of perspectives. The result was that feelings of powerlessness, folk theories of law and general factual inaccuracies played large roles in shaping attitudes on law. Firstly, respondents felt powerless in a system that was unresponsive to their demands. Notions of corruption, inefficiency and dissatisfaction with government led to a general distrust of institutions, of which legal institutions, both domestic and international, were just one example. Secondly, folk theories of law played a large element in legal reasoning, since respondents would often claim "not to be lawyers", only to use that statement as a premise for developing an opinion that would be consistent with it. This enabled them to say statements that were not consistent with the law, which partly reflects that they are not lawyers, but it also illustrates a more important notion: that politics, law and emotion work in tandem to create a general understanding of the situation. In other words, individuals use several narratives to build a picture of their personal world. Finally, factual inaccuracies were common among respondents. These are quite common in the interview and focus group setting, but some of these idiosyncratic images, such as the grandmother (*baka*) with the rifle, have a broader implication because they also justify narratives. The image of the *baka* helps make the point that civilians were not innocent and consequently crimes against them are permitted.

A period of transition offers an opportunity for an actor's identity to be defined or redefined, thereby creating the space for new norms to be incorporated into the new identity (Zambelli 2010). It is, however, possible that the everyday reproduction of the war narrative makes it difficult for the justice narrative to take hold and for associated norms to spread. Attitudes and perceptions towards the rule of law, as well as general understandings of the law, remain warped in Croatian society. The result is that some people think that certain crimes are acceptable in specific situations. By drawing on interview, focus group and survey data, this chapter seeks to answer questions, such as: Are convicted war criminals (at domestic or international trials) considered heroes or criminals? Does the public believe war crimes can be committed in a defensive war? And, how important principles such as the rule of law, human rights, cooperation with the ICTY and punishment of war crimes, among others, are to the Croatian public? These norms were, for the most part, discussed as a part of broader discussions on the topics of war crimes, Croatian war crimes (and associated topics, such as ethnic cleansing and command responsibility) and trials at the ICTY or domestic tribunals. Discussions surrounding mechanisms of transitional justice, such as tribunals, make it possible to also draw conclusions on the effects of such mechanisms on attitudes, perceptions and norms. The chapter is divided into three sections. The first deals with the general understanding of war crimes among participants and the public. The second analyses perceptions of the ICTY, which is seen as inefficient, politically biased, but also necessary. The third section looks at domestic war crimes trials, which are seen in a similar light, as slow, unjust and biased.

Understanding War Crimes

Attempts at discussing the general definition of war crimes often led to discussions of war crimes committed by Croatian forces. Consequently, most of the discussions on war crimes focused on what war crimes are *not* rather than what they are. Throughout the focus groups, crimes during the war (real or hypothesised) were discussed in different categories: those that were war crimes; those that were war crimes but were understandable or forgivable; and those that were not war crimes at all (if they were crimes at all, then they were "ordinary" crimes).

The most common narrative, especially with war veterans and pensioners, fits into the latter two categories: forgivable war crimes and "ordinary" crimes. This was based on the premise that crimes of passion or revenge were not war crimes. It was present in nearly identical format across all war veterans' and pensioner groups, but not at all with the teachers. Moreover, they were usually highly emotionally loaded, and in one instance, a participant had to remove himself from the group while discussing the concept. The two excerpts below are particularly representative:

> *Stjepan*: A colleague once told me that he saw them kill his whole family. He should not have gone there. And later he did that. When they later returned, he also killed them all. As a kind of revenge.
> All agree
> *Stjepan*: He experienced a breakdown. He had no purpose in his life, he had nothing.
> *Ivana*: His only real goal was revenge (focus group with non-urban pensioners).
>
> -
>
> *Marija*: In war someone can commit a crime of passion. This a crime in war. Or in the situation, when someone for example in Vukovar lost five or ten family members, who were massacred. And he finds himself, as a man, in a different region, defending a different part of Croatia, and in a certain moment it can happen that a person he comes across there, and maybe this person is not even armed, but they provoke him. In that moment he is not conscious, he is controlled by emotions. If someone at a certain moment says 'We will repeat Ovčara!', and his family were all killed at Ovčara, he may shoot and kill the person. According to me, this is not a war crime. This is a crime in war.
> Tomislav agrees
> *Marija*: What was targeted, consciously, be it rape, murder, massacres, liquidation, destruction of culture, that is a war crime.
> Alen agrees (focus group with Zagreb war veterans).

These passages suggest a distinction between individual acts and acts carried out in response to policy or orders, thereby distinguishing crimes by individual soldiers that do not implicate the army, since the army did not order them. They also show an apologetic attitude towards crimes committed as crimes of revenge or passion and a broader tolerance of deviance. Since war crimes were discussed in relation to Croatian forces, they were consequently broadly discussed in the context of a defensive war. Again, a categorisation was present: on the one hand, war crimes were considered possible in a defensive war (but that these crimes were sporadic), and on the other hand, war crimes were not considered possible in the context (but individuals did commit "crimes in war"). Moreover, when respondents considered such crimes to be possible, they were relativised to crimes by other armies (especially the US military), thereby removing responsibility from the Croatian state:

Moderator: Is it possible to commit war crimes in a defensive war?
Stjepan: It is. Surely.
Ivana: That is also possible. But I do not think there was much of that.
Stjepan: But this could have only happened sporadically. For example, individuals.
Ivana agrees
Stjepan: In every army. If we compare it to America, they recently admitted abusing prisoners. Our ones also exist, but in a different way (focus groups with non-urban pensioners).

These results have been replicated in numerous longitudinal studies over the years. A 2001 survey found that a large majority of the public did not consider the Croatian army (74%) or volunteers (69%) responsible for war crimes (Caritas Croatia and the Franciscan Institute for the Culture 2001). A 2011 study found that 44.9% of respondents did not believe it was possible for Croatian forces to commit a war crime in a defensive war, versus 29.8% who did (Kolstø 2011). Focus group participants reflected this survey result: 48% did not think it was possible and 38% did.

In addition to self-defence and emotion, the unpreparedness of the Croatian armed forces also presented a mitigating circumstance in the eyes of participants. These were most strongly expressed by all of the war veterans' groups who held a clearly different opinion compared to the other target segments that war crimes are not possible in a defensive war. Comments such as this were common among those groups:

Josip: During those times I do not think it was possible to commit a war crime against anyone because there was no war being conducted or directed at the territory of another state, where we could have led a war in which we could have killed Serbs on their territories. We waged a war only on our territories and this was a purely defensive war where Croats fought a war for the defence of their homeland inside their own borders (dyad with non-urban war veterans Slavonia).

More specifically, war veterans' groups and pensioners who took part in the war acknowledged that crimes of some kind were possible on the battlefield. Again, this was qualified in the case of Croatian crimes as either extremely rare or a result of emotion:

Goran: When someone is running away and you shoot him, like a rabbit, this is a crime. You do not even want to take something from him, you just kill him. You do not know him, he is innocent. This is a war crime. But when there are battles, this is different. Look. People go crazy. This is easy to talk about to you who were not in the war.

(The participant struggles to continue, pauses and removes himself from the group; focus group with non-urban pensioners).

-

Alen: A war crime can be committed on the frontline. Even in direct fights it is possible. But I cannot remember a single case, I mean in terms of alleged Croatian crimes, that would fit into that category. In principle it is possible, but I do not know of a single case (focus group with Zagreb war veterans).

The pause in the non-urban pensioners group also highlights the PTSD, trauma and emotion that can be triggered by questioning these narratives. The pause, or what is missing in this sequence of dialogue, shows the traumatic nature of the war narrative and how hard it is for top-down narratives to change everyday narratives. Further discussions on this topic led to a variety of elaborations of what war crimes were, but often with qualifications that the participants were not trained in law, which seemed to be viewed as a necessity in understanding the trials. This may be indicative of a failure of the ICTY Outreach Programme to make the institution more approachable to the publics in the target region. Equally, however, it may be a method for the publics to avoid dealing with ICTY rulings. Evidence for both was present in discussions:

Ana: They have their own lawyers, legal experts, a whole team working for them, with an insight into their business.

Lucija: We are just mere mortals (focus group with Sisak war veterans).

-

Dinko: I would, however, add, that I and Marko do not understand legal things much, we are not lawyers (focus group with Zadar teachers).

There was consensus across all groups, in one form or another, that international law or the Geneva Conventions defined war crimes. Among a long list of examples was the knowledge that medical personnel are protected under the Geneva Conventions (focus group with non-urban war veterans Banovina); that prisoners of war have special rights (focus group with non-urban pensioners); that these conventions were taught to officers in Yugoslavia (focus group with Sisak pensioners); that international human rights constituted a universal standard of some kind (focus group with Zadar teachers and dyad with Zagreb teachers); at the very least that some kind of broader international conventions existed (dyad with non-urban teachers); and in a minor example of dissent that the Geneva Conventions were still valid although The Hague's interpretation of them was incorrect (focus group with Zagreb war veterans). These often led to folk theories of law creating contradictions in respondents' understanding: respondents were aware of generally implicit norms of behaviour and even law but they still showed a tolerance for transgression.

On a more basic level, some participants and groups felt that war crimes were obvious and known to all before the war or the existence of the ICTY. For example, some expressed a feeling that war crimes were "that which could happen in any war, to come to something inhuman" (interview with Zagreb pensioner). A non-urban teacher believed it to be "any act in war, on any side, that is not in line with moral, human laws. Any actions outside of what we consider to be civilised behaviour" (interview with non-urban teacher). Again, this points to folk theories of law or even a type of *lex non scripta*; transgressions of human rights were intrinsically understood but their transgression was still tolerated.

Croatian war crimes, or alleged war crimes, were most often discussed in relation to Serbian war crimes. This relativity was brought up in numerous scenarios, so while Croatian crimes were considered sporadic, individual and unplanned, Serbian crimes were premeditated, planned and committed by the whole group. Serbs were seen as leaving Croatia willingly, rather than being forced out. In other words, the agency was on the side of the Serbs, who left willingly. Again, Croatian suffering was always compared to Serb suffering, using the logic that Croatia cannot be guilty since Serbia is much guiltier. This type of rhetoric could be found, sometimes less overtly, in nearly all discussions of Croatian war crimes across groups. As was already partly discussed in the previous chapter, there was a pervasive notion across all groups that crimes on the Croatian side were committed by individuals. This was expressed unequivocally across all groups and had several implications. Given that individuals had committed crimes, the Croatian army was not seen as responsible and individuals were seen as not being able to taint the war, the way generals or state policy could:

> *Petar*: On the Croatian side, if there were crimes, then they were committed outside the system of organised defence. They were committed by the horrible impulses of an individual. Like we have crimes today. A husband kills his wife. This involved these types of people. These types of people killed. And I cannot transfer this to the guilt of the entire Homeland War. This is the guilt of an individual and he should be harshly punished (focus group with Zadar war veterans).

Key elements of the war narrative, such as the unprepared and unorganised (even clumsy) defence, were expressed throughout. This further reinforced the notion that Croats did not commit crimes, especially compared to the organised Serbian ones:

> *Nikola*: Unfortunately I do not think we were capable enough to organise something (laughs).
> *Ivo*: Yes.
> *Nikola*: They are giving us powers we do not have.
> All laugh and agree (focus group with Sisak teachers).

The most striking juxtaposition with Serbian crimes was, however, the narrative of the *baka* with the rifle and other similar narratives of armed civilians. In discussions about war crimes, this basic notion was present in many more formats. It was used to relativise Croatian actions in the war and featured many of the most common elements of the Croatian war narrative. For example, the Zadar pensioners below first relativise using figures, then portray Serbs as universally and inherently armed (from children to old people) and finally contrast this with the image of Christ, a victim, speaking the truth, as Croats now must do. It was a particularly powerful symbol when expressing any kind of tolerance of deviance:

> *Fran*: Here they mobilised, I think about 50,000–100,000 of them. There was not a peasant that did not have a weapon. And today we talk about this and that. This is why Tuđman pardoned them, because he would otherwise have to punish even the simplest of peasants because the *JNA* armed them all.
> *Ognjen*: From children to old people.

Fran: That is right. Today we avoid this in discussion and in politics and so on. But this is a tragedy. As Christ said, the truth will set you free. And we have to speak the truth and only the truth (focus group with Zadar pensioners).

-

Josip: There is this mystery around the Zec family. If these people were really killed as civilians, then this was a war crime and we cannot run away from that. However, a lot is not known about what happened in the background. If someone from the Zec family picked up a weapon (dyad with non-urban war veterans Banovina).

This last quote is particularly interesting, since the participant used this to directly question a war crime case that has featured heavily in the Croatian press, but with no mention of any members of the family being armed. Such factual inaccuracies were quite common and not all too surprising with the lesser known cases, but their broader significance is that they help justify certain parts of the dominant war narrative. This helps justify the notion (much like the *baka* with the rifle does) that Serb civilians were armed and that their murder did not constitute a war crime. In fact, some groups across all target segments felt that Croatia had tried all of their war criminals and investigated all committed crimes, so it was common for participants in these groups to see no reason for further inquiries. A minority view expressed across all groups was that Croatian war crimes were a fabrication by the Serbian or former Yugoslav secret services in order to start the Serb rebellion or to equalise guilt.

The mention of ethnic cleansing inevitably led to a discussion of Operation Storm. This is representative of the Croatian public's view of war crimes since it contains the narrative of revenge and of sporadic crimes rather than organised ones. In numerous groups, the questions "can war crimes be committed in a defensive war?" and "what do you think about the claim that the Croatian state was responsible for ethnic cleansing during the war?" led to an immediate response about Operation Storm. This is not surprising given how the trial of Gotovina captured the attention of the public for so many years and the emotional attachment much of the public has to it, since it was seen as holding the potential to delegitimise the Croatian state. The degree to which Croatian war crimes are connected to Operation Storm is best captured by the response of a Sisak war veteran, who threatened to remove herself from the group if the moderator did not stop focusing solely on Operation Storm, even though the moderator had not mentioned the theme at all and the conversation at the time was about the crimes and trials in Bosnia:

Sara: You have once again focused on one detail from this complex war. The war did not start with Operation Storm. The war started far earlier. Theoretically it started long before 1991 (focus group with Sisak war veterans).

All groups agreed that crimes did happen on the Croatian side and that this happened especially during the period of this military operation. Again, however, there was a perception across all groups that these were not war crimes but "crimes in war" motivated by individual revenge or emotion. This view seems to be influenced by the connected, equally widespread, belief that Serb populations across all of Croatia and in particular in the region to be captured by the military action knew that it was about to occur and had time to leave. Participants often referred to personal stories or hearsay to bring up examples of how the Serb populations knew the attack was about to happen or how they were forced out by retreating Serb forces. This was a common pattern in sequences when Gotovina or Operation Storm was mentioned, as participants then often stressed that Serbs left willingly. This led to an impression that Croats were disadvantaged compared to Serbs, that judging them on an equal basis was unjust and that crimes were not possible or as severe:

Ivana: Everyone in Croatia knows that there was no ethnic cleansing because just before Operation Storm the Serbs went around chasing their own away. They prepared buses and chased them away.
Goran: They ran them over.
Ivana: They chased them away since they knew a military operation was being prepared. Someone told us, a Slovenian, but his wife was Serbian. He was in the military… Ordinary people knew that this was a show and was staged, and that the Serbs expelled their own people before our soldiers arrived. Gotovina could not then have even committed war crimes in Operation Storm, since there were no people.
All agree
Goran: The buses took them all (focus group with non-urban war veterans Banovina).

Across the board, there was, therefore, a feeling that Croatia did not commit any organised war crimes during the war generally and Operation Storm specifically. Numerous respondents felt that the

Croatian state gave enough guarantees to local populations for them not to have to leave. The juxtaposition between the situation of the Croats and the Serbs leaves an impression that legal understanding is being defined by the difference in playing fields for the two ethnicities and on emotional grounds. This is probably best exemplified in the recurring use of the concept of war crimes versus "crimes in war". Further support for this notion is present in survey results. Whereas the public does not believe it was possible for the Croatian side to commit *war crimes* in a defensive war (see above; Kolstø 2011), the Belgrade Human Rights Centre (2011) survey found that 66% of the public did believe it was possible to commit *crimes* in a defensive war, versus 29% who did not.

Participants regarded the doctrine of command responsibility, also a key feature of the Gotovina trial, with a mixture of disbelief and confusion. Numerous individuals admitted they were confused about the concept, although there was a view across all groups that the unorganised nature of the Croatian defence mixed with the inherent difficulty in controlling vengeful individuals meant that it was not correct to try commanders, since it was impossible to control all individuals in such a situation. This is another example of folk theories of law playing a large role in legal reasoning: respondents first admitted not understanding the concept and then outlined the premise for their definition of the concept, before arguing for why they believed Croatian generals were not guilty of command responsibility. They constructed their understanding of the situation through a mixture of law, politics and emotion:

Vedran: It is difficult to talk about command responsibility in 1995 in the Croatian Army, when a man after five years liberates his house and kills someone he found inside it. Of course he is guilty for that war crime and for the murder of a civilian, but it is hard to control him (interview with non-urban teacher).

-

Stjepan: [Norac] was a young boy thrown into huge responsibility, to lead those people there. He could not, so young, command those types of people in the army. Those were mainly people from that region, from that place. What we just discussed, revanchism. Here the Medak Pocket and all of that happened. He was tried mainly for that and sentenced. What did they call it? A massacre. Compared to Čavoglave, what they did there, this is not normal, it is not even comparable (follow-up dyad with non-urban pensioners).

Many of these attitudes are also present in narratives on the ICTY and domestic war crimes tribunals. As the following section will show in more detail, there is a sense that too few Serbs were put on trial compared to the number of Croats. Overall, all types of trials were considered too slow and there was a general feeling that many perpetrators of crimes are known but nevertheless free. Unsurprisingly, there is, therefore, an impression that no one has been held accountable for the crimes committed and that justice has not been done. Victims, therefore, felt unrepresented by all types of courts. The Croatian state in its current form was blamed for crimes committed against the victims. They connected the lack of trials to the state and to its perceived infiltration. The resulting universal view of courts is of inefficient and often biased institutions that were for the most part not fit for purpose. Most groups, however, concluded that it would have been difficult to come up with a better mechanism to achieve justice.

The ICTY—Slow, Inefficient, Unjust and Biased

The ICTY is and has been the primary, or at least the most visible, instrument of transitional justice in Croatia, as well as the region more broadly, since starting its work in 1993. It, therefore, had the potential to guide the whole process and to set the tone for the work of future institutions. It has, however, never been particularly popular in Croatia (in 2011, 65% of the public had a negative opinion of it and 24% a positive one, although this may have changed with the release of Gotovina in 2012; Belgrade Human Rights Centre 2011) and most focus group discussions reflected this.[2] The institution was generally seen as inefficient, political and biased against Croats and Croatia. This highlights how general distrust of institutions plays a role in shaping attitudes about law.

There was, however, a feeling that it was necessary and verdicts at the Tribunal, both in "favour" of Croats and against, seemed to influence the opinions of participants. This points to some level of credibility given to the institution, despite the poor public opinion.

The Inefficient ICTY

The ICTY was above all considered inefficient, and all groups spent some time discussing this topic. Survey research has reflected this in that 69% of respondents in the Belgrade Human Rights Centre (2011) study felt trials were needlessly long, as opposed to 25% who felt that trial complexity justified this. Given the crimes it was dealing with and the emotional nature of the memories involved, it is debatable if it could have ever been seen as efficient since justice may never seem swift enough. Many reasons were given for this inefficiency, for example that the institution lacked qualified professionals. War veterans considered it inefficient since it did not try the "aggressor" sufficiently, which it was in their eyes meant to do. All groups, but teachers in particular, felt the Tribunal was poorly implemented from its original design, which led to inefficiency:

> *Moderator*: Do you think it was a mistake to establish the Hague Tribunal?
> *Mario*: No.
> *Ivo*: No, it was established with a different intention.
> *Nikola*: As an idea it was good.
> *Mario*: As an international court of justice.
> *Nikola*: However, what kind of court of justice is it if the Americans do not recognise it?
> *Ivo*: That they do not respect.
> *Nikola*: This is an international criminal court for the second division. For those clubs who play county level matches. This is not a court for the top division, for the Security Council. Who would they prosecute on the Security Council, when they have the right to veto. No one. This is for us small ones. To give us some sense of justice and truth.
> *Mario*: Of international justice.
> *Nikola*: International justice, because we are fooled by terminology. International.
> *Ivo*: To show that we are not forgotten, that they are thinking of us (focus group with Sisak teachers).

This passage highlights another problematic aspect of the ICTY's work that it is frequently confused with the ICC. Given respondents were not particularly well acquainted with these legal institutions, this is not surprising, but once again factual inaccuracies in this instance served the purpose of reinforcing established narratives. This is significant since the institution is seen as highly political and influenced by larger, more powerful, states, which are seen as not being governed by the same rules as smaller states. The Sisak teachers, above, discussed the notion of "international justice" as an injustice towards Croatia and other small nations. Vukovar was seen as emblematic of ICTY inefficiency and unjustness. The view that no one has been sentenced sufficiently, if at all, for war crimes in the city was expressed in varying degrees across all groups. This was exacerbated due to the symbolic nature of the city:

> *Ema*: Has anyone been sentenced for Srebrenica and Vukovar?
> *Lena*: No one.
> *Ema*: What are we talking about here? This was a war crime, genocide was committed there.
> *Lara*: A hard to believe genocide in the twenty-first century.
> *Ema*: And no one has been indicted for that.
> *Lara*: If you tell your children, they cannot believe you. My grandchildren cry when they hear about the genocide against the Jews, not to mention if I speak about the Homeland War. Too horrific.
> *Mia*: That city was levelled to the ground. It is too horrific (focus group with Zadar war veterans).

Much of the above passage is factually incorrect (a number of individuals have been sentenced for crimes in both Srebrenica and Vukovar), but it does show how powerful this symbol of Vukovar is and how emotional it is. Other than a further example of factual inaccuracy being employed for the purpose of supporting the war narrative, this dichotomy points to a lack of Outreach or press coverage, since trials did take place (although it is debatable how happy the Croatian public is with their outcomes). The ICTY has in reality itself only sentenced Serbs for crimes committed in Croatia, whereas no Croats have been sentenced for such crimes (only for crimes in Bosnia). Efficiency was, however, often judged through the ratio of Serbs and Croats on trial. This undertone was always present in groups, sometimes through literal complaints about not enough Serbs being put on trial, at others more discretely by simply comparing the numbers without further comments. Other than the above views, respondents provided a vast range of other reasons for ICTY inefficacy, these included but are not limited to the institution being too complex, having no clear aims or being too opaque. Some felt this had the effect of raising tensions and digging wounds in the region, as well as portraying the institution as unjust.

The Biased and Political ICTY

Another recurring complaint about the ICTY was that it was biased against Croats and Croatia because it was attempting to equalise guilt between the warring factions, but especially between Croats and Serbs. Again, this has been shown in longitudinal research where it was found that 44.5% agreed and 11.8% disagreed that this was the aim of the Tribunal (Ipsos Puls 2012). The concept of equalisation of guilt has the potential to undermine the Croatian war narrative because respondents saw it as portraying the Homeland War as a civil war with no exclusively Serbian aggression, no exclusively Croatian defence and no unique Croatian victimhood. Participants felt this belittled victims and some consequently did not take the ICTY seriously since in their view it had a misconstrued notion of recent Croatian history. For example, a Zadar teacher claimed, "as soon as the stories started that Croatia committed some kind of crime and was being equalised with the aggressor, I immediately stopped following [the ICTY]" (focus group with Zadar teachers). This also highlights a connection between expressivist aspects of courts and their legal performance: as much as legal decisions can be perceived as unjust, thereby delegitimising expressivist messages, so can disagreement with the expressivist message (often based on emotion) delegitimise legal rulings.

War veterans saw "equalisation" as an attempt to equalise the aggressor and victims, as well as war crimes and crimes in war. This was attributed not only to the ICTY, but also to the Croatian government, civil society groups and the international community, further spreading a feeling of distrust of nearly all institutions, especially ones with a top-down approach to their work. There was a further notion that this attempt was a small element in a broader strategy of falsifying Croatian history:

> *Dalibor*: This criminal enterprise, which the Prosecution wanted to use to sentence the generals, which would have solidified this idea of equalising guilt, this is the elementary concept with which they wanted to falsify Croatian history (dyad with non-urban war veterans Slavonia).

Once again, discussions on this topic frequently compared the number of Croats and Serbs on trial to prove that the Tribunal was biased against Croats (in the sense that the ratio of trials was not reflective of the number of crimes committed). In one extreme instance, a participant claimed that Croats were the most punished ethnicity and this has also shown up in survey research over a number of years (see Belgrade Human Rights Centre 2011). Overall, however, there was an impression that this element of the ICTY trials damaged Croatia extensively. Participants also felt that the Tribunal and the international community thought of Croatia as an actor in a region that it wanted to portray as barbaric.[3] Some participants complained that this was demeaning since it equalised Croatia and Serbia, while others complained more about being portrayed as savage:

Moderator: Why do you think the ICTY had this approach [to equalise guilt]?

Nikola: So that they could prove that we are all some kind of Indians, savages, and that we every once in a while, every 30 or 40 years, slaughter each other. That it is nearly a part of our folklore and that we act like that (focus group with Sisak teachers).

-

Fran: This is the plan of the European Union, because even in the European Union all countries will not be the same. Of course on the one side we will have England, Germany and France. But this here will be the region South-Eastern Europe (focus group with Zadar pensioners).

Much of this was related to the generally accepted notion that the ICTY was politically motivated and controlled by big power politics. This is partly the result of political bargaining between Croatian governments and the EU, NATO and ICTY over accession conditionality. For example, Lamont (2010) identified Tuđman's bargaining with the ICTY as the major reason why the transfer of individuals to the ICTY was viewed as a political process rather than a judicial one. This not only blemished the ICTY, but also the Croatian government, which was seen as only transferring individuals who did not possess necessary political connections with the government. Moreover, since so much reporting on trials has occurred around the transfer of individuals, these events held more potential than others to influence public opinion. Conversely, so did judgements, such as the appeals decision in the Gotovina trial, which can make the ICTY look fairer in Croatian eyes. Trials, indictments and verdicts were across the board seen as politically motivated, and the institution was subsequently not considered to be independent:

Marko: I had this feeling as if Croatia was rewarded for admission to NATO and the EU by releasing the Generals. If that is true, then this is truly an embarrassment for the court and for international law.

Andriana: It looks like politicisation and no one can deny that.
All agree
Dinko: I want to add that there was a connection between the state and that court. The very extradition of the generals was a consequence of the fact that Croatia wanted to join the EU so they had to appease them, even though most of the *narod* was not in favour of extraditing the generals.
Andriana: Yes.
Dinko: In my opinion this is an embarrassment for Croatia.
Marko: Especially because the majority of politicians said one thing in opposition, and something different in power (focus group with Zadar teachers).

Overall, the ICTY was seen as closely related to the highly distrusted international community, another topic that features plenty of conspiracy theories. For example, 54% of respondents in the Ipsos Puls (2012) survey felt that some great powers tried to undermine the Croatian independence attempt in order to keep Yugoslavia intact, versus 5.5% who did not. This leaves the impression that the ICTY is seen as an institution created by big powers to dictate politics in the inferior Balkan region. This factor, possibly more than any other, contributes to the general distrust of the ICTY. Together with all the other factors in this process, it helps create a widespread feeling of powerlessness, which respondents frequently expressed.

The Necessary ICTY

Despite a range of critiques against it, the ICTY did attract a certain level of praise. The praise was not as universal as the criticism, for example war veterans had next to none. The only positive sentiment they expressed (other than that it did sentence some Serb war criminals) was that the institution initially had good intentions, which other groups agreed with:

Lucija: The worst part is that the late President Tuđman, as far as I remember, supported The Hague and was a founder of it. He supported the trying of war criminals more than anyone.
Ana: Of course (focus group with Sisak war veterans).

Pensioners and teachers, even in groups strongly opposed to the ICTY, also believed that in retrospect it was not a mistake. They believed that it did help Croatia, if not the region, and that it did punish crimes that ought to have been punished:

Moderator: Do you think it was a mistake to establish the ICTY?
Hrvoje: Maybe not. Because who knows when the war would have ended or how. The Americans got involved, and then the court came, so that it somehow ended up like this.
Fran agrees: I have personally changed my opinion.
Petar: The war happened and Tuđman was also an initiator of the idea…
Fran (interrupts): That is right.
Petar: And I saw what this should be, that criminals would be punished, that they would be stopped. However, later I saw that this had nothing to do with this. Nothing to do with this.

-

Moderator: Do you think it was a mistake to establish the ICTY?
Maja: No.
Mario: Perhaps it was not, I do not know, a mistake.
Maja: A war crime has to be punished.
Mario: Yes, in that light it definitely was not a mistake (dyad with Zagreb teachers).

Teachers stood out as the group that felt particularly positive about the ICTY. Other than the above opinions, teachers frequently expressed that it was better than no court at all and often it was compared to the domestic judiciary, which was seen as inferior. Some teachers also felt that the Tribunal was cathartic, or at least had the potential to be. The Belgrade Human Rights Centre (2011) survey found that the Croatian public was roughly divided on this issue: 44% felt it was the right decision to establish it compared to 45% who felt it was not.

For much of the Croatian public, the trial of Ante Gotovina at the ICTY defined the entire transitional justice process. Participants often admitted that they felt there were so many trials that Gotovina was just the easiest to notice or remember, which is not surprising given the predominance of reporting on the trial. All participants considered Gotovina to be innocent and believed the ICTY appeals chamber verdict to be correct. He was seen as standing out from other criminals because he was a professional soldier and was in the French Foreign Legion. Many shared the view of the Sisak teacher that you "never have crimes committed by the French Foreign Legion" (focus group with Sisak teachers). A recording of a speech Gotovina gave to his soldiers prior to Operation Storm, in which he warned them against committing crimes, was often cited as further proof of his innocence and military correctness. Finally, given that crimes were considered to have been crimes of passion, Gotovina was not seen as responsible for these or as being capable of preventing them.

The Gotovina trial taps into many of the problems about the ICTY discussed above. A guilty verdict had the potential to undermine the Croatian war narrative by falsely criminalising the Croatian state, people and history, worries which were explicitly expressed across all groups:

Lena: If Croatia, in other words if Gotovina, is sentenced for anything, that means that we are all criminals and that Croatia was created through crime.
All agree
Lena: That is our justified fear. That means that the person who killed her brothers (points at Eva) was right, who killed her husband. Is that what it means?
All agree vocally
Lena: That is what we are scared of. It means that the person who killed her brothers was right. That is how it ends, right?
All agree.
Lena: This is why we are scared. The objectiveness of the ICTY is such a fabrication.
Lara: A huge one.
Lena: We, as a *narod*, swallowed that bait. Politicians sold Croatia for 30 pieces of silver.
Ema: Our poet. 30 pieces of silver. We all know how Judas sold Jesus for that bag of coins (focus group with Zadar war veterans).

Moreover, the Zadar war veterans considered the Croatian government to be at fault, by selling the Croatian people out. They use biblical imagery to fortify the image of the Croatian *narod*'s victimhood (as Jesus), betrayed by its government (as Judas). War veterans and victims, therefore, feel unrepresented by the government. The ultimate verdict in the Gotovina case was seen as "correct" and as absolving the Croatian state of any guilt. The trial of Gotovina has come to represent ICTY bias in that it indicted Gotovina, inefficiency in that it had two wholly different verdicts, but also correctness since it did find him, and seemingly the foundation of the Croatian state, to be innocent.

ICTY verdicts in general did seem to leave some kind of impression on participants. Whereas the final Gotovina verdict can reinforce the war narrative, the guilty verdict for Kordić has the potential to undermine the war narrative and, therefore, erode trust in the ICTY. Teachers, but at times also pensioners, expressed the belief that ICTY verdicts were ultimately correct and viewed Kordić as guilty due to the ruling. These sequences also show there is acknowledgement of guilt, but that the political implications are seen as more important than the legal ones. Once again, the theme is ignored and participants tried not to discuss it at length:

Marko: Given he was sentenced, I suppose he was guilty. I do not think it is such a big problem not to agree with the verdict, maybe he is innocent but I do not know, but what was problematic was his reception when he returned as a positive individual, despite that he was sentenced. This can be compared to the reception of Gotovina, who was found innocent. It is not fair to Gotovina, or to the victims.

Andriana: I agree.

Dinko: Bosnia is quite a complex theme. I would not like to add much (focus group with Zadar teachers).

-

Marijan: I do not think it was fair that the Church went to welcome him and kiss him. He has served his sentence, so it was proven through a court decision. There is nothing else to consider. He should not have been welcomed like that (follow-up interview with Zagreb pensioner).

The last quote shows how an ICTY verdict can be seen as significant to individuals and that war criminals ought not to be accepted back into society as they previously were. At the very least, the guilty verdict seems to have generated some kind of debate over how convicted war criminals should participate in society. Despite the ICTY's huge unpopularity, this evidence shows that it may have some level of legitimacy in the eyes of the public and that, despite numerous criticisms, the verdicts it passed held some form of meaning with respondents.

Domestic War Crimes Trials: Just as Slow, Unjust and Biased

Trials in domestic courts are not as well known as those at the ICTY. Survey results have shown this, and the interviews, individual or group, reflected this (see Belgrade Human Rights Centre 2011). Overall, there was once again a lack of diffuse support and trust, leading to cynicism with the institution. This provides yet another source of institutional distrust to the public, which together with a range of others leads to scepticism regarding the whole process of transitional justice. Much like with the ICTY, domestic courts were also seen as lacking qualified personnel and as being slow. This was connected to a generally poor Croatian judiciary:

Stjepan: Our courts are worthless. Look at the statistics of unresolved cases. Last year they lowered them a bit. But until now they have been lagging. And now they have abolished county courts, they do not work well. They do not process people.

Ilija: Our paupers are not in prison, our rich people are. And they will bribe the judges. Corruption is like that in Croatia, that he who has money does not have to fear anything (focus group with non-urban pensioners).

-

Blanka: The institutions have failed because they have not dealt with all the crimes. The system has failed. From the police, to the public prosecutor.

Lara (interrupts): To the judiciary.

Blanka: The judiciary (focus group with non-urban war veterans Banovina).

-

Hrvoje: Here corruption and clientilism have taken over, so that our courts have stooped very low (focus group with Zadar pensioners).

This inefficiency of the Croatian judiciary was seen as emerging from several sources, such as corruption, broader institutional inefficiency and the legacy of communism. Some individuals also felt that it was not possible to question verdicts, since this could mark you as a communist sympathiser or as anti-Croat, depending on which verdict you question. In general, there was a feeling that the judiciary did not stand out from other state institutions, which were all developed in a poor climate. Similar as to the ICTY, a pervasive feeling was expressed that domestic courts were biased against Croats. War veterans felt that courts only processed Croats and that they would sentence a Croat quickly. The case of the Zec family was used across a number of groups, not only war veterans, as an example of bias against Croats and towards Serb victims. It was normal for the case to be directly contrasted with local crimes or with numbers of Croat victims, thereby discriminating against the Serb (or Orthodox) minority:

Blanka: Lara's parents were killed in Petrinja. Mother and father. When she went to the Republic of Croatia, she ended up having to pay court fees.
Lara: And Aleksandra Zec is the inspiration for plays and I do not know what else Frljić has done with her.
Blanka: And in Croatia 400 children were killed.
Lara: She is given rights simply because she is Orthodox.
Maja: And in our region we have a 16 year old girl who was raped and killed. Her, her parents, her grandmother and her grandfather (focus group with non-urban war veterans Banovina).

War veterans and some pensioners attributed this bias to the lack of lustration in the Croatian judiciary, which allowed judges from the Yugoslav system to remain in place in the Croatian one. This remains significant in modern-day Croatian politics since lustration laws continue to be discussed by political parties. It demonstrates how much sway that part of history holds over politics in Croatia today. Less common among these groups, but present, was the view that the judiciary was infiltrated by the UDBA or a communist mentality. The theme of infiltration was present more broadly across all groups in the sense that Croatian courts were seen as influenced strongly by the ICTY, Europe or big power politics.

Despite the range of criticisms levelled at domestic war crimes trials, positive views were present in several groups. Teachers and pensioners often expressed the view that these courts provided difficult, given the environment, yet correct verdicts. There was a view that they did as much they could have done:

Nikola: As much as they could, they did.
All agree (focus group with Sisak teachers).

-

Pero: In the last years, the last four years, the situation regarding war crimes here has changed drastically. It is unrecognisable now. People who have been sentenced in the last four years, it would not have been possible to even get them to a court four years before that (interview with Sisak pensioners).

As this last quote shows, there was a sense that domestic courts were improving. War veterans, however, did not share this notion as they felt the courts were biased against Croats. Much like with the ICTY, there was a pervasive view across all groups that not enough Serbs and too many Croats were processed (at least in relation to Serbs). All groups felt that most, if not all, Croat perpetrators had been dealt with at domestic trials. In reality, domestic courts had by 2014 processed 3,553 individuals and sentenced 589, predominantly Serbs.[4]

It is, however, questionable how well-known domestic war crimes trials are at all. The Norac trial was the best-known domestic trial across all groups, while most other cases were generally unknown. Domestic cases were frequently discussed in relation to the ICTY, sometimes because the two were confused and at other times because the ICTY seemed to embody the transitional justice process as a whole. Narratives about the ICTY and domestic courts were, therefore, at many junctures used interchangeably, and it was common for individuals to jump from court to court when making examples. For instance, a war veteran stated, "when the ICTY prosecution interprets things, I return again to the Zec family, to the ICTY it is all a war crime" (dyad with non-urban war veterans Slavonia). Another participant on the other hand felt that "domestic courts viewed things through the prism of the ICTY" (focus group with Zadar war veterans). Distrust of one institution, therefore, affected the other. It is questionable if a particularly negative view of one drags the other down with it, but pessimism regarding both reinforced the more general cynicism regarding transitional justice.

Despite the overall pessimistic view of domestic war crimes trials, verdicts discussed in groups seemed to have some effect on participants. Verdicts were viewed as valid, although the institution's credibility was often questioned. Some saw them as defining what constituted a war crime, others as a warning to future perpetrators. Teachers expressed this most consistently, although not exclusively, and when circumstances of trials were questioned, actual verdicts were nevertheless not (despite the usual relavitisation of crimes):

> *Marko*: I do not think a Croatian court would have sentenced [Norac] if he were completely innocent. In war both sides commit crimes. Everyone knows what the Americans did in Vietnam, but that does not mean that the Vietnamese side did not commit crimes (focus group with Zadar teachers).

Most striking was that war veterans also rarely questioned the validity of verdicts, despite numerous objections about the judiciary itself.

For example, the Zagreb war veterans group admitted that war crimes did happen on the Croatian side and that these have been dealt with. They continued to state that when people say "hero, not war criminal", they do not mean people like Norac, who was actually sentenced for war crimes.[5] This highlights the complexity of perceptions of transitional justice, since they are certainly not exclusively negative. Consequently, even by parts of society who have been traditionally opposed to trials of Croats, these institutions are seen as partially legitimate.

The case of Norac was, as previously discussed, also by far the best-known domestic war crimes trial. The case was mentioned frequently as proof of the quality of Croatian courts. Generally, he was considered guilty of the crimes committed, although participants across all groups felt the circumstances were unfair on the former general, due to the unprepared and unarmed nature of the Croatian defence in which revenge killings were a common problem. It would be interesting to see if such results would be equally reproduced outside of the group or follow-up interview setting. It is possible that a guilty verdict by a Croatian court means that individuals feel the need to show their respect for that in front of others, whereas individually they may doubt it more openly.

Conclusion

Respondents discussed and defined war crimes in relation to Croatian defence. They were across the board considered to be conscious, often planned, acts. This allowed for an apologetic attitude towards crimes committed in revenge, which were seen as crimes, but not quite war crimes and, therefore, viewed more leniently. Moreover, respondents frequently asserted that the killing of civilians was a war crime, but their definitions of ethnic Croat and Serb civilians differed. This justified the killing of Serb civilians by Croatian forces through folk theories of law and factual inaccuracies. For example, the image of the *baka* with a rifle was frequently used as a mitigating circumstance and led to a certain acceptance or understanding of Croatian crimes. The lack of preparation by Croatian forces meant that war crimes, defined as planned, were not seen as possible on the Croatian side of the conflict.

Overall, respondents in the study revealed a tolerance for deviance in the context of war crimes committed by Croats. Various factors of the dominant war narrative, such as the unorganised and unprepared defence, were seen as a mitigating circumstance to such war crimes. These crimes were often defined in relation to Serbian crimes, which were seen as a part of a planned aggression. War crimes in defence were seen as possible by teachers and some pensioners, but this did not happen with Croats or it happened sporadically. The "but" in these statements is crucial since respondents frequently used these contradictions, in tandem with a range of mitigating circumstances, to show that they were aware of what constituted a war crime but that tolerance for deviance in certain situations was acceptable.

Much like with the war narrative, there was a stark contrast between how teachers and war veterans perceived the law, while pensioners had mixed opinions (Fig. 4.1). The key difference was that although there was consensus across all groups that the ICTY was inefficient, teachers nevertheless thought the ICTY was necessary and attributed significance to their and domestic courts' judgements, whereas war veterans generally did not. Moreover, teachers had different understandings of what constituted a war crime and debated if Croatian war crimes were possible, while war veterans did not.

Transitional justice institutions, be they international or domestic, had to operate in the context of localised complexities and normative expectations in attempting to instil a rule of law norm in the public.

	Perception	Crimes of passions are war crimes (yes/no)	Crimes possible in defensive war (yes/no/both)	Croatian war crimes (silence or debate present)	ICTY (inefficient/ efficient)	ICTY (necessary/ unnecessary)	ICTY/Domestic trials have signifiance (yes/no)
Teachers	Zagreb	**Yes**	**Yes**	**Debate**	Inefficient	**Necessary**	**Yes**
	Zadar	**Yes**	**Yes**	**Debate**	Inefficient	**Necessary**	**Yes**
	Sisak	**Yes**	**Yes**	**Debate**	Inefficient	**Necessary**	**Yes**
	Non-urban	**Yes**	**Yes**	**Debate**	Inefficient	**Necessary**	**Yes**
War veterans	Zagreb	No	Both	Silence	Inefficient	Unnecessary	**Yes**
	Zadar	No	No	Silence	Inefficient	Unnecessary	No
	Sisak	No	No	Silence	Inefficient	Unnecessary	No
	Non-urban Banovina	No	No	Silence	Inefficient	Unnecessary	No
	Non-urban Slavonia	No	No	Silence	Inefficient	Unnecessary	No
Pensioners	Zagreb	**Yes**	**Yes**	**Debate**	Inefficient	**Necessary**	**Yes**
	Zadar	No	No	Silence	Inefficient	Unnecessary	No
	Sisak	No	Both	**Debate**	Inefficient	**Necessary**	**Yes**
	Non-urban	**Yes**	Both	**Debate**	Inefficient	Unnecessary	No

Fig. 4.1 Overview of perceptions of law

Respondents across the board regarded all domestic and international institutions, including legal ones, as corrupt and inefficient and were consequently dissatisfied with and distrustful of them. On the whole they, therefore, felt powerless in an unresponsive system where justice was imposed from above. In this sense, all legal institutions were painted with the same brush.

Localised folk theories of law also played a large role in the legal reasoning of respondents. This allowed for an apologetic attitude towards certain crimes, based on an understanding of the law that was not legally consistent but was consistent with emotional and political narratives. This means that in Croatian society the dominant war narrative plays a large role in shaping attitudes towards law. Finally, factual inaccuracies often served the purpose of justifying respondents' narratives. This involved several characteristic symbols, including core components of the war narrative, such as the *baka* with the rifle that vindicated Croatian crimes or at least lowered them to the level of common crimes, rather than war crimes. Croatian war crimes were seen as unexceptional crimes in war (to be punished more leniently), while Serb crimes are seen as exceptional war crimes (to be punished more harshly).

These factors led to an attitude in individuals that crimes are acceptable in certain situations or that they are, at least, not war crimes. Law is most effective when it takes into account the social norms that govern behaviour, including norms against disorder that may give rise to crimes (Meares and Kahan 1998). In this instance, institutional distrust coupled with the strength of the war narrative in society has led to a great deal of cynicism with the transitional justice process. Despite the ICTY and, especially recently, domestic courts providing legally sound judgements and strongly adhering to legal justice over political justice, this has not led to concurrent understandings of law. Localised narratives and normative processes have proven effective in undermining the potential trickle-down effects of rule of law norms.

This expectation may have been too high on legal institutions, but it does highlight the need for transitional justice efforts to take into account localised normative processes in their work and in their attempts at producing pedagogical effects. Arguably, it will simply take more time for these institutions, especially domestic ones, to achieve this effect and results from the focus groups are not exclusively pessimistic, far from it. Responses were different across target segments, and the youngest segment, history teachers, had a far more optimistic view of the ICTY and domestic courts than pensioners and war veterans' groups. Nevertheless, teachers also often displayed a tolerance for deviance, which may be a warning for the future if left unchanged. This is particularly important in relation to reconciliation, given that notions of legality are defined differently in relation to Croats and Serbs.

Notes

1. Diffuse support is defined as conferring legitimacy on an institution.
2. This has depended on who was being tried at any one time, so the initial Gotovina verdict and the appeals verdict may have influenced popularity. Similarly, more popularity may have come about from the Ovčara perpetrators trial, while less from the temporary release of Šešelj.
3. Croatian institutions have also reflected this feeling and fear of being grouped in a region considered to be inferior. For example, the Croatian Academy of Sciences and Arts (*Hrvatska akademija znanosti i umjetnosti* or HAZU) sent complaints to the ICTY, EU and Western European universities over reports intended for Croatia being in Serbian. This is discussed further in the following chapter.
4. See www.dorh.hr/fgs.axd?id=1841.
5. The "hero, not war criminal" (and derivations thereof) slogan was first used at public demonstrations in Zagreb and Split in 2001, in protest against the Croatian indictment of Mirko Norac for war crimes. It has since then been used mostly for Gotovina, but it has featured in many other protests in support of the generals as well.

References

Arendt, H. (2006). *Eichmann in Jerusalem: A report on the banality of evil.* London: Penguin.

Belgrade Human Rights Centre. (2011). *Informisanost i stavovi građana Hrvatske prema Haškom tribunalu i suđenjima za ratne zločine pred sudovima u Hrvatskoj* [Awareness and attitudes of the citizens of Croatia towards the ICTY and war crimes trials in Croatia].

Brodersen, K. H. (2014). The ICTY's conditionality dilemma. *European Journal of Crime, Criminal Law and Criminal Justice, 22,* 219–248.

Caritas Croatia and the Franciscan Institute for the Culture. (2001). *Peace in Croatia: Results of research.* Zagreb: CROPAX.

Elster, J. (2004). *Closing the books: Transitional justice in historical perspective.* Cambridge: Cambridge University Press.

Hagan, J., & Ivković, S. K. (2006). War crimes, democracy, and the rule of law in Belgrade, the former Yugoslavia, and beyond. *The Annals of the American Academy of Political and Social Science, 605*, 130–151.
Ipsos Puls. (2012, January). *Izbori 2011* [Elections 2011].
Karsai, L. (2000a). Crime and punishment: People's courts, revolutionary legality, and the Hungarian holocaust. *InterMarium, 4*, 1–13.
Karsai, L. (2000b). The people's courts and revolutionary justice in Hungary, 1945–1946. In I. Deák, J. T. Gross, & T. Judt (Eds.), *The politics of retribution in Europe: World War II and its aftermath* (pp. 233–251). Princeton: Princeton University Press.
Kolstø, P. l. (2011). *Strategies of symbolic nation-building in west Balkan states: Intents and results*. University of Oslo. Available at http://www.hf.uio.no/ilos/english/research/projects/nation-w-balkan/.
Lamont, C. K. (2010). *International criminal justice and the politics of compliance*. Farnham: Ashgate.
Luban, D. (2004). A theory of crimes against humanity. *Yale Journal of International Law, 29*, 124–131.
McAuliffe, P. (2010). Transitional justice and the rule of law: The perfect couple or awkward bedfellows? *Hague Journal on the Rule of Law, 2*, 127–154.
Meares, T. L., & Kahan, D. M. (1998). Law and (norms of) order in the inner city. *Law & Society Review, 32*, 805–838.
Panakova, J. (2011). Law and politics of universal jurisdiction. *Amsterdam Law Forum, 3*, 49–72.
Radbruch, G. (1946). Gesetzliches unrecht und übergesetzliches recht. *Süddeutsche Juristenzeitung, 1*, 105–108.
Sampson, R. J., & Bartusch, D. J. (1998). Legal cynicism and (subcultural?) tolerance of deviance: The neighborhood context of racial differences. *Law & Society Review, 32*, 777–804.
Sarkin, J. (2015). The interrelationship and interconnectness of transitional justice and the rule of law in Uganda: Pursuing justice, truth, guarantees of non-repetition, reconciliation and reparations for past crimes and human rights violations. *Hague Journal on the Rule of Law, 7*, 111–139.
Shklar, J. N. (1964). *Legalism: Law, morals, and political trials*. Cambridge: Harvard University Press.
Slaughter, A. M. (2004). *A new world order*. Princeton: Princeton University Press.
Spoerri, M., & Freyberg-Inan, A. (2008). From prosecution to persecution: Perceptions of the international criminal tribunal for the former Yugoslavia (ICTY) in Serbian domestic politics. *Journal of International Relations and Development, 11*, 350–384.
Stover, E. (2005). *The witnesses: War crimes and the promise of justice in The Hague*. Philadelphia: University of Pennsylvania Press.

Subotic, J. (2009). *Hijacked justice: Dealing with the past in the Balkans*. Ithaca: Cornell University Press.

Teitel, R. G. (2005). The law and politics of contemporary transitional justice. *Cornell International Law Journal, 38*, 837–862.

Tladi, D. (2012). Cooperation, immunities, and article 98 of the Rome statute: The ICC, interpretation, and conflicting norms. *ASIL Annual Meeting Proceedings, 106*, 307–308.

United Nations Security Council. (1993). *Resolution 827*. Document S/RES/827.

Zambelli, N. (2010). A journey westward: A poststructuralist analysis of Croatia's identity and the problem of cooperation with the international criminal tribunal for the former Yugoslavia. *Europe-Asia Studies, 62*, 1661–1682.

CHAPTER 5

Serbs in the Eyes of Croats

The predominant war narrative of the 1991–1995 conflict in Croatia has become an intrinsic part of how Croats view the Serb minority in Croatia. The key characteristics of this narrative are Croatian defence, survival, struggle and victimhood against a Serb, Serbian or Yugoslav (among a range of terms) aggressor, in a broken Yugoslav system (Banjeglav 2012; Jović 2009; Koren 2011; Pavlaković 2014; Peskin and Boduszynski 2003). Moreover, there exists a notion that the war is not over since it continues to form a key part of many individuals' lives and issues from it remain unresolved. Many of these issues are defined in relation to Serbs and Serbia. The situation with Cyrillic[1] signs in Vukovar exemplifies this since it has come to be seen by Croats as an aggression against them, rather than an issue of minority rights.[2] This chapter investigates how Croats view Serbs in Croatia and how the war narrative features in this attitude. It looks at how different types of institutions, such as the Church or the government, affected this. These issues in great part define how Serbs make up the "other" in Croat identity.

Serbs remain the largest ethnic minority in Croatia and make up 4.36% of the population, down considerably since the 1991 level of 12.2% and the 1971 level of 14.16% (Croatian Bureau of Statistics 2011). Moreover, although the numbers remain disputed, 217,000 Serbs were killed in Croatia during the Second World War by the Nazi collaborationism regime (Goldstein 2003: 310). The UN Human Rights Committee expressed concerns in 2015 over the level of discrimination

I. Sokolić, *International Courts and Mass Atrocity*,
Memory Politics and Transitional Justice,
https://doi.org/10.1007/978-3-319-90841-0_5

and violence against Serbs and Roma, in particular (United Nations, Office of the High Commissioner for Human Rights 2015). Moreover, Serb returnees continue to struggle to access government programmes aimed at facilitating their return. A Council of Europe Report (2016) expressed concern over: the surge of nationalism and political radicalisation having an impact on minority rights, especially in war hit areas; the small number of minorities employed in public service; the limited right to use minority languages and scripts in certain locations; the use of hate speech in media and political discourse; and the public debate concerning minorities being dominated by anti-minority rhetoric and prejudice.[3] Human Rights Watch has also consistently highlighted discrimination against Serbs in their world reports, most recently in 2018 (Human Rights Watch 2018).

The events in Vukovar originated with the 2011 Croatian census, which found that Serbs comprise over one-third of the population in Vukovar, thereby requiring bilingual signs in the city. This resulted in a series of demonstrations in Vukovar in late 2013, as well as some other Croatian cities, to protest this move. The initial rally involved over 20,000 individuals, featured slogans such as "*VUKOVAR, NE ВУКОВАР*"[4] and was likened to previous public shows of support for the Croatian generals in Split. The proposed bilingualism frustrated war veterans and many ordinary citizens due to the wartime experience of the city. Signatures were also collected across the country for a referendum to change the law on minority rights and bilingualism.

Identity, ethnic or national, involves both belonging and otherness, "there is no self without an other; no identity without alterity; no nation without rival foreigners" (Spiering 1999: 153). Individuals are conscious of belonging to an "ingroup" as opposed to another "outgroup", and their behaviour is often biased towards the ingroup and against the outgroup (Langston and Peti-Stantić 2014; Oakes 2001; Tajfel 1978). Moreover, stereotypes about the ingroup and outgroups are constituent parts of identity (Joseph 2004: 76). Serbs have composed the "other" to Croatian identity, and President Tuđman argued that this otherness was based on cultural, historical and geographical differences, which he used in his attempt to unify the Croatian people (Bellamy 2003: 68). Political elites since then have furthered this image of Serbs as Croatia's "radical other" and presented them as uncivilised, non-Western and savage (Zambelli 2010: 1664). Unsurprisingly, there is a high degree of xenophobia towards Serbs in Croatia, especially returnees, who are seen as embodying this otherness and the collective guilt of Serbian aggression (Leutloff-Grandits 2016). Serbs and Serbia were portrayed, often through historical revisionism, as oppressors of Croats and Croatia throughout history. This allowed domestic actors to argue that history was repeating itself and that Croatia must once again defend itself (MacDonald 2002).

Štiks (2010) and Jović (2017) argue that this has made Croatia into an ethnic democracy. Croatia has become democratic and liberal, but ethnicity continues to play a key role in Croatian politics. This political system is defined by the institutional dominance of one ethnic group, within a democratic framework (Štiks 2010: 93). In party politics, the Serb minority is tolerated, but not considered a political factor worth including in significant decision-making (Jović 2017: 268). Jović goes as far as to call this the "ethnototalitarianism of the everyday", in which minority expression is not only forbidden, but it is seen as a provocation and threat to the existence of the majority (ibid.: 314). He uses the example of Milanka Opačić, Vice-President of the Croatian parliament, who received threats after a doctored image of her was posted on an online portal, in which she was wearing a t-shirt with Serbian symbols. The ensuing public debate did not ask why she should not be able to wear such a shirt, even if she had, while symbols of the majority group are allowed and encouraged (ibid.). Jović argues that the public understanding is that other ethnicities do not exist, or if they do, then their public acknowledgement represents a provocation (ibid.: 314). In party politics, the Serb minority is tolerated, but not considered a political factor.

The picture is, however, more ambiguous. For example, in a study focused on the region of Slavonia, Croat respondents were for the most part prepared to reconcile with Serb returnees, other than those who had committed war crimes (Babić 2010: 221). Eastern Slavonia featured higher tensions than Western Slavonia, due to the severity of the war there, associated war memories and exacerbated present-day ethnic divisions, but primary social connections in local communities were being gradually rebuilt (Babić 2010: 222). The intensity and speed at which this was happening differed to Western Slavonia, but coexistence has once again become a part of local social fabric.

Participants in this study differentiated with Serbs predominantly in terms of religion and language. That is not to say that these are the only factors in defining modern, post-war Croatian identity, since the legacy of the Second World War and communism also contribute strongly to the Croatian sense of differentiation with Serbs. These different memories and associated debates have polarised Croatian society and more recent events such as the shouting of "*Za dom, spremni*" at football matches has highlighted this (Brentin 2016; Pavlaković 2008).[5] Moreover, human rights abuses from the communist period have been presented as attacks by one ethnicity on another and have never been analysed in a political vacuum, thereby being easily appropriated for nationalistic mobilisation (Subotic 2015).

National identity in Croatia is, nevertheless, strongly based on religion (Babić 2010; Smith 1991). Throughout the fieldwork, the notion of Croat Catholicism was commonly juxtaposed with Serb Orthodox Christianity. As much as Croats identified themselves as Catholics, they equally strongly identified Serbs as Orthodox. The importance of Catholicism to Croatian identity has been observed among elites and Prcela (2009: 211) has even argued that it has been overlooked as a factor in Croatian identity.[6] This identification stems from the 1945–1990 period, when Croatian Catholicism and Croatian national identity merged, as the Church presented itself as the only defender of the Croatian people's collective identity (Jakelić 2010: 118). In Croatia, as well as in Bosnia–Herzegovina, Catholicism became an identity marker for Croats (Sells 2003). It became collectivistic and public; emphasised tradition and ascription; and defined group boundaries towards the "other" (Casanova 1994: 217; Jakelić 2010: 197).[7] During the Homeland War, many volunteers in the Croatian Army saw military deployment as more than just their national duty, but as a religious calling to defend Croatia and in some rural areas facets of Catholicism continue to provide a basis for resistance to centralisation and economic change (Schäuble 2014). This union is probably best exemplified in the expression "*bog i hrvati*" (God and the Croats) that is built on a shared Croat feeling of suffering (Schäuble 2014: 262). Today, these elements are recurring features in political speeches, religious sermons and in public discourse more broadly.

Language is seen as fundamentally linked with the history of the Croatian people, and language is another large differentiator between Serbs and Croats (Fishman 2006). How people identify themselves is in many ways language and culture specific, so identity can be viewed as a key function of language, equal to those of representation and communication (Joseph 2004). To legitimise modern Croatian language (especially as a language planning project) and a distinct Croatian national identity, Croatian linguistic identity has been presented as reaching far into the past (Langston and Peti-Stantić 2014: 45). The aims of language planning in Croatia since the 1990s have been exclusively symbolic in order to enhance this identity, in large part because ethnic foundations and identities in the region have been so hotly contested over time (ibid.: 57). Language policy was used exclusively in the service of national projects, and purity of the language was argued to be essential for the survival of the *narod* (Kordić 2010: 9). This was the case not only in Croatia, but in the region as a whole. Elites in the region believed it to be important for each nation to have its own language in order to differentiate it from other nations (ibid.: 167). Language purism was the consequence of nationalist understandings of language. In the 1990s, the HDZ became an active agent of language change since they saw language as the main point of differentiation with other Balkan nations, especially Serbs (Bellamy 2003: 146). In an effort to legitimise the Croatian nation, an attempt was made to erase anything from the language that could associate or remind Croats of their shared past with Serbs (Richter Malabotta 2004: 80). Croatian and Serbian were now different languages, and if this difference was not visible, then it had to become so (Kordić 2010: 47).

Langston and Peti-Stantić (2014), however, argue that in Croatia the government itself has not been the primary vehicle of language change; instead, this was achieved through non-governmental institutions with similar goals, but greater ambitions. The government rarely seemed eager or willing to introduce legislation or regulations to control language policies, even when the HDZ was in power (Langston and Peti-Stantić 2014: 145).[8] Laws that did and do exist were rarely enforced and allowed for exceptions, while even less was done regarding the norms of the language (ibid.: 145). Institutions that have been actively involved in this process and that propagated language planning most successfully functioned in a similar way to language academies in other states, both before and after independence (ibid.: 171). These primarily included but are not limited to the Croatian Academy of Sciences and Arts (*Hrvatska akademija znanosti i umjetnosti* or HAZU), the Council for the Norms of the Croatian Standard Language (*Vijeće za normu hrvatskog standardnog jezika*), the Institute for the Croatian Language and Linguistics (*Institut za hrvatski jezik i jezikoslovlje* or IHJJ) and *Matica Hrvatska*. These are not strictly government institutions, but they do all have significant connections (institutional or financial) to the state, so they do not form a part of civil society either. The government thereby did influence language change through sponsorship of practice rather than by law. The paradox here is that the reason that the issue of a "minority language" has arisen in Vukovar at all is because Croatian as the official state language has been defined by law and, therefore, defined Serbian as a different language in need of protection. This would not be the case if the law regarded the two as different variants of the same language, since there would be no argument for the representation of multiple languages.

In the 1990s, the above-mentioned institutions started to encourage an exclusive view of the Croatian standard language that actively looked to eliminate anything related to the "East" (Langston and Peti-Stantić 2014: 277). This exclusivity defined Croatian identity based on religion (Western Christian and Catholic), language (Croatian and not Serbian) and alphabet (strictly not Serbian Cyrillic). Croatian alphabets were defined as Latin, Glagolitic and Croatian Cyrillic (Horvat 2009: 18).[9] HAZU even complained in 2007 to the ICTY about their reports intended for Croatia being written in Serbian, along a range of other complaints to the European Union and Western European universities (HAZU 2007). The HAZU called on the government to take more action to prevent Europe from introducing a single regional language for Croatia, Serbia and Montenegro. This can be interpreted as reflecting either the Croatian public's or elites' fear that Europe and the West were treating Croatia as a part of an inferior region together with its neighbours. Whose fear it represents is debatable and indicative of the strange position of HAZU, since they and other similar institutions occupy a grey area between government institutions and civil society.

These notions of identity sit alongside the dominant war narrative, which frames the relationship as one of aggressor and victim. In this sense, the Serbian Orthodox Church is seen as inherently aggressive, as opposed to the forgiving and compassionate Roman Catholic Church in Croatia. The Serb community is seen as taking advantage of their unique status in Croatia, granted to them by an open multiethnic state. These attitudes, however, feature a range of contradictions. The situation with Cyrillic in Vukovar, discussed at the end of this chapter, exemplifies this best. The Serb community feels the effect of these discourses, since they are seen as undeserving of some of the rights granted to them by the Croatian state. The issue of Serbs in Croatia is made into an issue of security to the Croatian state (Jović 2017: 254). The implications of this can be exacerbated during turbulent times, such as war, where ingroup and outgroup relations are potentially dangerous and even a matter of life and death (Dugandžija 2006). They become a matter of self-defence and, especially because of this notion, in Croatia they can be related to the feeling that the war is not over.

This chapter unpacks these contradictions, as expressed by participants, and connects them to representative survey results. The first section outlines how Serbs represent the embodiment of collective Serbian guilt and Croatian suffering. Guilt is not individualised to any significant level. The following section examines the role of religion in this relationship: Catholic Croat is forgiving; Orthodox Serb is aggressive. Finally, the issues of Serb language rights and Cyrillic signs in Vukovar are used to illustrate these attitudes. Serbs are tolerated, but increasing their rights is seen as a threat to the Croatian nation and state.

Contradictory Attitudes Towards Minorities

Survey results on attitudes towards minorities in Croatia are ambiguous and point to a generally positive view of them, whereas the focus group and interview data point to a far more pessimistic view of the Serb minority specifically. Three general trends are apparent in surveys: that the Croatian public claims to view ethnic minorities in Croatia favourably, that they rank harmony between ethnic minorities as a low priority, and that they do not believe localities with significant Serb populations should have signs in Cyrillic. Participants in this study reflected this, when asked to rate the importance of three principles of the Croatian constitution, ethnic equality scored lowest. Surveys by Ilišin (2011) conducted in 1999 and 2004 support these findings.

The Ipsos Puls (2012) survey found that the Croatian public generally looked favourably on different ethnicities living in Croatia (Fig. 5.1) but less favourably on coming into familiar contact with members of those ethnicities (Fig. 5.2).

What is striking here is not only the negative opinion of Serbs, but of all ethnicities listed. This calls into question the centrality of Serbs; they appear to be liked and disliked as much as other groups. Participants in this study also displayed ambiguous opinions in the survey element. For example, a survey question regarding Serb minority involvement in the development of museums dealing with twentieth-century Croatian

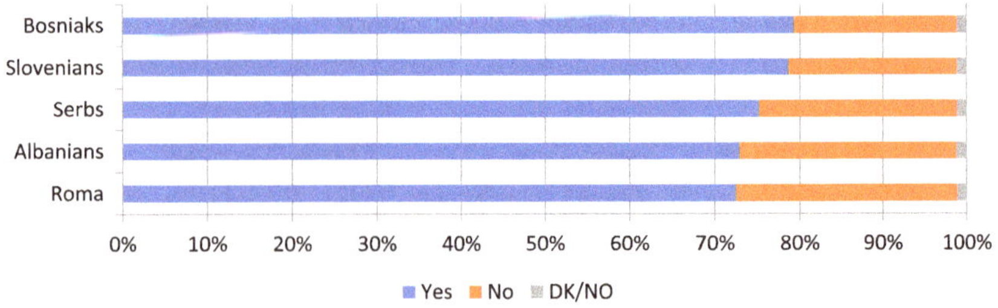

Fig. 5.1 Members of different ethnicities frequently come into close interpersonal contact. What form of interpersonal contact would you find acceptable with the following groups? To live in Croatia (Ipsos Puls 2012)

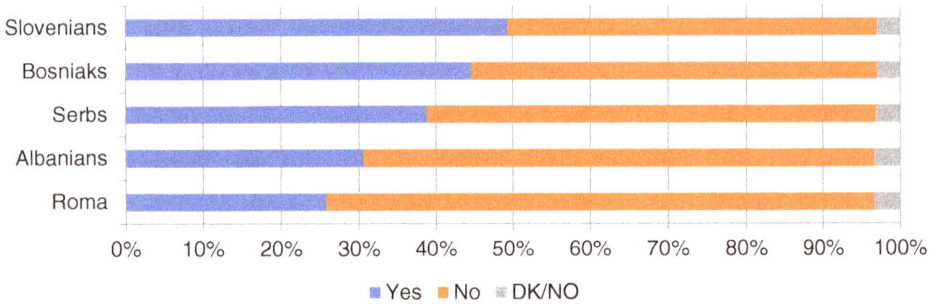

Fig. 5.2 Members of different ethnicities frequently come into close interpersonal contact. What form of interpersonal contact would you find acceptable with the following groups? To be a member of your family (Ipsos Puls 2012)

history received a generally positive response, but as the below passages will show, strong negative opinions of the minority were present in focus groups, dyads and interviews. This presents another instance of contradiction where narratives of inclusivity, expressed by the public, meet a relatively strong war narrative by which issues of minority rights are instead interpreted as an attack on the Croatian people. Moreover, this highlights the conflicting nature of quantitative and qualitative research methods. Quantitative methods can miss narratives that influence behaviour and individuals may be aware of the social expectations to express openness towards Serbs, although they may not act consistently with this opinion in specific situations (such as Cyrillic in Vukovar).

Throughout all the group discussions related to Serbs in Croatia, war veterans and pensioners were exceptionally vocal, while teachers were quiet. The two target segments spent much time discussing the Orthodox Church and the current position of Serbs in Croatia, in particular. Across all groups, however, discussion centred on the war and the role of the Croatian Serbs in it. Much of this focused on the notion that there was no expulsion of Serbs from Croatia (that they left willingly), that they committed more crimes than Croats, and that they knew the war was coming and were, therefore, prepared for it.[10]

All groups felt that Serbs and Serbia had not punished their own criminals the way that Croatia had. Various reasons were given for this, from the strength of nationalism in Serbia to conspiracy theories concerning political elites in the region:

> *Marko*: The problem in Serbia is that it has not come to terms with the role she has played [in the war] and now the current government is quite radically nationalistic… (pauses) They allow them to be Greater Serbs, chetniks, nationalists, this and that (follow-up interview with Zadar teacher).
>
> -
>
> *Domagoj*: Courts in Serbia have not convicted a single officer. They have sentenced a few regular soldiers, volunteers. Courts in Croatia have convicted highly ranked officers from colonels to generals in the Croatian Army (focus group with Zagreb war veterans).

There was, however, disagreement over exactly what was necessary by the Serb side to be seen as trying their own. In the below passage, one participant felt that Serbia was doing enough by cooperating with the ICTY, which another participant saw as a defence of Serbian aggression. Accusations such as this can limit the potential for constructive debate about interethnic relations or even the past more generally:

> *Ante*: Who sent [Milošević] to The Hague?
> *Mladen*: That is what I wanted to say, in the end the Serbs sent him.
> *Vlasta*: Well yes, they sent him, they had to.
> *Ante*: What more do you want?
> *Mladen*: Do not argue.
> *Vlasta*: You are defending Milošević and the Serbian aggression.
> *Ante*: No!
> *Vlasta*: If I need to discuss this with you.
> *Ante (interrupts)*: This is our Croatian politics.
> *Vlasta*: Do not teach me about Croatian politics, I have seen it all up close.
> *Ante*: Do not teach me, I am older and I took part in the Second World War! I can read between the lines quite well (focus group with Zagreb pensioners).

Pensioners and war veterans felt that Serbs, as an ethnicity, were inherently aggressive and hateful. Again, this was closely connected to the predominant war narrative and the feeling that the war is not over. In extreme cases, Serbs were seen as teaching their children to hate. This was compared to the peaceful nature of the Croat people:

Ivana: Us Croats are that kind of *narod*. Even though the wounds are deep and it is difficult for someone who has lost someone, but reconciliation will come from our side before it comes from theirs. Although they maybe say it is not so. They are simply that kind of *narod*.
Stjepan: They would wage war now.
Ivana: Yes, they are like that. It is in their blood.
Vladimir: Since they teach them to hate (focus group with non-urban pensioners).

This is closely related to how respondents viewed the Catholic and Orthodox Churches, the former as peaceful and the latter as aggressive (discussed below). It is also linked to the general view of the Greater Serbian plan. Respondents believed that "Greater Serbia is an idea that lives on and will live on in many Serbs and generations to come" (focus group with Zadar war veterans) and attempts to introduce Cyrillic signs in Vukovar were at times seen as an attempt to implement this plan.

Not all comments directed at the Croatian Serb community were negative. Since discussions predominantly focused on the Homeland War, there were admissions across all groups that Serbs, although only a minority, did fight on the Croatian side in the war. Croatia was by some also seen as the homeland of the Serbs. Teachers generally felt that it was hard for Serbs during the war, while war veterans considered "good" Serbs to be the ones that fought on the Croatian side and used stories about their neighbours to show evidence of this (including how they personally helped each other during the war). This is indicative of the strength of social ties in the local community, and the results have been replicated in survey research (Babić 2010). Despite so many communities being destroyed, neighbours did protect each other and such memories have survived through the war narrative. This provides hope for the rebuilding of local communities, especially in war hit areas, where interethnic tensions are particularly high.

All target segments believed that Serbs overall were manipulated by Greater Serbian politics. This creates yet another contradiction with the war narrative's notion of exclusively Croat victimhood and Serb aggression. Instead, it reformulates it into Serbian state aggression and manipulation of all ethnicities in Croatia, painting them all as victims:

> *Nikola*: The Serb minority currently has a very interesting situation. I think they were manipulated in this whole story. They were a tool of Greater Serbian politics and Milošević used them for his own interests (focus group with Sisak teachers).

On the other hand, the Zadar teachers, for example, thought that Serbs considered themselves to be eternal victims and that they were only affected by the war on the frontline. Serb returnees were, however, only brought up and discussed by war veterans, who debated the topic at length. They universally saw them as accomplices to war criminals:

> *Blanka*: So I told [a Serb returnee], this war criminal, I told him 'in you, in every person who returns from Serbia, I see the potential killer of my husband.' He responded 'please madam do not be like that.' So I responded, 'until you tell me who killed my husband, I have the right to think so. I can walk through the town with my head raised high. I have the right to say this. You are the killer of my husband until you reveal who actually is' (focus group with non-urban war veterans Banovina).

To many in Croatia, Serbs are seen as the embodiment of collective Serbian guilt and collective Croatian suffering (Leutloff-Grandits 2016). Individuals have all too frequently employed notions of collective guilt, especially since guilt has not been individualised to any significant extent. Moreover, the previously cited Babić (2010: 137) survey found that a majority of the public was only prepared to forgive Serbs who were not criminals. The combined implication of this is that if many Serbs are seen as criminals due to their ethnicity (especially returnees), then readiness for forgiveness can be interpreted as low in Croatia.

The Forgiving Catholics and the Aggressive Orthodox

National and ethnic identity in Croatia is closely linked to religion and the Catholic and Orthodox Churches featured in all group discussions. They were discussed as a source of information on the war, and the Catholic Church specifically was seen as educational and reliable. For example, a non-urban teacher believed the Church to be more consistent than any state, since it had been with the Croatian *narod* for 13 centuries. In many instances, however, the topic was laughed off.

The two churches came up in other parts of discussions as well. These can be divided into four separate categories: opinions about both overall; the Church as a key component of identity; the Catholic Church specifically as forgiving; and the Orthodox Church specifically as aggressive. Overall, teachers saw all Churches as politically biased (towards the right), political or corrupt, although this did feature some disagreement within groups. Pensioners also discussed the Church, but they were not as critical, while war veterans generally avoided the topic. The Church was seen as identifying ethnicity in a number of ways. War veterans especially, but not exclusively, did not consider only Croatia and the Croat *narod* to have been attacked, but also the Catholic Church. On the other hand, they used the term Serbs (*Srbi*) and Orthodox Christians (*pravoslavci*) interchangeably to refer to Croatian Serbs:

> *Lara*: For [the murder of] my parents Tarbuk gave the order. The Serb, Orthodox, leader (focus group with non-urban war veterans Banovina).
>
> -
>
> *Lucija*: People of the Orthodox faith, Serbs, were informed when to leave before the artillery fire started (focus group with Sisak war veterans).
>
> -
>
> *Goran*: The Church protected its Catholic *narod*. It knew who attacked the Catholics (focus group with non-urban pensioners).
>
> -
>
> *Josip*: Today they talk about Serb villages, but these are not Serb villages, but Croatian villages with Orthodox inhabitants (dyad with non-urban war veterans Slavonia).

War veterans and pensioners saw the Catholic Church as forgiving and, therefore, Croats as a forgiving *narod*. This notion came up exclusively in a spontaneous fashion in those groups and never came up with teachers. Forgiveness was discussed through the use of Catholic symbols and language. Moreover, the topic was frequently associated with reconciliation in the region:

Lana: In our Catholic country they say that, in order to forgive someone, that someone has to ask for forgiveness. They have to be aware that they sinned. If I hurt someone, who will forgive me anything if I am not first aware that I have hurt them. Only then can I ask them for forgiveness. I also need to repent and be aware that I have truly hurt them and I never want to do that again. [...] If someone truly apologised to me, maybe I would have that feeling. They have repented and I will forgive them.

Ema: You would, because you are Catholic (focus group with Zadar war veterans).

-

Goran: I am a believer. How can I forgive a criminal who does not seek forgiveness? This is a question of faith (focus group with non-urban pensioners).

This has the implication that forgiveness, in the eyes of these individuals, is interpreted as religious and specifically Catholic. The would-be sinner must, therefore, ask for it. Given there is a slight preponderance of citizens who believe that the Catholic Church is the predominant moral authority in Croatia (41% agree versus 33% who disagree), this can have far-reaching consequences (Fig. 5.3).

Fig. 5.3 The Catholic Church is the moral authority whose opinions should be adhered to by all citizens (Ipsos Puls 2012)

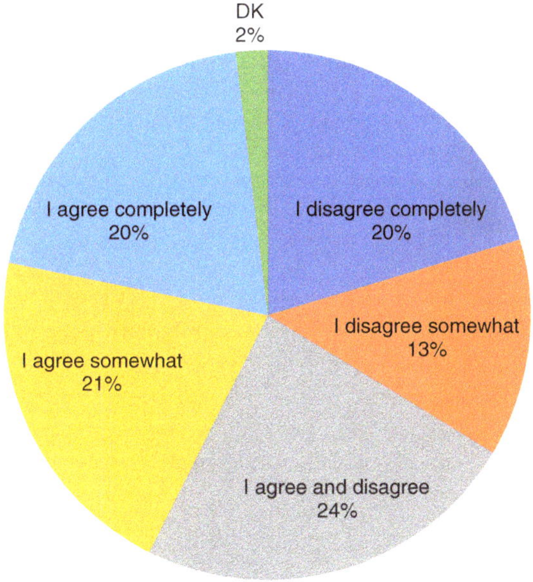

Whereas only some target segments saw forgiveness as exclusively Catholic or Croat, there was much wider agreement across groups that the Orthodox Church was inherently aggressive. Consequently, there was consensus that the Orthodox Church was involved in the war, directly or indirectly. For example, the Zadar war veterans described coming across Orthodox Churches being used as ammunition storage and a non-urban teacher noted, "I know the role of the Orthodox Church in the war, it is well known" (interview with non-urban teacher).

The special place that the Serb minority holds in Croatia, due to the legacy of the war and the large size of it, was reflected in discussions. Respondents felt that the minority was unique and that it received more rights than other minorities, as well as more rights than Croats in Serbia. The Serb minority was considered unique for a range of reasons: for getting special treatment as victims; for their perceived self-imposed segregation; for having to suffer for others' crimes; due to the Law of General Pardon (Narodne Novine 1996)[11]; and so on:

> *Silvio*: I think that today, some 15 years since Operation Storm,[12] they are given such rights and benefits that barely any other minority gets in Croatia (interview with non-urban teacher).
>
> -
>
> *Dario*: We cannot talk about any kind of reconciliation because [the Serbs] are equal citizens of the Republic of Croatia. No one belittles them. Just read an issue of the Serb *Novosti*,[13] by the Serb National Council, and you will see what kind of articles are put in there. Can you in any other country write such articles about the country you live in, to smear it, and to still receive funds from the government (focus group with Sisak teachers)?

Passages such as these were common. Veterans complained a great deal about the Law of General Pardon, which they felt gave Serbs special rights, while on the other hand teachers felt that the general Serb population was unique in that a few "bad apples" had made it difficult for the whole ethnicity to live in Croatia. Generally, however, as in the above passages, the ethnic group was often compared to others, especially Italians in Istria:

Ilija: Because they did not stab the Croatian man in the heart or the back. No Croats attacked these poor Serbs, but they attacked us. But with the Italians it was different. When I was in the army, I was told not to sing the songs about our conquest of Trieste. And we gave Trieste back. There is no more war. In Istria there are many Italians. But they have not hurt Croatia in any way, but the Serbs wanted to put all of Croatia under the boot (focus group with non-urban pensioners).

At times, the position of the Serb minority in Croatia was compared to the Croat minority in Serbia and, again, there was a feeling that Croats were worse off than their Serb counterparts. These comparisons between the Serb minority and other minorities led to a feeling that the Serb minority should not, but does, receive more rights than other minorities. The reasons for this can be divided into four broad categories, each of which features many examples. First, because of what they have done and the legacy of that, so they do not deserve more rights until the country is de-mined or the missing persons are found. Second, because of what they do today, such as voting based on ethnicity. Third, because of what they may do in future, for example to attack once again (this is connected to the notion that the war is not over). Finally, they should not receive more rights because Croats in Serbia do not.

Cyrillic

The issue of Cyrillic signs in Vukovar illustrates the inherent contradictions present in how Croatia and Croats deal with the Serb minority in the country. While nearly all respondents felt that Serbs should have the right to Cyrillic signs, they also felt that it was too soon to put them up in Vukovar. No date was, however, given for when the right time might be. While the Serb minority was for a variety of reasons seen as undeserving of this right, all segments agreed that the government created the issue in the first place. Survey results point to similarly contradictory outlooks.

Across a range of longitudinal measures, attitudes towards ethnic minorities can be interpreted as open and positive. The Kolstø (2011) survey asked a range of questions related to this topic and found that:

- Ethnic identity and civic identity were of nearly equal importance, although civic identity ranked higher than ethnic.
- Respondents felt they had the most in common with inhabitants of Croatia, regardless of ethnicity, rather than members of their ethnicity living abroad.
- There was some disagreement over whether ethnicities in Croatia were treated equally (44.3% felt they were, 45.7% felt they were not), although this does not indicate if respondents were unhappy with how Serbs, Croats or any other ethnicity were treated. Results from focus groups and interviews in this study indicate that it may be the case that Croats are being seen as treated unfairly. On the other hand, the regions that felt strongest that treatment was unequal (and therefore answered "no") were Zagreb, Hrvatsko Primorje, Gorski Kotar, Rijeka and Istria, regions that also displayed the most openness towards Croatian Serbs in the rest of the survey. Slavonia, which on the other hand did not display this, featured the most respondents who felt that treatment was equal. Babić's (2010) longitudinal results further support this difference between the regions.
- Both majority and minority groups were strongly (79.8%) seen as deserving equal rights. In other words, that no one deserved special rights.
- For the most part, interethnic relations were regarded as positive or at the very least rarely negative (Fig. 5.4).
- Interethnic relations were also seen as having improved in the last ten years (Fig. 5.5).
- The Ipsos Puls (2012) survey also found that respondents overwhelmingly felt that ethnicities should not live alone in their own states.

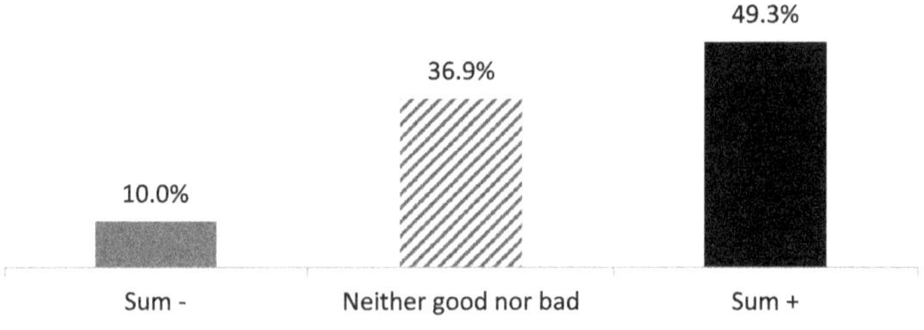

Fig. 5.4 How do you evaluate interethnic relations in Croatia. Do you think they are... (Ipsos Puls 2012)

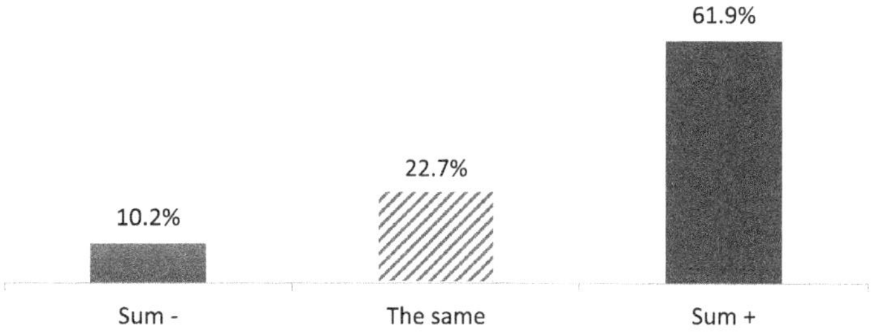

Fig. 5.5 How do you compare current interethnic relations in Croatia compared to ten years ago? Are they now… (Ipsos Puls 2012)

The above stand in stark contrast to the strong objection to Cyrillic signs in Croatia. The same Kolstø (2011) survey found that respondents were predominantly opposed to the introduction of such signs in villages and towns with significant Serb populations (Fig. 5.6). Participants in this study reflected this nearly universally.

That is not to say there was consensus among participants or groups on the issue as a whole, but all participants agreed that this policy ought not to be implemented at the time. Respondents universally argued that introducing Cyrillic signs in Vukovar and in Croatia more broadly was not the same. Vukovar as the "hero city" was frequently raised as the reason for why it was too soon to do so:

Mirna: But we all forget that Cyrillic is also a Croatian alphabet.
Iva: Yes. And formally as well, but this means something different to them.
Mirna: Something different, that is right.
Iva: Those wounds are still too fresh. I do not know, if I were from there, to have lived through it, I do not know how I would react. Currently I have no dilemmas about Cyrillic in Vukovar, just like Istrians have no problems with Italian. And they should have because the Italians occupied them, they depopulated them and everything. But they do not have a problem, 40 years have passed, and they do not have a problem.
Mirna: Yes, yes.
Iva: Maybe in 50 years in Cyrillic in Vukovar will also not be a problem (dyad with non-urban teachers).

-

Mario: To me it is absurd that, not to mention so recently after the end of the war, in our hero city they are trying to force this. These are political games, but it is absurd. Horrible (dyad with Zagreb teachers).

Fig. 5.6 Do you think that the names of villages and towns with significant Serb populations should be also written in Cyrillic? (Kolstø 2011)

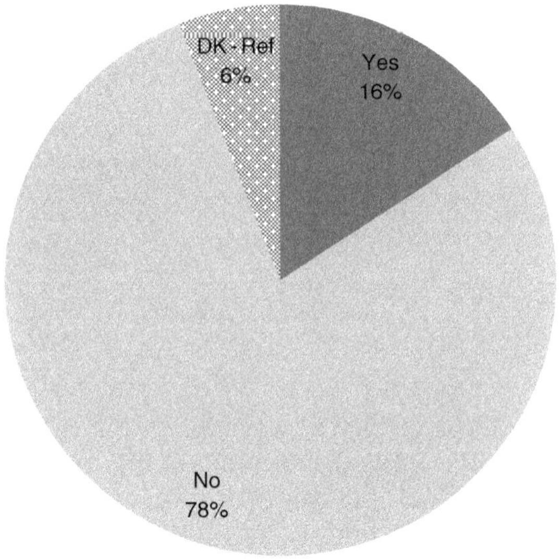

At times, this was seen as a continuation of the war and an act of aggression. It, thereby, fit into the dominant war narrative:

Andriana: They are pouring salt on people's wounds. I do not know how someone even came up with the idea to put [the signs] right there.
Marko: Someone wrote that law and they knew that is could be used in Vukovar. Obviously whoever was making this law was not aware of the geography and population, or it is simply a case of negligence.
Andriana: Yes.
Marko: The state is at fault (focus group with Zadar war veterans).

-

Ana: This is a provocation! They are even waging war in peacetime (focus group with Sisak war veterans).

-

Goran: If I were in power, I would put this Cyrillic on two signs, one at the front of [a group of Serbs], one at the back. And then send them over the Danube. Who knows how to swim, who does not (focus group with non-urban pensioners).

The language employed in many of these passages is highly symbolic ("hero city"), accusatory ("this is a provocation"), emotional ("blood from the war has not dried yet") and at times aggressive ("and then over the Danube"). This highlights the significance of the issue and of the potential for Vukovar and Cyrillic to stir up emotions. As already noted in some of the above passages, the introduction of Cyrillic signs in Vukovar was across all groups seen as the fault of the government and as a political game of some kind. In extreme instances, it was seen as a provocation or even an attack from Zagreb:

Kate: Cyrillic in Vukovar and Cyrillic in Croatia is not the same thing. Cyrillic in Vukovar is a grenade from Zagreb directed at Vukovar. Zagreb is attacking Vukovar (focus group with Zadar war veterans).

Hrvoje: The blood from the war has not dried yet, from the killing of the people in Vukovar and they are bringing, the Prime Minister is bringing signs with Cyrillic to put on… Even a blind man can see that this is a first-class provocation. A provocation (focus group with Zadar pensioners).

All target segments connected the issue of Cyrillic in Vukovar primarily with the Croatian government, at least as the initiator of this effort, and not necessarily with the Serb minority. Overall, it was seen as proof of special treatment of the Croatian Serb community. At times, they were seen as a victim to party politics and at other times as an ally of the "infiltrated" government. Some saw it as a method for politicians to hide real problems, such as the economy, while other saw it deeply mired in party politics and blamed either the SDP or the HDZ:

Dario: This is political.
Nikola: Against the current government.
Dario: Yes, the current government is using Cyrillic to annul greater problems than Cyrillic.
All agree.
Nikola: It is cheaper to put up 100 signs than to remove loss making companies and to revitalise economic life.
Ivo: You need to know that here, as soon as big problem arises.
Dario: A smaller one appears.
Ivo: A media war starts. A new Cyrillic! A new Milošević!
Nikola: Pure politicisation.
All agree
Ivo: Always (focus group with Sisak teachers).

One group of war veterans even saw it as a method for preventing Croats from getting jobs. In this discourse, Cyrillic in Vukovar is interpreted as much more than an issue of minority rights, but instead it is seen as a threat to Croatian jobs and as a continuation of the Croatian struggle for independence. Despite that all groups acknowledged Cyrillic was also a Croatian alphabet and formed a part of the Croatian cultural heritage, many nevertheless felt it had been misappropriated and had become dangerous, since it could and was separating people. Given that both the SDP and HDZ were at times blamed for language problems, it is possible that what started as a 1990s HDZ policy of language change has come to be accepted by the majority of the mainstream political spectrum. The Croatian language and associated alphabets may have become one of the primary sources of national and ethnic identification across the majority of Croatian society.

Conclusion

Participants in the study reflected the notion that Croatian identity is largely defined by religion and language. These elements are contrasted with the "other" to Croatian identity, Serbs. Whereas Croats see themselves as Catholic, speaking Croatian and writing in Latin, Serbs and Serbia are seen as Orthodox Christian, Serbian speaking and writing in Cyrillic. This "other" is also greatly defined by the war narrative, so the Orthodox Church is seen as aggressive, as opposed to the forgiving Catholic Church. Not only were Croats attacked during the war, but also so was the Catholic Church, and general notions of reconciliation are seen as highly based on religion. Croatian identity is, however, based on a much broader set of historical factors and especially the legacies of the Second World War and communism. Together, they help construct how Croats view Serbs.

All participants agreed on only two notions: that Serbs fought on the Croatian side (and do not, therefore, all constitute the enemy) and that Cyrillic signs should not be put up in Vukovar (summarised in Fig. 5.6). This exemplifies the core contradiction in the Croat view of Serbs. On all other issues, the same pattern as before was present, teachers and war veterans generally disagreed, while pensioners showed mixed opinions. It is, however, worth noting that teachers stood out in their lack of debate on this topic, whereas war veterans and pensioners discussed it at length. Serbs were not seen as deserving more rights, despite respondents expressing openness towards minorities in general. This is a type of role reversal from Yugoslavia: because Croats now have certain rights, "others" are not allowed those same rights (Jović 2017: 255). Much of this dynamic was embodied in discussions about Cyrillic signs in Vukovar. A range of survey results and participants' comments across all groups indicated that ethnic minorities had a right to their own language, but that Serbs could not receive this right in Vukovar at the present time. This created a stark contradiction between general openness towards minorities, but no openness towards Serbs right now, with no indication of when the time might be right. This echoes Jović's (2017) observation that Serbs are tolerated, but not given any significant rights or power. Participants across many groups, in a narrative that featured numerous facets of the war narrative, interpreted Cyrillic in Vukovar as an aggression against Croatia, instead of as an issue of minority rights. This narrative offered no rational solutions or visions of the future; instead, it was dominated by emotion and, in particular, anger (Fig. 5.7).

Some individuals are still reliving the war on a daily basis, and alarmingly, this same group also felt their old neighbours, now back, were all potential perpetrators at worst and witnesses at best. Participants overall distrusted institutions meant to protect them and, as if by association, also their Serb neighbours, the Serbian state and the Serbian Orthodox Church. Their memories were not only laced with emotion, they were defined by it.

	Issue	Cyrillic signs in Vukovar (yes/no)	Serbs fought on Croatian side (yes/no)	Much or little debate on ethnic issues	Cyrillic a provocation/attack	Church (Ignored/political/debated)	Serbs inherently aggressive (yes/no)	Returnees are accomplices (yes/no)
Teachers	Zagreb	No	Yes	Little	No	Political	No	No
	Zadar	No	Yes	Little	Yes	Political	No	No
	Sisak	No	Yes	Little	No	Ignored	No	No
	Non-urban	No	Yes	Little	No	Debated	No	No
War veterans	Zagreb	No	Yes	Much	Yes	Ignored	Yes	Yes
	Zadar	No	Yes	Much	Yes	Ignored	Yes	Yes
	Sisak	No	Yes	Much	Yes	Ignored	Yes	Yes
	Non-urban Banovina	No	Yes	Much	Yes	Ignored	Yes	Yes
	Non-urban Slavonia	No	Yes	Much	Yes	Ignored	Yes	Yes
Pensioners	Zagreb	No	Yes	Much	No	Debated	No	No
	Zadar	No	Yes	Much	Yes	Ignored	Yes	Yes
	Sisak	No	Yes	Much	Yes	Ignored	No	No
	Non-urban	No	Yes	Much	No	Political	Yes	Yes

Fig. 5.7 Comparison across groups of attitudes on Serb minority

The ingroup versus outgroup dynamic in this instance has an implication for the Croatian Serb minority in the country, which in the eyes of the majority Croat public continues to be defined by the war narrative. They are defined and discussed as an issue of security (Jović 2017: 254). The introduction of Cyrillic signs in Vukovar seems to have had the effect of simultaneously reducing trust in government institutions and making Croats feel threatened by a perceived Serb threat. The implications of this become more dangerous and pronounced in any instance of higher tensions, violence or war, when outgroup membership can become life threatening.

Notes

1. The Cyrillic alphabet originated in the ninth century with the disciples of Saints Cyril and Methodius, who brought Christianity to the region to south-eastern Europe. In Serbia, it forms a large part of the Serbian literary heritage and is today one of the two alphabets used to write standard modern Serbian. In Croatia, on the other hand, only the Latin alphabet is used.
2. The Croatian city of Vukovar, on the Serbian border in the north-east of the country, was the scene of an 87-day siege by the Yugoslav People's Army (*JNA*) and Serbian paramilitary forces in 1991. It was the most badly damaged Croatian city during the war and following its fall, a number of war crimes took place in and around it. Prior to the war, it was one of the most ethnically diverse parts of Croatia.
3. For more information on the current status of the Serb minority in Croatia, also see the Serb National Council (*Srpsko narodno vijeće or SNV*) sponsored *SNV Bulletin #6*, available at http://snv.hr/file/attachment/file/bilten6-compressed.pdf.
4. This translates to "Vukovar (in the Latin alphabet), not Vukovar (in Cyrillic)".
5. "*Za dom, spremni*", literally translated to "for the home, ready", was the official salute of the NDH (*Nezavisna Država Hrvatska* or Independent State of Croatia), the Croatian fascist puppet state during the Second World War. It was led by the Ustasha movement and was responsible for the mass killings of a high percentage of Croatian Serbs, Jews, Roma and political opponents (most notably Partisan fighters). Chief among the incidents of the salute being used in public events was the shouting of the salute by a Croatian national team football player, Josip Šimunić, to a crowd of 25,000 spectators in Zagreb in November 2013. For an overview of the incident and all of the extensive reactions to it (including by media, elites, sports governing bodies and so on), see Brentin (2016).

6. *Matica Hrvatska*, the institution behind the cited publication, is a non-governmental organisation devoted to Croatian literature and culture. Its aims also include the promotion of Croatian national and cultural identity, and it has played an important role in the history of the standard Croatian language.
7. It is important to note that this is not universal among the Croatian public or political elites. In 2009, President Stjepan Mesić had a highly public dispute with the Croatian Catholic Church over the place of Catholic symbols in public institutions.
8. Langston and Peti-Stantić (2014) base this analysis on a model that divides level of language planning into macro (government) and micro (academic institutions; scholarly literature; and, communication with society) levels.
9. "Croatian" Cyrillic is also known as "Bosnian" or "Western" Cyrillic. It was used in Bosnia–Herzegovina from the eleventh until the eighteenth century and saw resurgence in the 1990s, amid various nation-building aspirations. It is similar to Serbian Cyrillic, although it was never standardised, and has featured in debates over its historical origins (Bosnian, Croat or Serb).
10. The idea of Serb preparation was partly based in fact, since arms shipments from the Yugoslav People's Army were prior to the beginning of the conflict, in October 1991, rerouted and left unlocked in Knin so that local Serbs, informed of this in advance, could obtain them (Ramet et al. 2008).
11. The Law of General Pardon (*Zakon o općem oprostu*) was passed in 1996, following the end of the war. It protected former members of Serb forces from prosecution, other than for serious human rights violations (Narodne Novine 1996).
12. This is factually incorrect, since Operation Storm had (at that stage) taken place nearly 20 years prior to the interview.
13. *Novosti* is a weekly magazine published by the Serb National Council (SNV).

References

Babić, D. (2010). *Etnonacionalizam i rat u Hrvatskoj: Teorijski aspekti i istraživanje međunacionalnih odnosa u lokalnim zajednicama* [Ethnonationalism and war in Croatia: Theoretical aspects and investigation of interethnic relations in local communities]. Zagreb: Plejada.

Banjeglav, T. (2012). Conflicting memories, competing narratives and contested histories in Croatia's post-war commemorative practices. *Politička Misao, 49*, 7–31.

Bellamy, A. J. (2003). *The formation of Croatian national identity: A centuries-old dream?* Manchester: Manchester University Press.
Brentin, D. (2016). Ready for the homeland? Ritual, remembrance, and political extremism in Croatian football. *Nationalities Papers (web)*. Available at http://dx.doi.org/10.1080/00905992.2015.1136996.
Casanova, J. (1994). *Public religions in the modern world*. London: University of Chicago Press.
Council of Europe, Advisory Committee on the Framework Convention for the Protection of National Minorities. (2016, May 30). *Fourth opinion on Croatia adopted on 18 November 2015*.
Croatian Bureau of Statistics. (2011). *Census 2011*. Available at http://www.dzs.hr/default_e.htm.
Dugandžija, N. (2006). Od nacije do reakcije: Nacionalne manjine i nacionalni agnostici (From nation to reaction: Ethnic minorities and ethnic agnostics). Zagreb: Srpsko kulturno društvo "Prosvjeta".
Fishman, J. A. (2006). *Do not leave your language alone: The hidden status agendas within corpus planning in language policy*. Mahway: Lawrence Erlbaum Associates.
Goldstein, I. (2003). *Hrvatska povijest* [Croatian history]. Zagreb: Novi Liber.
HAZU. (2007). *HAZU o hrvatskom jeziku u europskim integracijama* [HAZU on Croatian in European integration]. Available at http://www.hkv.hr/kultura/jezik/962-hazu-o-hrvatskom-jeziku-u-europskim-integracijama.html. Accessed 11 Apr 2016.
Horvat, R. (2009). *Hrvatski identitet* [Croatian identity]. Zagreb: Matica Hrvatska.
Human Rights Watch. (2018). *World report 2018*. Available at https://www.hrw.org/sites/default/files/world_report_download/201801world_report_web.pdf.
Ilišin, I. (2011). Vrijednosti mladih u Hrvatskoj [Values of young people in Croatia]. *Politička Misao, 48*, 82–122.
Ipsos Puls. (2012, January). *Izbori 2011* [Elections 2011].
Jakelić, S. (2010). *Collectivistic religions: Religion, choice, and identity in late modernity*. Farnham: Ashgate.
Joseph, J. E. (2004). *Language and politics: National, ethnic, religious*. New York: Palgrave Macmillan.
Jović, D. (2009). Croatia after Tudjman: The ICTY and issues of transitional justice. *Chaillot Paper, 116*, 13–27.
Jović, D. (2017). *Rat i mit: Politika identiteta u suvremenoj Hrvatskoj* [War and myth: The politics of identity in contemporary Croatia]. Zagreb: Fraktura.
Kolstø, P.l. (2011). *Strategies of symbolic nation-building in west Balkan states: Intents and results*. University of Oslo. Available at http://www.hf.uio.no/ilos/english/research/projects/nation-w-balkan/.

Kordić, S. (2010). *Jezik i nacionalizam* [Language and nationalism]. Zagreb: Durieux.

Koren, S. (2011). "Korisna prošlost"? Ratovi devetesetih u deklaracijama hrvatskog sabora ["Useful past"? The wars of the ninites in the declarations of the Croatian Sabor]. In Cipek, T. (Ed.), *Kultura sjećanja: 1991. Povijesni lomovi i svladanje prošlosti* [Culture of memory: 1991. Historical breaks and overcoming the past] (pp. 123–156). Zagreb: Disput.

Langston, K., & Peti-Stantić, A. (2014). *Language planning and national identity in Croatia*. London: Palgrave Macmillan.

Leutloff-Grandits, C. (2016). Post-Dayton ethnic engineering in Croatia through the lenses of property issues and social transformations. *Journal of Genocide Research, 18,* 485–502.

MacDonald, D. B. (2002). *Balkan holocausts? Serbian and Croatian victim-centred propaganda and the war in Yugoslavia*. Manchester: Manchester University Press.

Narodne Novine. (1996). *Zakon o općem oprostu* [Law on general pardon NN 80/96]. Available at http://narodne-novine.nn.hr/clanci/sluzbeni/265079.html.

Oakes, L. (2001). *Language and national identity: Comparing France and Sweden*. Philadelphia: John Benjamins.

Pavlaković, V. (2008). *Red stars, black shirts: Symbols, commemorations, and contested histories of World War Two in Croatia*. Seattle: The National Council for Euroasian and East European Research.

Pavlaković, V. (2014). Fulfilling the thousand-year-old dream: Strategies of symbolic nation-building in Croatia. In P. Kolstø (Ed.), *Strategies of symbolic nation-building in south eastern Europe* (pp. 19–50). Farnham: Ashgate.

Peskin, V., & Boduszynski, M. (2003). International justice and domestic politics: Post-Tudjman Croatia and the international criminal tribunal for the former Yugoslavia. *Europe-Asia Studies, 55,* 1117–1142.

Prcela, F. (2009). Polog katoličkoga u Hrvatskom identitetu [The role of Catholicism in Croatian identity]. In R. Horvat (Ed.), *Hrvatski identitet* [*Croatian identity*]. Zagreb: Matica Hrvatska.

Ramet, S. P., Clewing, K., & Lukić, R. (2008). *Croatia since independance: War, politics, society, foreign relations*. München: R. Oldenbourg.

Richter Malabotta, M. (2004). Semantics of war in former Yugoslavia. In B. Busch & H. Kelly-Holmes (Eds.), *Language, discourse and borders in the Yugoslav successor states*. Buffalo: Multilingual Matters.

Schäuble, M. (2014). *Narrating victimhood: Gender, religion and the making of place in post-war Croatia*. Oxford: Barghahn.

Sells, M. (2003). Crosses of blood: Sacred space, religion, and violence in Bosnia-Hercegovina. *Sociology of Religion, 64*(3), 309–331.

Smith, A. D. (1991). *National identity*. London: Penguin.

Spiering, M. (1999). The future of national identity in the European Union. *National Identities, 1,* 151–159.
Subotic, J. (2015). Genocide narratives as narratives-in-dialogue. *Journal of Regional Security, 10,* 177–198.
Štiks, I. (2010). Uključeni, isključeni, pozvani: Politike državljanstva u postsocijalističkoj Europi i Hrvatskoj. *Politička Misao, 47*(1), 77–100.
Tajfel, H. (1978). Social categorisation, social identity and social comparison. In H. Tajfel (Ed.), *Differentiation between social groups: Studies in the social psychology of intergroup relations* (pp. 61–76). London: Academic Press.
United Nations, Office of the High Commissioner for Human Rights (OHCHR). (2015, April 30). *Concluding observations on the third periodic report of Croatia.*
Zambelli, N. (2010). A journey westward: A poststructuralist analysis of Croatia's identity and the problem of cooperation with the international criminal tribunal for the former Yugoslavia. *Europe-Asia Studies, 62,* 1661–1682.

CHAPTER 6

War Veterans in Croatia

Under Tuđman, war veterans had a privileged position in society and their associations enjoyed special benefits, as well as extensive financial backing by the government (Fisher 2003). The rest of Croatian civil society has since 1991 been plagued by personality conflicts and fragmentation (Fisher 2003). Support for the war veterans proved useful to the HDZ's discourse of defence and victimisation, while human rights focused NGOs were called "anti-Croatian" by the HDZ and were generally perceived in a negative light (Fisher 2003: 79). Veterans' associations have and continue to enjoy prominent media coverage, since the media have used these issues to boost sales (Fisher 2003: 76). The cumulative effect of the close connection between the HDZ and war veterans' associations is that they are not wholly independent from political institutions and that their actions are, therefore, tied to the performance of the HDZ and similar parties. They still form a part of Croatian civil society, but they also remain distinct from many other parts of it due to this close connection to state institutions. This is reflected in how war veterans' associations act and how they are perceived by the public.

War veterans from the Homeland War have undergone four distinct phases of reporting in the Croatian media, all of which were reflected in the focus groups and interviews by all target segments. The first phase was one of war veteran self-sacrifice and willingness to give their lives for the freedom of Croatia; the second was of war veterans as victims in a society that did not know what to do with them; the third

I. Sokolić, *International Courts and Mass Atrocity*,
Memory Politics and Transitional Justice,
https://doi.org/10.1007/978-3-319-90841-0_6

was one of war veterans as frauds, stealing money from the state; and, finally, the last one was that of enemies of the state and threats to society (Car 2008). War veterans' associations are believed to have prevented the transmission of international human rights norms to the public by fortifying non-compliance preferences in transitional justice (Lamont 2010: 42). Civil society, more specifically war veterans' associations, provided a space where the mobilisation against transitional justice was allowed to flourish (Lamont 2010: 42). The overall picture is, however, ambivalent since human rights NGOs did play a role in catalysing the growth of human rights norms. War veterans' associations remained dependent on state funding, thereby tying their fate to the HDZ whether they were in power or not, which translated into how they acted as a grouping (Rangelov 2013). Civil society actors have, therefore, often exerted pulls in opposing directions, and the outcomes of their efforts have been equally ambiguous. Public protests over the indictments and trials of General Norac and Generals Gotovina, Čermak and Markač exemplify this.

The scale of the 2001 public demonstration against the trial of General Norac took the Croatian media and government by surprise. This showed the potential for civil society actors to challenge the state. In 2004, however, war veterans' associations struggled to reach the same level of mobilisation to protest the indictments of Generals Gotovina, Čermak and Markač without government support. Ivo Sanader, who in 2001 had helped organise the Norac protests as leader of the opposition, had become prime minister and become more committed to cooperation with the EU and the ICTY to further Croatian EU integration (Rangelov 2013: 81). Without his support, only 50,000 people attended the largest event in Split, with only minor crowds elsewhere (Rangelov 2013).

War veterans' associations and nationalistically oriented political parties, especially the HDZ, have since Croatian independence been able to use the memory of the Homeland War in order to legitimise their efforts (Peskin and Boduszynski 2003: 1123). War veterans' associations have had nearly exclusive access to state funding and have since then continued to enjoy relatively positive views in the eyes of most media outlets, while human rights NGOs remain dependent on international funding and are often branded as "communist", even after 2000 (Lamont 2010: 45–46). Because the war narrative has proven to be so enduringly influential in society, war veterans' associations have been able to exploit related symbols to more effectively further their political aims, often ideological ones not specifically related to war veterans' direct interests.

This has two implications. First, it allows the HDZ (or any other political party) to easily appropriate such groups for their own means, by strongly opposing any supposed attacks on the legitimacy of the Homeland War and calling them to arms when needed. This does not, however, mean that war veterans do not also use the HDZ to assure their own continued influence. Second, it means that political aims of war veterans' associations come to overshadow the humanitarian and therapeutic aims of such groups.

Given the prominent role of war veterans' associations in Croatia and in the sphere of civil society, it is important to understand how others in society see them, how they see themselves and how they interact with civil society more broadly. Moreover, in Croatia war veterans' protests receive much press coverage and public interest, potentially diverting attention from larger problems in the country. While the bond between the HDZ and war veterans' associations has certainly grown weaker since 2000, recent protests have once again shown how symbols of the Homeland War can be appropriated in order to mobilise protests around political causes and parties. What briefly stopped in 2000 seems to have now returned to Croatia, and protests in Vukovar and *Savska* seem to exemplify that. Politicians, such as Tomislav Karamarko when he was leader of the HDZ, have openly stated that the law should apply differently to war veterans (Jović 2017: 334). At a more everyday level, in 2018 protests by a widows of war veterans' association regarding the film *Ministry of Love*, a romantic comedy about two men investigating fraud among war widows, resulted in several reschedulings of the movie premiere (Milekić 2018). This was the last in a series of protests about films related to the Homeland War.

This chapter begins by outlining how participants constructed the image of war veterans as a problem. The position of war veterans is seen as dire: they are being manipulated, they have become political, there are too many of their associations and they are fragmented. Because of this, their associations are not trusted, while war veterans themselves are exalted and seen as the embodiment of the war narrative. The chapter then turns to the position of war veterans' associations in Croatian civil society and how they interact with it. Finally, the chapter looks at how war veterans experienced the twin transitions: from conflict to peace and from authoritarianism to neoliberalism. These concepts are semantically linked in the eyes of war veterans. The overall effect of this is that war veterans' associations often have political aims, related to maintaining their status in society, which are prioritised over their rehabilitating aims.

The Problem of the *Branitelji*

War veterans were discussed at length in all focus groups. Generally, there was an impression across all groups that the actual number of war veterans was unknown and that they were hard hit by unemployment and poor pensions, in other words, that they returned to a dire situation. A large part of these discussions focused on the problems with war veterans. This construction of war veterans as a "problem", by both participants and the researcher, is itself problematic. It makes their situation in society difficult by portraying them in a negative light and, therefore, making them unwelcome (which they feel they are). Instead of highlighting that they may have out of the ordinary but manageable needs (as any former combatants do), they are branded as the sick child of Croatian society:

> *Dragan*: I have first-hand experience. My sister in law's son was in the war. From his unit, half later committed suicide, only a couple landed on their feet and now have decent assets. He never wanted to deal with any of it. He was a bit messed up and he did not want to go around to all of those offices, to write those applications and so on. And he now lives in poverty and no one cares (focus group with Sisak pensioners).
>
> -
>
> *Mladen*: My opinion of *branitelji* is that it is a catastrophe because firstly they have no place to work, their jobs are gone. Then young people, 35 or 40, who had jobs, had to get sent into retirement. These people now have nowhere to go so they gather, not all of them, in cafes, in bars, and that is all they do. And what can they do when they meet? They all have the same opinion; they are upset with everything and everyone. I think it would have been healthy for society if it upheld production, that people were given jobs, and not to have to live off the war, which has passed. It has contributed a lot to Croatia, it freed Croatia, but now they need normal jobs. It is catastrophic to retire a boy of 35 or 40. He will remain unemployed until the end of his life. That is horrible.
>
> All agree (focus group with Zagreb pensioners).

War veterans expressed this notion in the broader context of coming back to nothing and of currently having nothing. They linked this problem to their lack of unification and misrepresentation:

Kate: Currently there are 37 *branitelji* in parliament, and they have never had a shared idea, despite their party allegiances, to solve something for the Croatian *branitelji*. This has not happened a single time. Not in a single session of parliament. This means that there is not even a reason to talk about the war. Why should we talk about the war? This is something ugly, dark.

Lana: It is the past.

Lara: It is not the past to me. To me it was yesterday. My husband is gone. I am putting on a uniform, I am carrying a rifle, I am firing.

Kate: This is all done by people who do not have a single wound from the Homeland War. They live comfortably on the cross of these *branitelji*. They cannot see the cross from some cosy office, who would see the cross? But we carry it every day. We live with these people, especially those who also took part. Now this happens on *Savska* and it is some kind of world wonder. Maybe someone has really had enough.

Lana: I do not like to compare, but it really bothers me that the dignity towards the Second and First World Wars has to be sown into younger generations as something that needs to stay with the *narod*. And the feeling that you need to respect that (focus group with Zadar war veterans).

-

Ana: As I said, we came back to nothing. It is different if you return, if you wage a war in another country against someone else, and then you return to your family, your home. Many came back here and no longer had a home. Had nothing. They came back to poverty (focus group with Sisak war veterans).

The above passages illustrate the preoccupation with the memory of the war, or in other words, the preoccupation with not letting it be forgotten since this would mean that the war veterans would be forgotten. In their eyes, they are not only defending the existence of Croatia, but also themselves and their status in society. The Zadar war veterans again highlight the use of Christian symbols to discuss their victimhood, but also how real the war remains to these individuals. To them, it is still a part of everyday life, which creates a distinction between them and the non-veteran population. It also creates a distinction between them and veterans of the Second World War, who they see as revered, rather than forgotten, in society. The war veterans interviewed in the study all felt that they were not unified and that they wanted to have more of a say in Croatian society and politics. They felt manipulated (a common theme) and excluded. Within these discussions, a distinction was often made, explicitly or implicitly, between the "veteran" (*branitel-jska*) population and the rest of the "civilian" population. The Zagreb war veterans below attributed different values to these populations, thereby creating a stratification in society. Again, many respondents felt that the "veteran" population should unify in order to gain a stronger voice and to influence societal values:

Marija: They say there 500,000 *branitelji* in the register, minus the 80 or 90,000 who are buried, but add to that their families, their friends, a range of citizens. When in this country they will have the right, when they will have the right, although they are a minority. When they will have the right to participate, not to decide, but to participate in the defining of what are positive and negative values in this society, then we open the path towards reconciliation. Dialogue is required for reconciliation.

All agree

Domagoj: Absolutely.

Marija: There has to be reconciliation between a civil sector, which has power and money, and it decides.

Alen: And arbitrates.

Marija: What are negative and positive values. And it completely ignores a large part, multiply 500,000, every person has three or four dependants in his family or wherever.

Alen:Half of Croatia really.

Marija: So two million people have a system of values that are based on the values of the people who created this state (focus group with Zagreb war veterans).

The other groups agreed that war veterans suffered from a lack of pensions and that they wanted to be listened to; they wanted the rest of the public to hear their "truth". The other groups also, however, felt that it was difficult to comment on the war veterans since they did hold a special status in society, for better or for worse. They were seen as possibly holding too much power, preventing anyone from speaking out against them:

Vedran: The veteran scene is very strong, and rightfully so, they sacrificed a lot for the state, they created it, but this does not mean that they do not serve it. This does not mean that they can dictate the political picture of Croatia and if someone who was a war criminal on our side has to be tried, they do not have the right to organise protests and I do not know what. When in 2000 the politics of the current government, as they call it in Croatia the Yugonostalgics, the SDP, did not suit them, they then organised a demonstration of 200,000 people with the right wing parties in order to topple the government. Of course it is legitimate to protest and demonstrate, however, we know the underlying reasons. When someone today supports the current government, then he is a Yugonostalgic. If I wanted to prosecute a *branitelj*, then I would be a Serb lover (interview with non-urban teacher).

Dragan: Now a small joke. Ante Tomić wrote in Jutarnji List, about the *branitelji*. Imagine a situation where a *branitelj* wants the service of a woman for sex. And he calls and says "I want this and that". She asks what he wants, oral or what. He asks for the price and she says 500 kunas. He says this is a bit steep. And Tomić started a story that *branitelji* who are *branitelji*, in this society with its unemployment and so one, ask for a bit too much in relation to those who have practically nothing. So the *branitelj* asks for a discount and she says no. So he says, what if someone from the other side now called you. She says the price would stay the same. So the *branitelj* accuses her of equalising the victim and the aggressor (focus group with Sisak pensioners).

Teachers and pensioners felt that a range of sources was manipulating war veterans, including all governments to date. War veterans expressed this more strongly. They believed that because of this manipulation they were repressed and that their "truth" was not heard. This highlights the notion that war veterans, the state and the war narrative represented as "the truth" are all interconnected, not only in academic analyses, but also in the eyes of the public:

Lucija: Those who were participants of the partisan (*narodno oslobodilačka*) fight, or war. They had memorials. They were praised. Today you cannot even say that you have a medal or that you were a *branitelj*, they all spit on you. That is what the Homeland War is to us.

Ana: Politics made it so.

Lucija: Yes.

Ana: Now who is behind the politics? Maybe we are at fault. I especially blame us *branitelji*. This is what I have always been saying.

Sara I agree. I agree that we should have been louder (focus group with Sisak war veterans).

All of the interviewed veterans' groups agreed with the Sisak veterans, that it was their own fault for this state of affairs since "they did not fight enough". This leads to a permanent call to arms by the veterans, who feel they have to not only continue to defend Croatia, but also Croatian values and their own rights within the Croatian state. Much like with the war narrative or Cyrillic signs in Vukovar, war veterans more so than any other group interpret their position in the state as under attack.[1] This is made starker in the context of their perceived diminished rights in post-Tuđman Croatia, and it does offer a higher potential for manipulation. Moreover, they felt that the media misrepresented them and contributed to this state of affairs:

Ema: And how much does the media contribute to this insulting of the *branitelji*? Jure Jurić has killed Pero Perić. It will say that a Croatian *branitelj* killed Pero Perić.

All agree

Ema: Or a Croatian *branitelj* beat his wife. But recently we had an incident here, where a drug addict attacked his girlfriend with a knife. And a Croatian *branitelj* was passing by and he jumped to the girl's rescue. He got stabbed and I am not even sure if he survived.

Lana: He did survive.

Ema: It did not say anywhere that a Croatian *branitelj* saved a woman from a drug addict, it said that Jure Jurić saved a girl. If it is anything negative then, poof, Croatian *branitelj*.

Kate: This is called, in the former UDBA or KOS, linguistic terror. Linguistic terror. Constantly someone is bombarding you with certain words and this goes into the consciousness of people. This has come into the consciousness of people. And it now causes fear (focus group with Zadar war veterans).

As previous chapters have shown, PTSD was present among participants. All groups considered PTSD to be prevalent, hard to diagnose and permanent among the war veteran population. These individuals continue to face great psychological pains, but this also further reinforces the notion of perpetual victimhood in which events are often interpreted as further attacks on the war veteran population. War veterans admitted they suffered from it openly, talked about it at length and alluded to PTSD being a further manner in which their struggle or war was not yet over:

Ana: The world powers, you, Europe, you are playing with us. You are forgetting that we lived through this and that we are still here.
Lucija: And we are still experiencing it.
Sara: It is still not over.
Ana: We are all on pills (focus group with Sisak war veterans).

Such exchanges were common, together with admissions of diagnoses. Moreover, they have the effect of making the notion of conflict or war current and ongoing, since the suffering has not stopped. Children and future generations were also mentioned as the individuals who will continue to suffer from the effects of their (war veteran) parents' suffering from PTSD. The other two target segments predominantly shared these opinions as well.

The war veterans' associations, also known as *udruge*, were seen as predominantly untrustworthy and a blight on war veterans, especially by the interviewed war veterans' groups. A Zagreb war veteran's view was that "the associations are numerous, but there are few associations that I take seriously. They are very rare. The others were formed in order to socialise" (follow-up interview with Zagreb war veteran). Other than showing a general dislike of war veterans' groups, this individual believed their aim should not be socialisation. Given how often group discussions focused on a persistent defence, it is possible this is seen as a more appropriate aim of associations. The defence is centred around pervasive political and societal complaints. Overall, how all of the interviewed war veterans' groups viewed other groups was best described in a long passage by the Zadar war veterans. They were seen as fragmented, too numerous, politically motivated and manipulated. Additionally, these sequences (such as below) often moved from discussions of veterans' issues to politics and how corrupt the world around them is[2]:

Lara: I was in a war veterans' association in Sveti Filip Jakov, but it fell apart. These people had PTSD, they did not like to talk about war, they had receded into themselves and they are easily manipulated. For example, when the presidential elections were on, the head of our group wanted Bandić for President. And we said that we should not discuss politics in the group. He was handing out t-shirts and so on. We did not like that so we parted and have not met since. Only when we need flowers or so on.
[…]
Ema: There is no umbrella organisation that keeps them all organised.

Lana agrees

Ema: They are all over the place. As they say, divide and rule. Well that is what they did with the war veterans associations.

All agree

Lara: I think all of the presidents of these associations just fight for their seat and nothing else. I was a member of a group for PTSD sufferers and I did not get any care, any attention or anything that would help *branitelji* know their rights or get help. I left the group and I joined this one.

Lana: I just wanted to add that a real cancer has started, a disease, when they allowed 200 umbrella associations to be established. This is the folly of the century. It is as if you are saying that you are building a house that will have 200 roofs. If the Croatian *branitelji* exist, if their families exist, who were hit directly or indirectly by war, there exist civilian victims, then I do not see a fourth option. What is this fourth option? It does not exist! But it is allowed, in the name of politics. This is done on purpose. 200 umbrella organisations, and I do not know how many small ones. A million small ones. Why? Because that is how you can manipulate (focus group with Zadar war veterans).

War veterans are seemingly aware of the political manipulation they are subject to. Other segments for the most part agreed with this view of war veterans' associations. They also found them too numerous, politically motivated and fragmented. This led to the view that while war veterans were respected a great deal, their associations were not.

In the eyes of all participants in this study, the war veterans' associations were not representative of war veterans as a whole and were linked with ulterior motives. They were seen as giving war veterans a bad name and were not even considered serious by war veterans themselves. Furthermore, the protests at *Savska* were not wholly supported. While all groups agreed that war veterans had problems they had to tackle, the protesters and groups at *Savska* were generally seen as attempting to divide Croatia for political or corrupt purposes. In some ways, therefore, the perceived connection between war veterans' associations and the government has damaged their image in the eyes of the public. Even honest plights for better treatment may, therefore, be seen as merely political posturing on behalf of party politics.

A recurring topic in discussions was that of victims of the war. A "victim" was not only someone who was physically or mentally injured during the war; instead, it was the whole Croatian population in varying degrees since the war narrative victimises all Croatians. The narrative, therefore, featured a type of stratification, where some victims were seen as more typical of the category than others. In this sense, war veterans were at the top of the hierarchy due to their sacrifices for Croatian independence. Below this were victims on the frontline or in occupied territories and victims who were directly hit by the fighting. Below this was the rest of Croatia, for example residents of Zagreb who were victims, but not as much as residents of Sisak. Finally, there were Croats who fled Croatia to go abroad, who were victims but only to a minor degree.

In Kosovo, a similar hierarchy of victims is semi-legally enshrined and allows for higher benefits and lower eligibility criteria for military victims (Ströhle 2013: 252). The effect of this is that military victims hold higher social value and their calls to arms are legitimised (Ströhle 2013). Competition over the "purest" commitment to the nation has also been contested among politicians and war veterans (Ströhle 2010: 501). In that case, the heroic self-representation of these groups allowed them to make claims for power and to establish clientelistic networks around them (Ströhle 2010: 501). Hints of this are apparent in Croatia, for example with the HDZ presenting themselves as the war veterans' party or business owners using their status as war veterans to further business interests. These types of formal and informal practices can segment social citizenship, as they have done in Kosovo, thereby creating social divisions (Cocozzelli 2009: 119; Ströhle 2013: 259). Entitlement claims premised on heroism or victimhood have also been shown to challenge democratic principles of equality and citizenship, potentially undermining peace and social justice (Bayer and Pabst 2017).

During the fieldwork, war veterans' groups frequently made two specific distinctions: between war veterans and other members of society ("civilians"), and between war veterans who fought on the frontline and those who did not. War veterans in the non-urban and Sisak pensioner groups also admitted that those working behind the scenes during the war were equally responsible for Croatian independence, although this notion never came up with the war veterans' groups. The below are only some examples of this stratification:

> *Ana*: I know what the Homeland War was, I know why I went to war, and I know how we conducted the Homeland War. And everyone who conducted the war, who was in the war, who took part, especially on the battlefields know what the Homeland War is. It is a different question

for those who were here, but who were not on the battlefield. This means they were not directly involved in the action (focus group with Sisak war veterans).

Davor: The defence of this Homeland War is attributed to one side, to one group. It is not attributed to all citizens. But my opinion is that all citizens who lived here, who produced oil, who produced iron, who produced other things, but I mention only these two strategic aspects, they are all participants of the Homeland War. Because they worked under artillery fire, which was worse than being in a shelter. Even on the frontline it was easier, since you had some shelter. They had bunkers there. In the workshops, in INA, you had nothing but work. Production had to continue (follow-up dyad with Sisak pensioners).

All participants, and especially those who were direct victims of the war (the non-urban war veterans' group in Banovina stood out in this regard), felt abandoned by authorities, such as the government, ICTY, judiciary and international community. Victims levelled complaints at the ICTY because none of them had been called to participate in any trials, despite feeling that they had valuable information to present to authorities. Similar complaints were made regarding Croatian authorities. Moreover, war veterans' groups complained of a monopoly on victimhood by certain victims, especially Serb ones, which prevented others from being heard. The other groups also directed similar complaints at war veterans, since they saw that this segment of society was louder than civilian victims. This collective feeling of underrepresentation seems to have led to a degree of finger pointing between the various stratifications.

The Role of Civil Society

War veterans' groups, in particular, felt that civil society in Croatia, meaning human rights NGOs, was dysfunctional and looked to divide Croatian society. This is a common notion in Croatia and also in Serbia, especially with the right-wing press. Despite the proportionately small size of human rights NGOs in both countries, they have often been seen in a negative light, particularly due to their relative success in attracting Western funding, which war veterans' associations have not been able to do. The constant theme in this narrative was that someone or some kind of entity, working in the background, was attempting to divide civil society and war veterans' associations, as well as to equalise guilt or portray the war as a civil war. Some attributed this to an unknown entity, others to infiltration of associations by unwanted elements and others to influence by the international community that was attempting to equalise crimes:

Jasna: It obviously suits someone that they are all separated and act alone. Because if they were united then they would be too strong. I think that if *Documenta*[3] and the war veterans' associations and the civilian associations, and other associations that exist, were to unite and to start working on collective questions, then everything would be solved quickly. But obviously this does not suit someone. There is a constant need to interfere and to instil some kind of hatred. There was a war. It is a fact that that the *JNA* and the Serbs wanted to occupy Croatia, but the Croats rose up and did not allow it.

Lara agrees

Jasna: It was not a civil war, it was a war, there was aggression. Aggression by one state on another.

All agree (focus group with non-urban war veterans Banovina).

-

Tomislav: You will most likely speak to various non-governmental organisation, maybe you already have. I wanted to say what I think would be good. When you are speaking to me or to them. You should consider who comes from where. In terms of family. Not ethnicity. You can then get a complete picture of the truthfulness of my or their dialogue (focus group with Zagreb war veterans).

-

Dalibor: The international community protects certain so called non-governmental organisations, world famous ones. The proof of this is *Documenta*, which as an international institution conducts certain investigations and their aim is the absolute, so-called, equalisation of guilt (dyad with non-urban war veterans Slavonia).

Members of war veterans' associations felt that they and NGOs such as *Documenta*, the Centre for Peace, Nonviolence and Human Rights, the Civic Committee for Human Rights and the Centre for Peace Studies had a basic disagreement over the war narrative and the notion of a defensive war. This meant that NGOs were seen as trying to criminalise the Homeland War. The Zagreb group, in particular, also felt that these human rights NGOs actively prevented other groups, specifically war veterans' associations, from participating in the activities they undertook, thereby creating a monopoly in the space. There is not much support for this in the survey research. The public is relatively divided over the issue, but many respondents did not have an opinion at all (Fig. 6.1).

Other target segments generally did not comment on this topic. Only the Zadar pensioners strongly agreed with the war veterans. They shared their opinion that civil society had been infiltrated (specifically by UDBA) and that they were aiming to write a false history. War veterans expressed a range of other opinions about civil society more broadly. Some believed that at the very least some human rights NGOs and especially *Documenta* had a similar aim to war veterans' associations in attempting to record an oral history of events. Others believed that the fight for monopoly in the sector was due to funding and that human rights NGOs were much better at attracting the significant international funding available, giving them an advantage. The non-urban war veterans in Banovina, for example, felt that although they disagreed with *Documenta* and other local organisations (most notably a local human rights NGO), they agreed that they also had the right to participate in the debate and provide their own view. Finally, and specifically with regard to transitional justice, some felt that only human rights NGOs had access to justice, since they had the necessary funding to engage with courts.

Other target segments did not comment on civil society nearly as much, nor were they asked as many questions on the topic. The one general thread that was common is that they believed that civil society groups, both war veterans' associations and human rights NGOs, do not communicate effectively despite having the same aims:

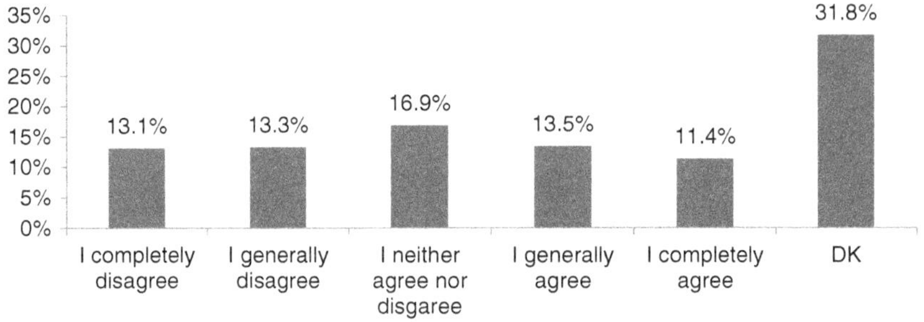

Fig. 6.1 Do you agree with the following statement: the most dangerous enemy of Croatia are so-called fighters for human rights, who come from the ranks of Yugonostalgics and members of foreign agencies (Ipsos Puls 2012)

Marko: I think both sides do a good job, but that the problem is more in communication rather than in the actual work. Both are trying to help people who have been suffered and are trying to get to the truth about the war (focus group with Zadar teachers).

This teacher went on to say that lack of communication was also the problem with RECOM.[4] In a follow-up interview, he elaborated that he felt RECOM suffered from horrible leadership, despite being an initially sound idea. He felt that the far right in Croatia had, therefore, managed to convince the public that RECOM is an attempt to falsify the truth. This does highlight the two-sided nature of the project, which identifies with and involves many human rights groups that war veterans are highly critical of, such as *Documenta*, while also including war veterans' associations in the coalition. This novelty makes it both remarkable and confusing to outsiders. Overall, however, this was the only mention of RECOM throughout the fieldwork.

Twin Transitions—Neoliberal and Post-conflict Transition

During and since the Homeland War, Croatia experienced two simultaneous transitions, that of transitional justice and of a shift to the neoliberal economic model. Croatia's economic transition was marked by widespread corruption led by an elite class of businessmen and politicians. As a consequence, Croatians do not make a semantic distinction between the two transitions, "capitalism" is linked to "democracy", which is linked to the "European Union", which is linked to the "ICTY" and so on. The dynamic between the twin transitions has broad societal implications. It shows the inconsistency between how a period of change is greeted and how it is experienced. It shows how war veterans, as a disproportionately influential part of civil society, do not only remove space for action from human rights NGOs, but also from more economically focused groups, such as unions. Finally, core parts of the war narrative, such as the notion that the aggression has continued, can be used in order to divert attention from economic problems in the state. The cumulative effect of this is that the transitional justice process could be suffering from an image problem associated with an economic transition marked by corruption, since they are seen as linked.

The two older target segments, pensioners and member of war veterans' associations, discussed at length the period during the war as one of hope, unity and harmony, which they juxtaposed with the post-war (and current) period where this hope was lost. The new situation was characterised by a loss of employment opportunities and a rise in corruption. For some, the memory of the war was characterised by this loss. The examples were numerous:

Moderator: Has your opinion of the Homeland War changed since the end of the war?
Vladimir: Yes, for the worse.
Stjepan agrees
Goran: It all started so well. Together. The *narod*, the people, there were Serbs there as well, people were coming from abroad. And in the end the representatives of the state trick you. This one starts to steal. From the President to whomever has an opportunity.
Stjepan: The difference [since the war ended] is huge. A lot of people expected to have a job, but they stayed on the street (focus group with non-urban pensioners).

-

Dragan: Many people were previously successful in the industry here, which was large here. Unfortunately today it is gone (focus group with Sisak pensioners).

-

Ana: Our companies have all disappeared. Or in our place there are now Serbs who conveniently stayed behind, who were not allowed to go to war.
Sara: They had work duties.
Ana: While we had rifles on our shoulders, they got work duty through their connections, so they were not allowed to go to the battlefield, instead they were in the companies. So you come back and you do not even have the company. You are killed by the poverty and misery. By the time you realised what they are doing to your state, you are old and sick. Young people came, like you new historians, who are now telling us what we should do. INA is failing. We remember 1995 when we had to work hard for INA. Do I remember? And what about those people who were left here with these work duties, who remained behind to care for the city, for my companies. Where have the companies gone? I defended my state. And now I should cower. They should call me up again, because jobs are disappearing. By the time we realised that it is not good to let someone else run your state… If you knew how to create it, then you also know how to run it.

Lucija agrees

Ana: If you know how to guard your house, then you know how to run the family in that house. By the time we realised this, they had already ruined it for us (focus group with Sisak war veterans).

To the Sisak war veterans, Serbs and those who did not fight in the war represented two groups of people who were less deserving and less able to run the state, in comparison with those who literally fought for the country. They connect the disappearance of jobs to the Serb minority, specifically those who did not fight, and even feature a type of call to arms ("they should call me up again"). They not only ignore the economic reasons for unemployment, but also place blame on the Serb minority in the state. The closing down of the INA oil refinery was a relevant topic at the time and discussions in the predominantly industrial city of Sisak, where the refinery is based, saw much discussion about jobs as a consequence of this. This feeling was, however, expressed across all geographic locations to a certain extent. Corruption was seen as the embodiment of this loss of hope and harmony. The concept of a job was seen as one of the aims of the war; in other words, people fought and died for jobs:

Goran: In the beginning there was faith and hope.

Stjepan: That people got what they fought for. Their jobs. For no one to prevent that. If they had received that, that would be dignity, gratefulness for this Homeland War.

Goran: That war would have at least brought you what you fought for. To have a job, for your child to get an education and to know that you will have work (focus group with non-urban pensioners).

As far as pensioners and war veterans were concerned, the legacy of the conflict and the transition to neoliberalism were inextricably linked. The Croatian government was seen as selling out the Croatian soldiers by not giving them a job to return to. There is a structural fault in the Croatian state underpinning this: the high pensions awarded to war veterans, in relation to other citizens, have made it difficult for war veterans to reintegrate into the labour market (European Commission 2018). Unemployment and economic struggle were discussed through the use of symbols of the Homeland War and, thereby, connected to the continuing need for defence. Additionally, all target segments saw reconciliation and the economy as connected. They regarded a strong economy as the key to reconciliation and saw some transitional justice issues as means to divert attention from the economy (such as the issue of Vukovar discussed in the previous chapter):

Dinko: And now it is getting to Croatia and Serbia throwing insults at each other. One complains about Šešelj and the others retort about ten Cyrillic signs. So this is being kept up.
Marko: I think it is much more important for Croatia and Serbia to find ways to cooperate better economically, Vojvodina and Slavonia, so then people who would have work to do would be less burdened by these problem. It is the worst when a person is disempowered, humiliated and unemployed.
Andriana: It is toughest economically. They would be much happier in their situation without that (focus group with Zadar teachers).

-

Ivan: Ordinary people. Now ordinary people do not need to reconcile, since they never fought. Just like someone mentioned, the economy. The airport in Osijek was approached by the Serbian side, they want to use the services of the Osijek Airport for their purposes. The economy will reconcile this, it has to.
Pero and Davor agree.
Ivan: Common interests will be found in the economy, in investment (focus group with Sisak pensioners).

-

Marijan: People [in Vukovar] are under heavy tensions and frustrations. If they were not frustrated, then none of this would be happening. But many are frustrated. Frustrated because someone is fuelling the fire. And this is causing the bigger problem. If it were not so then everything would be fine. Instead of opening factories, instead of focusing on employment, they are doing this (follow-up interview with Zagreb pensioner).

Evidence that economic concerns are related to the legacy of conflict and socialism by certain parts of the public was found in the focus group discussions. War veterans and some pensioners' groups connected economic failures to the lack of lustration in Croatia following the war and the long-term effects of Yugoslav socialism. These two elements are merely two examples of a variety of reasons given by these target segments, as the reasons for Croatia's poor economic performance:

Josip: The Great Serbs, Yugonostalgics, people who persecuted Croatia and Croats throughout history. Today they have infiltrated all parts of the Croatian administration and politics, all parts of life. That great idea of reconciliation, and thank God for Dr. Tuđman's great idea, since it is a major reason for today's freedom of the Croatian *narod*. However, after the war ended, I am absolutely for it, I was then and I am now, to undertake some kind of lustration. Why? What is happening in Croatia today, it is coming exactly from those cadres, those people, those currents of Croatian political life. They just have to work a bit for people to forget about the serious topics, like why is our economy like this, why is our economy in recession for 12 quarters, why despite joining the European Union Croatia has the worst European economy, why we do not see economic improvement in the near future. Those same currents, today and before, their aim is to remain in power and to destroy the pan-Croatian national spirit. The pan-Croatian national spirit was present in the war, in the defence and so on. And today it would be unique in the economic recovery, if it were not for these people (dyad with non-urban war veterans Slavonia).

-

Vlasta: I think [the other focus group participants] are people from an old environment of fear of communism. You cannot freely say that they wanted a Croatian state, you saw how they always kept on finding negative things. It really struck me when I told them we were craftsmen, for two generations now, my parents and now me. We truly could not wait for private capital to finally come, for entrepreneurship to start moving forward. But yesterday they started spitting on this "what are you business owners? You stole! You bought a yacht by cheating on taxes!" I do not have a yacht, my daughter lives downstairs. At the end of the day, if we have two generations, and we had many workers, we worked hard, and we were big. But I am not an enemy of the state. That communist mentality has remained in some people, with the older generation. That all those who have something robbed the state (follow-up interview with Zagreb pensioner).

-

Domagoj: In Croatia the situation with the economy, finances, the administration of resources—Croatian waters, the floods—is poor. Poor administration of the sea. Of sources of oil, gas and energy. These are consequences of a catastrophic approach and running of the economy during the 50 years of socialism (follow-up interview with Zagreb war veteran).

It is easy to see how the above war veterans' passages can easily be interpreted as forming a part of their desire and attempt to return the HDZ to power, by using economic concerns as the reason. The intertwined narratives on what can broadly be described as transitional justice issues[5] and economic concerns can mean that transitional justice efforts suffer from being seen as related to economic grievances. Moreover, self-conceptions of defence and victimisation in Croatia against larger, foreign powers may now be set against neoliberal globalisation instead (Schäuble 2014). The disparity between how the period of change was greeted and how it was experienced is, therefore, also associated with any actors involved in transitional processes. Arguably, this stems from the failure of transitional justice institutions to make it clear who they were designed to deal with and how, leaving other plights for justice to different actors. The cumulative effect is that some segments of society see economic failures as caused by issues in the realm of transitional justice, while others see transitional justice as a means to divert attention from economic failures.

Conclusion

War veterans and their associations, staunchly opposed to the transitional justice process, continue to be the most influential part of Croatian civil society. War veterans remain preoccupied with the war narrative and continue to see a need to defend Croatia, the values of the Homeland War and their own rights in society. They feel like "the radical losers in the war" (Schäuble 2014: 201). This makes it easy for political actors to manipulate them, especially right-wing parties, like the HDZ, who have in the past given war veterans special benefits due to their shared priorities regarding the Homeland War. Veterans might associate the HDZ with protection of the war, but they might also see it as a means to once again gain more funds and powers. This creates tensions between how war veterans are seen as individuals and how their associations are seen.

While war veterans remain respected by the Croatian public, war veterans' associations are on the whole distrusted and viewed as fragmented, politically manipulated and too numerous. War veterans share this belief about their own associations. Given the preoccupation of war veterans with political and social issues, it is not surprising that socialising and humanitarian services of war veterans' associations are ignored and seen as inferior. It is also then easy to imagine why others see them as politically manipulated. It is possible that what started as a means for the large associations to keep or get the HDZ in power, with the aim of maintaining or returning to a Tuđmanist state of affairs, has had a spill-over effect on the smaller associations that took part in this study. Only one group seemed to have an overt connection to the HDZ, while the others seemed dissatisfied with the political system as a whole, including the HDZ. Despite this and possibly inadvertently, their narratives featured symbols from the Homeland War, calls to arms, nostalgia over the Tuđman regime and so on; all mannerisms associated with war veterans' associations of the 1990s.

A comparison of views across groups (Fig. 6.2) shows a high degree of unanimity on this topic, especially in comparison with others. All groups agreed that war veterans were being manipulated, that the war veterans' associations were not to be trusted and that the key to reconciliation was in the economy. Transitional justice and neoliberal transition were semantically linked by war veterans and pensioners, while teachers generally distinguished between the two. War veterans expressed a worry

	Issue	War veterans are being manipulated	Are the udruge trustworthy?	Key to reconciliation is the economy	Transitional justice and neoliberalism are linked	Main issue facing war veterans is	View of NGOs
Teachers	Zagreb	Yes	No	Yes	**No**	**Jobs/pensions**	**Neutral**
	Zadar	Yes	No	Yes	**No**	**Jobs/pensions**	**Neutral**
	Sisak	Yes	No	Yes	**No**	**Jobs/pensions**	**Neutral**
	Non-urban	Yes	No	Yes	**No**	**Jobs/pensions**	**Neutral**
War veterans	Zagreb	Yes	No	Yes	Yes	Being forgotten	Look to divide
	Zadar	Yes	No	Yes	Yes	Being forgotten	Look to divide
	Sisak	Yes	No	Yes	Yes	Being forgotten	Look to divide
	Non-urban Banovina	Yes	No	Yes	Yes	Being forgotten	Look to divide
	Non-urban Slavonia	Yes	No	Yes	Yes	Being forgotten	Look to divide
Pensioners	Zagreb	Yes	No	Yes	Yes	**Jobs/pensions**	**Neutral**
	Zadar	Yes	No	Yes	Yes	**Jobs/pensions**	Look to divide
	Sisak	Yes	No	Yes	Yes	**Jobs/pensions**	**Neutral**
	Non-urban	Yes	No	Yes	Yes	**Jobs/pensions**	**Neutral**

Fig. 6.2 Comparison across groups of attitudes on war veterans

that they and their sacrifices were being forgotten. This feeling was also shared by the other two target segments, but they discussed this more in terms of jobs and pensions, while war veterans had more emotional preoccupations about their position in society. Finally, the greatest difference in opinion was over what the role of human rights NGOs was, who war veterans and a group of pensioners saw as looking to divide Croatian society, while other groups were neutral on the topic.

What does this high degree of unanimity over war veterans mean? The narrative surrounding war veterans, their sacrifice and the problems they face seems to be unifying. They embody the spirit of the war narrative since they are seen as the truest victims of the Homeland War, the ones who made the greatest sacrifices. Alternatively, it could also be that, because of their place in the war narrative, it is considered socially unacceptable to critique their position and actions (something that would be reflected in the focus group setting in particular). Others may have a fear of speaking out at all, which was reflected in some interviews with teachers, who alluded to negative aspects of the special status war veterans have in Croatian society. The position of war veterans also highlights the need for social justice, alongside restorative and transitional justice, in the aftermath of conflict (Cocozzelli 2009). This often takes the form of a comprehensive social welfare system, which if neglected, can create social divisions, as it has in Kosovo (Ströhle 2013: 247). This means that transitional authorities, be they internal or external, need to pay careful attention to the social divisions and structural inequalities that are the result of different war narratives and memories (Ströhle 2013: 264).

At the time of the fieldwork, the HDZ was not in power, but with an election on the horizon, it had started to frequently employ nationalist symbols to raise their popularity among voters. War veterans' associations proved to be a useful ally since they fervently rally behind such causes. The relationship between Croatian economic transition and transitional justice highlights this, since the two are semantically identical in much of the public's eyes, and this allows issues between the two to be used interchangeably, easily diverting attention from one area by emphasising issues in the other. For example, calls for jobs for war veterans can be used to divert attention from broader issues of unemployment. This also shows the inconsistency between how a period of change can be greeted and how it can be experienced, with a stark contrast between hope and despair. The cumulative effect is that while war veterans' associations hold an influential position in society, they have been opposed to transitional justice and, given their preoccupation with the Homeland War, they can be manipulated by political actors. This allows political actors to divert attention from, for example, economic issues to issues related to the war narrative, which are seen as much more imminent in an atmosphere of perpetual defence.

Notes

1. In reality, however, war veterans receive a large number of benefits and vast quantity of monuments have been built and continue to be built across the country. These pay tribute to their sacrifices and reflect their role in society.
2. The official number of war veterans' associations according to the Croatian Ministry of War Veterans' Affairs is roughly 6300. See https://registri.uprava.hr/#!udruge.
3. *Documenta* aims to foster dialogue that focuses on interpretations, rather than dispute, of facts. Other key aims are: fostering public dialogue and judicial processes (including regional truth commissions and teaching of history); documentation of human losses; and improvement of judicial standards through monitoring.
4. The initiative for RECOM is a regional attempt to establish a commission for the establishment of facts about human rights violations committed in the former Yugoslavia from 1991 to 2001. It is a regional coalition formed of various human rights NGOs, war veterans' associations and victims' associations.
5. Lustration, the legacies of socialism and the Homeland War, perceived infiltration of Croatian institutions by unwanted elements, the need for a continued defence and so on.

References

Bayer, M., & Pabst, A. (2017). Heroes and victims: Economies of entitlement after violent pasts. *Peacebuilding, 29*(1), 49–64.

Car, V. (2008). Myths in media texts: How media in Croatia treats veterans and tycoons. *Medianali, 2*, 145–163.

Cocozzelli, F. P. (2009). *War and social welfare: Reconstruction after conflict.* Basingstoke: Palgrave Macmillan.

European Commission. (2018). *Country report Croatia 2018.* Available at https://ec.europa.eu/info/sites/info/files/2018-european-semester-country-report-croatia-en.pdf.

Fisher, S. (2003). Contentious politics in Croatia: The war veterans' movement. In P. Kopecký & C. Mudde (Eds.), *Uncivil society? Contentious politics in post-communist Europe* (pp. 74–92). London: Routledge.
Ipsos Puls. (2012, January). *Izbori 2011* [Elections 2011].
Jović, D. (2017). *Rat i mit: Politika identiteta u suvremenoj Hrvatskoj* [War and myth: The politics of identity in contemporary Croatia]. Zagreb: Fraktura.
Lamont, C. K. (2010). *International criminal justice and the politics of compliance*. Farnham: Ashgate.
Milekić, S. (2018). *Croatian war widows slate HRT 'insulting' comedy film*. Balkan Insight. Available at http://www.balkaninsight.com/en/article/war-widows-pressure-croatian-public-tv-over-film-01-12-2018.
Peskin, V., & Boduszynski, M. (2003). International justice and domestic politics: Post-Tudjman Croatia and the international criminal tribunal for the former Yugoslavia. *Europe–Asia Studies, 55,* 1117–1142.
Rangelov, I. (2013). Contesting the rule of law: Civil society and legal institutions. In B. D. Vesna, J. Ker-Lindsay, & D. Kostovicova (Eds.), *Civil society and transitions in the western Balkans* (pp. 71–84). Basingstoke: Palgrave Macmillan.
Schäuble, M. (2014). *Narrating victimhood: Gender, religion and the making of place in post-war Croatia*. Oxford: Barghahn.
Ströhle, I. (2010). The politics of reintegration and war commemoration. The case of the Kosovo Liberation Army. *Südosteuropa, 58,* 478–519.
Ströhle, I. (2013). Kosovo Liberation Army veterans' politics and contentious citizenship in post-war Kosovo. In S. Pavlović & M. Živković (Eds.), *Transcending fratricide: Political mythologies, reconciliations, and the uncertain future in the former Yugoslavia* (pp. 243–264). Baden-Baden: Nomos.

CHAPTER 7

An Atmosphere of Pessimism and Distrust: Comparison of Results

The interaction between different narratives and memories, produced and reproduced at different levels of society, is complicated and confusing. The preceding chapters have shown the structure of narratives associated with the transitional justice process in Croatia and how they interact with each other in some detail. It is, however, difficult to distinguish patterns across all of the investigated themes and target segments. This chapter will highlight some of these patterns by using Qualitative Comparative Analysis (QCA).

The main purpose of QCA is to take in-depth analyses of single cases and systematically compare them across a larger number of cases, often to ascertain causal factors. In this study, however, the purpose of QCA was to illustrate and to validate. QCA helped illustrate patterns that occurred across the interviewed target segments and to help ascertain why they occurred. For example, how did teachers express different attitudes towards transitional justice and specifically where did their views differ from other target segments? Moreover, the method can more clearly illustrate where the war narrative is particularly strong and where there is some debate. QCA can also help validate results, by systematically showing how certain discussions recurred across groups and how debate over certain topics may have led to a different understanding of transitional justice. The purpose of the QCA was, therefore, not to ascertain causality or causal paths, but to look for patterns.

I. Sokolić, *International Courts and Mass Atrocity*,
Memory Politics and Transitional Justice,
https://doi.org/10.1007/978-3-319-90841-0_7

The analysis used crisp set QCA for the sake of simplicity, in terms of both analysis and visualisation. This means that the various factors were, for the most part, dichotomised. The analysis of the whole set of factors showed no patterns, so the factors were divided along thematic lines (as they were discussed in the chapters). Themes that saw total agreement were removed from the QCA, but are discussed below. Logical remainders, such as parsimonious and intermediate solutions, which form a crucial part of QCA, were ignored since the aim was not to ascertain causality. QCA also uses the terminology of necessary and sufficient conditions. A sufficient condition is one that, if satisfied, guarantees a certain outcome. A necessary condition, on the other hand, is one that *must* be satisfied in order to achieve the outcome. For example, it is *sufficient* to skip a final exam to fail a course, but it is not the only way to fail a course; it is *necessary* to be female to be pregnant (Goertz and Mahoney 2012: 21). These are important in QCA to draw conclusions about causality, but in this study necessary conditions were particularly illustrative of patterns, while sufficient conditions for the most part highlighted the complexity of the narratives. They are included below only if they had high coverage of cases.

The analysis aimed to explain whether the transitional justice process in Croatia was successful in achieving some of its stated goals. This is based on the theory of deliberative justice, which argues that transitional justice is successful if it leads to a debate on topics relevant to the process. The analysis, therefore, looked for areas where debate or questioning over themes in the dominant war narrative occurred. The chosen "outcome" for the QCA was whether deliberation happened on the key topics that transitional justice deals with.

The following sections outline the results of the QCA theme by theme. Each section provides the relevant data used, the necessary conditions and the sufficient conditions, if any. Only conditions with significant coverage are included, meaning that a set of conditions had to cover more than one case (group) to be included. A presentation of the outcomes and the areas of universal agreement (those that featured no debate whatsoever) across groups precede these analyses. Together these also highlight potential future areas for study. Finally, the results are amalgamated and, through the use of focus group quotes, connected to the prior chapters.

Outcomes

It is debatable if it is at all possible to talk about "success" of transitional justice, since such a high degree of ambiguity is attached to the goals of the process. For the purposes of the QCA analysis, the outcome of transitional justice was assumed to be the presence, or not, of a debate on transitional justice issues. This outcome was drawn from six topics taken from the focus group discussions that were defined as "aims" of transitional justice, for the most part relating to understandings of the rule of law. They are both factual questions (such as the first two, based on belief in ICTY rulings) and value questions (the remaining four). These highlight how transitional justice is concerned with both the transmission of facts and with normative change:

- Did only Serbia commit aggression during the war? This is contradicted by ICTY rulings on Croatian involvement in Bosnia.
- Was there Croatian involvement in Bosnia? Again, ICTY rulings relate to this.
- Are crimes of passion war crimes?
- Are war crimes possible in a defensive war?
- Did Croatian forces commit war crimes? Domestic war crimes trials proved this to be the case.
- Did trials at the ICTY or domestic courts have any significance in the eyes of participants?

The outcome was reduced to a binary 0 (if three or less of the topics saw debate) or 1 (if four or more topics saw debate). In other words, transitional justice was adjudged to have been "successful" in initiating a debate if four or more areas of the six featured debate (Fig. 7.1).

It is possible that on the topics that featured debate, individuals already disagreed due to their existing orientations, which was reflected in results. In other words, that debate was not a result of transitional justice, but of existing social divisions. Given the difficulty in ascertaining causality, it is hard to decisively dispute such an explanation, other than to highlight that the survey results showed no clear distinctions between groups that would point to inherent social divisions. For example, university education seemed to only make a small difference in attitudes, but not independently of other factors. Moreover, the lack of representativeness means it is not possible to generalise with this data.

		Aggression (any debate over if it was only Serbian or if it is a war crime)	Croatian involvement in Bosnia had negative elements (yes/no)	Crimes of passions are war crimes (yes/no)	Crimes possible in defensive war (yes/no/both)	Croatian war crimes (silence or debate present)	ICTY/Domestic trials have signifiance (yes/no)	Deliberation present (yes=1, no=0)
Teachers	Zagreb	**Some debate**	**Yes**	**Yes**	**Yes**	**Debate**	**Yes**	1
	Zadar	**Some debate**	**Yes**	**Yes**	**Yes**	**Debate**	**Yes**	1
	Sisak	No debate	No	**Yes**	**Yes**	**Debate**	**Yes**	1
	Non-urban	**Some debate**	**Yes**	**Yes**	**Yes**	**Debate**	**Yes**	1
War veterans	Zagreb	No debate	No	No	**Both**	Silence	**Yes**	0
	Zadar	No debate	No	No	No	Silence	No	0
	Sisak	No debate	No	No	No	Silence	No	0
	Non-urban Banovina	No debate	No	No	No	Silence	No	0
	Non-urban Slavonia	No debate	No	No	No	Silence	No	0
Pensioners	Zagreb	**Some debate**	**Yes**	**Yes**	**Yes**	**Debate**	**Yes**	1
	Zadar	No debate	No	No	No	Silence	No	0
	Sisak	No debate	**Yes**	No	**Both**	**Debate**	**Yes**	1
	Non-urban	No debate	No	**Yes**	**Both**	**Debate**	No	0

Fig. 7.1 Overview of QCA outcomes

Fig. 7.2 Comparison of group outcomes

Deliberation Present	Deliberation Not Present
Zagreb teachers	Zagreb war veterans
Zadar teachers	Zadar war veterans
Sisak teachers	Sisak war veterans
Non-urban teachers	Non-urban Banovina war veterans
Zagreb pensioners	Non-urban Slavonia war veterans
Sisak pensioners	Zadar pensioners
	Non-urban pensioners

Across groups, the difference between the war veterans and teachers becomes obvious, whereas pensioners show mixed opinions (Fig. 7.2).

This simplification is useful for illustration, but it does miss nuances. For example, the groups of pensioners displayed mixed opinions compared to the overall less ambiguous teachers and war veterans; the Sisak teachers stood out compared to teachers in other locations; and the Zagreb war veterans did feature some discussion, at least compared to other war veterans' groups. Finally, the theme of the ICTY being seen as necessary or not has been excluded in this part of analysis since it correlates exactly with the outcome of debate over transitional justice. In other words, groups that felt the ICTY was necessary also featured debate on transitional justice. This most likely indicates that both outcomes are the result of a third factor, but ultimately this study cannot ascertain the exact significance of this. It is possible that individuals who see a purpose to the ICTY may also see a reason to question recent history and dominant narratives.

Before outlining the key differences between and among target segments, it is important to note the high degree of agreement across groups. In many ways, the most striking feature of this analysis is how much agreement is present across target segments and locations on key parts of various narratives (Fig. 7.3). This highlights that some narratives are too strongly ingrained in society to be easily undermined or even debated.

Within the predominant war narrative, the key notion of Croatian self-defence is not questioned at all, although all other elements are at least debated somewhat. Likewise, all participants discussed this in a local and personal manner, which hints at the everyday nature of this

Theme		
Sources of information	Participants and television highly trusted.	The ICTY, domestic courts, political parties and war veterans' associations highly distrusted.
The war narrative	Agree that the war was in self-defence and a struggle for survival.	The war narrative is discussed in a local and personal manner.
The rule of law	The ICTY is regarded as inefficient.	
Serbs in the eyes of Croats	Agree that there should not be Cyrillic signs in Vukovar.	Acknowledge that Serbs fought on Croatian side.
War veterans	Agree that war veterans are being manipulated, that war veterans' associations are corrupt and untrustworthy and that the economy is the key to reconciliation.	

Fig. 7.3 Topics of agreement across all groups and target segments

particular narrative. The ICTY is regarded as inefficient, although as subsequent sections will show, this does not mean their verdicts do not hold any significance. The view of the Serb minority, however, highlights the contradictions present among the Croatian public. Whereas there is widespread acknowledgement that they did fight on the Croatian side, there is also total agreement that there should not be Cyrillic signs in Vukovar. Given Vukovar's unique position in the Croatian war narrative, it is possible that views on Cyrillic in Vukovar are not necessarily also views on the Serb minority in Croatia. It is also possible that views on the Serb minority vary according to where people live, more so than this study has been able to highlight. Survey data support this notion (Fig. 7.4).

QCA of the participant survey results (handed out prior to focus groups) found no significant patterns. A simplification of the data showed some rough patterns. Many groups where debate took place did not place a lot of emphasis on the fate of their nation or did not take an interest at all; did not consider Croatian individuals indicted by courts to be heroes; did not consider it important to demonstrate their national belonging; and did have university degrees.

The War Narrative

The raw data regarding the war narrative (Fig. 3.2) was dichotomised as follows:

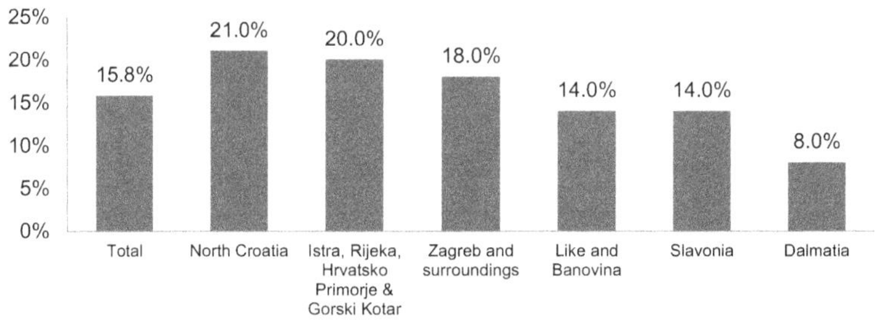

Fig. 7.4 Respondents who think that names of villages and towns with significant Serb populations should also be written in Cyrillic (Kolstø 2011)

- Vukovar (VU): elements over the Vukovar narrative were questioned (1) or they were not (0).
- Yugoslavia (YC), Milošević (MC) or both (BC) were seen as criminal: this condition was not dichotomised, but was split into three possible options: that Yugoslavia was criminal, that Milošević was or that both were. In the table, this is presented as binary, where 1 stands for the belief being present and 0 not. This was done because this view was expressed in such distinct ways and the criminalisation of one system or the other implies an important contrasting view of the past.
- The war is not over (WO): a belief in this notion (1) or not (0).
- Other conditions are present in the raw data table, but these make up a part of the outcome (TJ) (Fig. 7.5).

The analysis of necessity shows that only one condition was necessary (wo), so all groups that believed the war not to be over also did not deliberate on transitional justice issues, and vice versa. In other words, "wo" was the only necessary condition with 100% coverage that led to a deliberation on transitional justice. The sufficiency analysis highlights the importance of which system is considered to be criminal[1]:

VU*yc*mc*BC*wo	Zagreb teachers; non-urban teachers; Zagreb pensioners
vu*yc*MC*bc*wo	Zadar teachers; Sisak pensioners
vu*YC*mc*bc*wo	Sisak teachers

	VU	YC	MC	BC	WO	*TJ*
ZGT	1	0	0	1	0	*1*
ZAT	0	0	1	0	0	*1*
SIT	0	1	0	0	0	*1*
NUT	1	0	0	1	0	*1*
ZGV	0	1	0	0	1	*0*
ZAV	0	1	0	0	1	*0*
SIV	0	1	0	0	1	*0*
NUVB	0	1	0	0	1	*0*
NUVS	0	1	0	0	1	*0*
ZGP	1	0	0	1	0	*1*
ZAP	0	1	0	0	1	*0*
SIP	0	0	1	0	0	*1*
NUP	0	0	0	1	1	*0*

Fig. 7.5 War narrative set data table

Again, the Sisak teachers stand out since they were the only group to deliberate on transitional justice and believe Yugoslavia to be criminal. All other groups considered either Milošević to be criminal or both Yugoslavia and Milošević. Overall, however, the key difference regarding the war narrative is related to how relevant the war remains in individuals' lives. While it is factually inaccurate to claim the war is not over, what these individuals are most likely trying to say is that issues emerging from the war remain unresolved and that the war continues to pay a significant role in their personal lives.

Serbs in the Eyes of Croats

The conditions for how Croats viewed the Serb minority were dichotomised from the raw data table (Fig. 5.7) as follows:

- Debate on ethnic issues (MD): much debate (1) or little (0).
- Cyrillic is a provocation or an attack (CP): agreement with the statement (1) or disagreement (0).
- The role of the Church (RQ): the role was questioned or seen as political (1), or it was ignored (0).
- Serbs are inherently aggressive (SA): agreement with the statement (1) or disagreement (0).
- Serb returnees are accomplices (RA): agreement with the statement (1) or disagreement (0) (Fig. 7.6).

A calculation of necessary conditions highlights two factors with 100% coverage together and independently of each other:

Serb returnees are NOT accomplices (ra)

Serbs are NOT inherently aggressive (sa)

Serbs are NOT inherently aggressive

AND

Serb returnees are NOT accomplices (sa*ra)

In other words, groups that deliberated on transitional justice did not believe Serbs to be inherently aggressive and did not see Serb returnees as accomplices. Analysis of sufficiency did not reveal any significant patterns. Overall, these results highlight the unanimity of opinions across groups and that what sets war veterans and the Zadar group of

	MD	CP	RQ	SA	RA	*TJ*
ZGT	0	0	1	0	0	*1*
ZAT	0	1	1	0	0	*1*
SIT	0	0	0	0	0	*1*
NUT	0	0	1	0	0	*1*
ZGV	1	1	0	1	1	*0*
ZAV	1	1	0	1	1	*0*
SIV	1	1	0	1	1	*0*
NUVB	1	1	0	1	1	*0*
NUVS	1	1	0	1	1	*0*
ZGP	1	0	1	0	0	*1*
ZAP	1	1	0	1	1	*0*
SIP	1	1	0	0	0	*1*
NUP	1	0	1	1	1	*0*

Fig. 7.6 Serbs in the eyes of Croats set data table

pensioners out from the rest is a higher degree of distrust and suspicion of returnees. The higher level of distrust is, however, also present in many of their other views and seems to define a large part of their worldview.

War Veterans

The topic of war veterans in Croatian society saw a high degree of unanimity across the various topics. The raw data table (Fig. 6.2) was, therefore, reduced to only three conditions (Fig. 7.7):

- Transitional justice and neoliberalism seen as linked (TN): the group did not make a semantic distinction between the two processes and saw them as linked (1) or they did make a distinction between them and did not see them as linked (0). It is included in this section since most groups, but especially pensioners and war veterans, saw the legacy of the conflict and the transition to neoliberalism as inextricably linked. Their discussions of the position of war veterans in Croatian society frequently referred to neoliberal transition.
- Main issue facing war veterans (MV): the main issue facing war veterans is being forgotten (1) or the main issues facing war veterans are a lack of jobs and pensions (0).
- View of NGOs (VN): belief that NGOs look to divide the Croatian public (1) or a neutral opinion of them (0).

Fig. 7.7 War veterans set data table

	TN	MV	VN	TJ
ZGT	0	0	0	1
ZAT	0	0	0	1
SIT	0	0	0	1
NUT	0	0	0	1
ZGV	1	1	1	0
ZAV	1	1	1	0
SIV	1	1	1	0
NUVB	1	1	1	0
NUVS	1	1	1	0
ZGP	1	0	0	1
ZAP	1	0	1	0
SIP	1	0	0	1
NUP	1	0	0	0

The analysis of necessary conditions once again highlights distrust as the main differentiator between outcomes:

Main issues facing war veterans are a lack of jobs and pensions (mv)
Neutral view of NGOs (vn)

Main issues facing war veterans are a lack of jobs and pensions AND neutral view of NGOs (mv*vn)

It is not surprising to see that war veterans worry about being forgotten, but these groups that do not deliberate on transitional justice (except the Zadar war veterans) also believe that the NGO community in Croatia is looking to divide Croatian society. In the case of teachers, a sufficiency analysis also shows that they all make a semantic distinction between transitional justice and neoliberal transition (tn*mv*vn). In other words, they deliberate on transitional justice issues and see a difference between the two processes. Overall, although the topic predominantly featured agreement, the differences between outcomes are focused on general pessimism and distrust, on the one hand, and a generally better understanding of what transitional justice is, on the other.

Overall Comparison

Is a general sense of distrust within society the key factor to deliberative justice succeeding or occurring? These analyses cannot ascertain that, but they do highlight a certain correlation. A comparison of all of the above-mentioned areas also provides an interesting result. This analysis reduced each separate theme into a binary outcome. It included the areas of agreement and the area of disagreement to get an overall picture of each area. This method captured further nuances missed in the theme-by-theme analyses. The conditions in this analysis were:

- Sources of information (SI): given the general level of distrust, this was divided into higher levels (1) and comparatively lower levels (0).
- The war narrative (WN): whether there was any debate at all on issues (1) or not (0).
- Serbs in the eyes of Croats (SE): if four of more of the 7 factors were predominantly debated (1) or not (0).
- War veterans (CY): was there a high degree of pessimism (1) or a lower degree (0). Pessimism is defined as groups who believed the main issue facing war veterans is being forgotten (MV) and that NGOs look to divide the Croatian public (VN).
- Transitional justice and neoliberalism seen as linked (TN): this was included to check if it holds any significance. Again, either the group did not make a semantic distinction between the two processes and saw them as linked (1) or they did make a distinction between them and did not see them as linked (0).
- Outcome (TJ): the outcome was kept the same (Fig. 7.8).

The analysis of necessary conditions highlights two areas that receive good coverage across groups:

Low degree of pessimism regarding war veterans (cy)
Comparatively lower levels of distrust of sources of information (si)

Comparatively lower levels of distrust of sources of information
AND
A low degree of pessimism regarding war veterans (si*cy)

Groups with lower levels of distrust regarding sources of information and war veterans also tended to deliberate on transitional justice issues, whereas those with particularly high levels did not. An analysis of sufficiency highlighted similar areas, in addition to the importance of debate over Serbs in Croatia:

si*SE*cy*tn	Zagreb teachers; Zadar teachers; non-urban teachers; Sisak teachers
si*SE*cy*WN	Zagreb teachers; Zadar teachers; non-urban teachers; Zagreb pensioners

Condition	SI	WN	SE	CY	TN	*TJ*
ZGT	0	1	1	0	0	*1*
ZAT	0	1	1	0	0	*1*
SIT	0	0	1	0	0	*1*
NUT	0	1	1	0	0	*1*
ZGV	1	0	0	1	1	*0*
ZAV	1	0	0	1	1	*0*
SIV	1	0	0	1	1	*0*
NUVB	1	0	0	1	1	*0*
NUVS	1	0	0	1	1	*0*
ZGP	0	1	1	0	1	*1*
ZAP	1	0	0	1	1	*0*
SIP	0	0	0	0	1	*1*
NUP	0	0	0	0	1	*0*

Fig. 7.8 Comparison set data table

Amalgamating the Results

The focus groups, dyads, individual interviews, QCA and survey data point to a number of attitudes and perceptions among participants that may also be reflective of the wider public. Despite concerns about the representativeness of the sample, the combination of the various interviews with QCA adds more depth to how transitional justice issues are being deliberated in Croatian society. Most striking was the agreement across target segments on certain topics, which were rarely questioned, if they were questioned at all. For example, the notion of Croatian and Croat self-defence, as a part of the predominant war narrative, was universally accepted. Nearly all participants expressed it in a similar manner to Silvio, "For Croatia it was a true defensive war against the neighbouring *narod* who was not allowing us our freedom and who wanted to conquer us militarily, subdue us and force us to stay in the failed state of Yugoslavia" (interview with non-urban teacher). There was, however, no unanimity over whether it was the Croat *narod* that was attacked or the Croatian state, meaning there was no consensus over if the conflict was seen as ethnic or political.

The war narrative is very much an "everyday" narrative, and all participants discussed it in a local and personal way. Individuals on the frontline felt they knew it first hand, "About [the war's] general characteristics, from people who experienced it as such. I can only say what I saw and what I experienced" (dyad with Sisak pensioners). Individuals who were not on the frontline spoke of it in a similar fashion, "I personally think I do [have an understanding of the Homeland War]. Not only from written sources, but also from my conversations with people.

When I put all of that together then I think I have a fairly complete picture" (dyad with Zagreb teachers). Despite discrepancies in attitudes about the ICTY, there was agreement (strongly supported by survey data) that the ICTY was at the very least inefficient:

Marko: Some big fish avoided justice in the end.
Andriana: Or did not live long enough to see the trial end.
Marko: Either they did not live long enough or they died before making it there (focus group with Zadar teachers).

Many areas, however, were marked by differences in opinion. At times, these were relatively nuanced. For example, all target segments trusted participants and television pictures as a source of information and distrusted other sources. What set apart those who did deliberate on transitional justice issues and those who did not, however, were the levels of distrust. Those that deliberated simply distrusted the non-television media, "I have the impression that unfortunately we do not have any newspapers that are serious, where you can with certainty read something smart" (focus groups with Zadar teachers). Those that did not saw them as attempting to divide the Croatian public and especially war veterans from the rest:

Jasna: The demonstration on Savska has lasted for 60 days. In the news it gets a minute or not even a minute.
Blanka: What minute?
Lara: This is already old news, it does not exist anymore.
Jasna: They are once again trying to create a barrier between the civilian victims and the *branitelji* (focus group with non-urban war veterans Banovina).

Likewise, all groups distrusted the government. They distrusted an incompetent and selfish set of institutions and individuals that are no different to other governments through time:

Nikola: No government will say everything it knows. Only what suits them.
Dario: Yes. And this is normal for every government. In the future they will not release any more information.
Ivo: Throughout history it has always been like that. It has never changed, from Rome until now (focus group with Sisak teachers).

Those who did not deliberate on transitional justice saw a government that was infiltrated by "Greater Serbs, Yugonostalgics, persecutors of the Croatian national spirit throughout history, UDBA members. Today they have completely infiltrated all the pores of Croatian economic, political and daily life" (dyad with non-urban war veterans Slavonia). Likewise, the war narrative, despite universal agreement on certain facets, exhibited a key differentiator in groups of whether participants felt the war was over or not. The war remained a central theme to some participants' lives, and they saw issues from the war as unresolved:

Ilija: It is important for us to say what we think of our neighbours, the Serbs, how we now view them. In no way and never will we once again look at each other the same. Even if we lived another 100 years. They will come again. They said that even our great-grandchildren will fall victim to the Serbs.

Vladimir: They learn that. But we do not. Our future generations will not hate. They are vengeful. If there is a war, they will attack (focus group with non-urban pensioners).

The war did not hold the same central position in the lives of those who did deliberate on transitional justice. Whereas the above pensioners saw insecurity, a Zadar teacher merely saw tensions, "What is happening now is that Croatia is attacking Serbia over Šešelj, and Serbia is attacking Croatia over Cyrillic, because it cannot keep ten signs safe. Tensions are being kept high" (focus group with Zadar teachers). Many of those individuals believed tensions related to the war were still present in Croatian society, they adjudged much of politics and society around them based on the war, but this did not define their lives in the same manner.

Groups that deliberated on transitional justice also saw the ICTY as necessary or not as a mistake, despite its many flaws:

Moderator: Do you think it was a mistake to establish the ICTY?

Maja: No.

Mario: Perhaps it was not, I do not know, a mistake.

Maja: A war crime has to be punished.

Mario: Yes, in that light it definitely was not a mistake (dyad with Zagreb teachers).

Those who did not deliberate, on the other hand, saw the ICTY as a mistake. They also exhibited far more distrust of Serbs. Here, the key differentiators between those who deliberated and not were whether Serbs are seen as inherently aggressive or not. These types of exchanges were common with groups that saw Serbs as inherently aggressive:

Ivana: They are simply that kind of *narod*.
Stjepan: They would wage war now.
Ivana: Yes, they are like that. It is in their blood (focus group with non-urban pensioners).

These groups also viewed Serb returnees as accomplices to crimes committed by Serb forces during the war. One participant recounted a story of how she told a Serb returnee "in you, in every person who returns from Serbia, I see the potential killer of my husband" (focus group with non-urban war veterans Banovina). Finally, the QCA and discussions showed how groups differed in their view of war veterans. While those that deliberated on transitional justice considered the main problem facing the population of war veterans to be a lack of jobs, those who did not deliberate (including all five of the war veterans' groups) were more preoccupied with the war veterans being forgotten or misrepresented in society:

Kate: Currently there are 37 *branitelji* in parliament, and they have never had a shared idea, despite their party allegiances, to solve something for the Croatian *branitelji*. This has not happened a single time. Not in a single session of parliament. This means that there is not even a reason to talk about the war (focus group with Zadar war veterans).

Again, the differentiator is associated with different levels of distrust. Pessimism that certain individuals experience when interpreting the world around them seems to also be linked to a lack of deliberation on topics related to transition justice.

Conclusion

The purpose of QCA was to illustrate and to validate results. The purpose was not to ascertain causality or causal paths; rather, it was used to highlight patterns. By dichotomising factors or conditions, nuances of narratives were lost but certain aspects of them were better exposed. Necessary conditions identified key patterns, while sufficient conditions at times proved useful in emphasising the complexity of narratives across groups.

Groups deliberated on transitional justice issues if they thought the ICTY was necessary, and conversely did not deliberate if they felt it was not. Those who felt it was necessary also questioned or debated over recent history and dominant narratives. Other themes also stood out, as Fig. 7.9 outlines.

Issues of distrust are present under all of the different themes as the key factor that differentiates between where deliberation over transitional justice issues took place and where it did not. It is on this level that war veterans, in particular, stand out. For example, all target segments distrust most sources of information, but war veterans and the Zadar

Theme	Necessary Conditions	Sufficient Conditions
Survey responses	Individuals and officials convicted at the ICTY and domestic courts to be considered criminals, *not* heroes. Little importance attached to demonstrating national belonging. Little interest in national history and the fate of the nation. University education.	N/A
Sources of information	Government distrusted, but *no* need for lustration. Non-television media distrusted, but *not* considered to be aiming to cause splits in the public.	N/A
War narrative	War considered to be over.	Milošević or both Milošević and Yugoslavia considered to be criminal.
Serbs in eyes of Croats	Returnees *not* seen as accomplices. Serbs *not* seen as inherently aggressive.	N/A
Veterans	Main issue with war veterans are a lack of pensions and jobs, *not* that they are being forgotten. Neutral view of NGOs, *not* seeing them as aiming to divide Croatian society.	Only teachers: semantic distinction between transitional justice and neoliberal transition.
Overall comparison	Role of Serbs in Croatia debated. Lower levels of distrust.	N/A

Fig. 7.9 Overview of key conditions that lead to deliberation on transitional justice issues

pensioners also felt that some parts of the media and government had been infiltrated by unwanted elements. Equally, these segments felt that the war was not over. These highly suspicious groups also happened to not deliberate on transitional justice issues and see no need for the ICTY, whereas the other groups at least featured some debate.

The QCA confirms a number of points made in the prior chapters. Mainly, it shows the general agreement across all target segments in several areas, such as high distrust of media; perceptions of ICTY inefficiency; that Cyrillic signs should not be put up in Vukovar despite Serbs deserving equal rights; that war veterans are being manipulated but that their associations are corrupt; and that the economy is the key to reconciliation. As in most chapters, teachers stood out from the other target segments. The QCA also raised a number of further points. Statistical indicators, at least in this study, were not particularly indicative of patterns. War veterans' views and attitudes were nearly completely uniform, while teachers and, especially, pensioners showed variation. A key differentiator between whether groups deliberated on transitional justice issues or not was the perception of whether the ICTY was necessary or not. Those who felt it was necessary also questioned or debated over recent history and dominant narratives. Levels of distrust, however, proved to be the most common differentiator across the groups in this study. For example, is the Croatian government simply distrusted or is it also infiltrated and looking to split the public? Are Serbs inherently aggressive? Are all returnees accomplices to war crimes? This list also includes views on NGOs, non-television media and feelings of the war not being over. Overall, QCA highlighted that those with lower degrees of distrust and pessimism with these institutions also deliberated on transitional justice issues. While the analysis hints at a certain atmosphere of pessimism that is impacting the transitional justice process across all groups, it is also important to keep in mind that transitional justice is a process and that maybe the fact that issues related to it are being deliberated at all means that transitional justice institutions have succeeded in their work.

Note

1. These solutions have not been expanded for the sake of brevity and clearer illustration.

References

Goertz, G., & Mahoney, J. (2012). *A tale of two cultures: Qualitative and quantitative research in the social sciences*. Princeton: Princeton University Press.

Kolstø, P. I. (2011). *Strategies of symbolic nation-building in west Balkan states: Intents and results*. University of Oslo. Available at http://www.hf.uio.no/ilos/english/research/projects/nation-w-balkan/.

CHAPTER 8

Bosnia in the Croatian War Narrative: A Missed Expressivist Opportunity?

The in-court suicide of Slobodan Praljak at the ICTY is perhaps the most incontrovertible proof of expressivist effects of war crimes trials. The theatre of the trial took on a Shakespearean dimension. Whether or not the architects and staff of the ICTY intended for it to have expressivist effects, it will be remembered in great part based on the images and video of a defiant Praljak declaring his innocence and resistance to an unjust court, before drinking a vial of poison. These images made headline news worldwide. The incident encapsulates the anger many in Croatia felt with the court; the feeling that it was victimising certain groups; and the impression that it was incompetent. The shock of the suicide shows that expressivist messages can be positive or negative, that emotions play a key role in how the court is presented and that the theatre surrounding it all is of paramount importance.

This chapter differs from previous chapters, since the suicide of Slobodan Praljak occurred after the fieldwork was conducted. Participants discussed the conflict in Bosnia and Herzegovina, including Croatia's perceived role in it, but they did not comment on the trial directly, nor were they asked about it. They were, however, asked about other trials concerning the conflict in Bosnia. This chapter examines how these views fit into the Croatian war narrative, which is premised on self-defence and victimhood. It then looks at what narratives media and political elites in Croatia used to react to the suicide of Praljak, in order to validate the findings of previous chapters. Do everyday narratives of

I. Sokolić, *International Courts and Mass Atrocity*,
Memory Politics and Transitional Justice,
https://doi.org/10.1007/978-3-319-90841-0_8

participants reflect elite narratives? Have elite narratives changed since 2000? And, has the judicial narrative of the ICTY influenced the dominant war narrative in Croatia?

Slobodan Praljak was a HVO General in Herzeg-Bosnia, the self-proclaimed Croat state in Bosnia. He was an engineer, sociologist and theatre director (which may explain his understanding of dramatic effect) before the conflict. He volunteered to the Croatian army in 1991 and asked to be transferred to Bosnia and Herzegovina in 1992. He was posted to an area that covered his native Čapljina, and in 1993, he became a General in the HVO.

Praljak stood accused and was convicted of implementing a system of forced deportations of Bosniaks in the Herzeg-Bosnia entity, together with five co-conspirators, in a case known as Prlić et al. (IT-04-74). He was found to be aware of: deportations and detentions of the Muslim population; crimes committed in and around Mostar; destruction of buildings in East Mostar (most notably mosques and the Old Bridge); and attacks on international organisations. He facilitated the murder of civilians and made no significant attempts to stop such murders. This included the running of concentration camps (such as Dretelj) and the use of civilian detainees as slave labour and human shields. Most significant for the Croatian state, however, was the finding that the state, led by President Franjo Tuđman, carried out a joint criminal enterprise with the leadership of Herzeg-Bosnia. This was the greatest fear of consecutive Croatian governments, since the conviction implicates the Croatian leadership, including President Tuđman, and is perceived as a criminalisation of the war and, thereby, the nation state. It undermines claims that Croatia led an exclusively defensive war within its own borders and that it was not possible for it to commit war crimes in Bosnia. It also directly contradicts the dominant war narrative.

The Croatian government reacted defiantly to the verdict and death. Prime Minister Andrej Plenković; President Kolinda Grabar-Kitarović; and all parties in Parliament, except the Social Democratic Party (SDP) and the Civic Liberal Alliance (GLAS), called the verdict unjust and erroneous (HRT 2017). Croatian parliament also held a minute of silence for Praljak, held an extraordinary meeting to discuss a response and ended a session of parliament early as a mark of protest. An official commemoration for Praljak's death was organised by the Croatian Generals' Assembly at a concert hall in Zagreb (Milekić 2017). The commemoration was attended by 2000 people, including a number of MPs (mostly from the HDZ) and once-influential members of politics (ibid.). A large number of former generals also attended, including convicted war criminals, such as Mirko Norac and Dario Kordić. The City of Zagreb organised free bus transport to the commemoration, and, later in the day, a religious ceremony was held at a Catholic Church in Zagreb. A number of Croatian cities and towns also held commemorations and the national broadcaster aired documentaries and films that the general made. An alternative counter-commemoration was also organised by a Zagreb NGO, the Youth Initiative for Human Rights, to commemorate victims of Croat forces during the 1990s war (ibid.). President Grabar-Kitarović faced some pressure to take away Praljak's wartime decorations and general status, as had been done to generals convicted by Croatian courts, but refused to do so (Večernji List 2017).

The dramatic manner in which the trial of Praljak concluded holds significant lessons for international criminal law and its institutions. It shows that expressivist effects of trials are real and need to be taken into account. The ICTY may be remembered based on these events. To those who felt threatened by its verdicts, this can be seen as final proof of its partiality. To victims, their moment of justice is taken away from them. Both are left disappointed by the institution and become ever more cynical with the world around them. Political elites are the only perceived winners, since they can successfully manipulate the verdicts for political gain. The suicide diverted attention, especially for local publics and politicians, from a legally sound and significant judgement. It also showed that expressivist effects of trials can be positive or negative; they can be pedagogical, but they can also breed cynicism and distrust among local publics.

The ICTY's sometimes clumsy approach to public engagement allowed indictees to use their own trials as pulpits (Praljak, Karadžić, Šešelj are probably the three most memorable; Steflja 2017). Detailed legal arguments have little effect on publics or media that are not aware or interested in the legal intricacies of a hybrid international war crimes trial. General interest in trials peaks at key moments, such as when verdicts are read and when the indictees are presented in their most emotional and vulnerable state. Gordy (2014) argues that in Serbia these moments represented lost opportunities for societal reckoning with a violent past. In the context of a war crimes trial, they also represent crucial, brief moments laden with expressivist potential. Praljak used this moment to cause shock and anger, which bred confrontation and diverted the judicial narrative. The significance of the court's findings is ignored, while the cynicism and distrust associated with the court are fortified. This hampers the spread of human rights norms, and it fails the victims. Slobodan Praljak is seen as a victim of the ICTY; the many victims of his concentration camps and killing campaigns remain ignored; and their quest for justice remains unfulfilled.

The chapter begins by outlining the results of the focus groups. It analyses how participants constructed their narrative of Croatian involvement in the Bosnian conflict and compares this to elite narratives. Both are based on a framework of nesting orientalism, which sees Bosnia as an inferior "Other". The chapter then turns to Praljak's death as a key expressivist moment. This section validates the fieldwork results discussed in this chapter, as well as previous chapters. It looks at media and elite responses to the death in order to confirm that the war narrative remains unchanged. The conclusion discusses the implications of this: that the ICTY's expressivist effects matter and that they matter in key dramatic moments.

Focus Group Results—The Narrative of Croatian Involvement

The Bosnian conflict has the potential to provide a powerful counter-narrative to the Croatian war narrative, since it involved Croatian aggression in a foreign state. This has not happened. The case of the Bosnian conflict in the eyes of the Croatian public also provides an interesting comparison to the local and personal way that the war narrative is discussed, since it was not experienced directly. Despite the geographical removal, the conflict is still referred to in much the same way as the Homeland War: personally and, when possible, locally. As a theme, it provides an example of the inherent contradictions present in the war narrative.

A 2001 parliamentary exchange between Vesna Pusić,[1] at the time of the Croatian People's Party (HNS), and several members of parliament[2] encapsulated a range of these themes. The heated exchange began when Pusić proclaimed that she personally, not on behalf of her party, believed the Homeland War waged in Croatia was positive, but that it should not have been fought outside of the territories of Croatia, namely in Bosnia. This resulted in an avalanche of retorts, with one Member of Parliament quoting the Declaration on the Homeland

War, stressing that it clearly states that Croatia led a defensive and liberating, not an aggressive and conquering, war. Another Member of Parliament complained that she was incorrect on the basis of the Tuđman–Izetbegović agreement, which made Croatian military action in Bosnia legitimate. A number of members agreed with this, to which Pusić responded that she has the right to her own opinion, including on the Declaration, and that she believed the HDZ government waged an aggressive war in Bosnia. The reaction by others to this was possibly most telling of all: Vladimir Šeks requested the parliamentary session to be paused due to the insults of Pusić, and the Speaker of the Parliament asked Pusić to apologise to all of parliament for belittling the Declaration on the Homeland War, which was agreed upon through a vote. She refused and was given an official warning. The incident is emblematic of the war narrative's predominance and its commonly used symbols. It also shows the interaction between an emotional narrative and legal reasoning.

The Croatian political leadership, even post-2000, was always acutely aware of the potential for Croatian involvement in Bosnia to disrupt the dominant war narrative. This, together with Operation Storm, could undermine the crucial notion of self-defence that underpins the narrative. It would criminalise the war. This is why Bosnia featured so clearly in the 2006 Declaration on Operation Storm, which attempted to create an official version of Croatian involvement in Bosnia, within a framework of self-defence (discussed in more detail in Chapter 3). Article 2 stresses the cooperation between the governments of Croatia and Bosnia and Herzegovina, ignoring the role of Herceg-Bosna, and Article 5 portrays Croatia as the saviour of Bosnia through Operation Storm, which prevented a repeat of Srebrenica (Narodne Novine 2006). This narrative is not only elite: Croatia as the saviour of Bihać (Article 5) was reproduced nearly word for word in focus group discussion. Croatian elites not only care about this topic; the narrative they advocate has also had an effect.

Given the lack of personal experience of the conflict in Bosnia, most participants simply found it hard to comment on or explained that they did not know much. This was usually explained in terms of not having been present there or how the only source available was the media and the general opinion of the media remains low:

Mladen: I do not know much about it.
Vlasta: That is why I think we should limit ourselves to Croatia. Bosnians can talk about Bosnia. We do not know enough about it. War hit us and Slovenia and Croatia.
Mladen: But it is closely related. Croatia and Bosnia and Herzegovina.
Vlasta: But we in Croatia are not familiar enough with the situation in Bosnia to be able to talk about it.
Ante: That is what I tried to say I do not have the right information!
Vlasta: But if you lived in Croatia then you can talk, since you know what happened in Croatia (focus group with Zagreb pensioners).

The Zagreb pensioners also provide an example of how many participants and groups dealt with this thorny issue of negative Croatian involvement—by claiming to be ignorant of it. The conflict was seen as grotesque and extreme, especially when compared to war in Croatia. This is an image that respondents still held for Bosnia today: that it is savage and chaotic. Some even held the view that historically this has been Bosnia's, as opposed to Croatia's, role in the Balkans:

Goran: It was hard to live in Bosnia, there are three nations there. And these are half-wild people (focus group with non-urban pensioners).

-

Mario: Bosnia has always, from its establishment, not as this republic of Bosnia and Herzegovina, but from before the Romans, the area was like this. There were always conflicts between different factions (focus group with Sisak teachers).

By painting the Bosnian conflict as extreme, chaotic and unknown, individuals are able to more easily distance themselves from the reality of the situation. Bosnians (of any ethnicity) are likened to savages, much likes Serbs, distinguishing them from Croats. They, therefore, do not belong to the same state or nation, nor is their role one of innocent victims. The fact that the Bosnian conflict is considered unknown also helps explain why it has not come into a significant conflict with the premise of a wholly defensive war.

Most of the public in Croatia did have direct contact with the war in Bosnia through the huge influx of refugees into Croatia from the conflict. Of all of the topics concerning the Bosnian conflict, this one was present most consistently across the groups. Moreover, it was often discussed in a positive light, in terms of Croatia taking these refugees in:

Vlasta: Half of Bosnia, maybe not that much, was here. In my house, I have a big one, I took a whole family. We helped, seeing as we had good connections abroad, for example with women in Vienna, they were collecting for them. I personally took things to the refugee camp. Took them to the hospital. We were helping them. You cannot say that we wanted this war. But if we had let all of these refugees over the borders, to go, then the world would have thought differently. Croatia carried on its own back half of the Bosnian war and the armament of itself (focus group with Zagreb pensioners).

Illicit Croatian involvement in the Bosnian conflict was, however, generally ignored or denied. In the most extreme instance, the Sisak war veterans group refused to speak about the conflict at all or related ICTY trials, further showing the amount of suspicion present, especially given this group hinted that they required approval from a local party leader to take part in the group discussion. Moreover, the defensive war is itself used as a defence mechanism by the group to avoid difficult topics:

Moderator: What do you think of the trial of Dario Kordić?
Ana and Lucija vocally protest
Lucija: I would not like to answer that question.
Moderator: Could I then ask about the related trial of Tihomir Blaškić?
Ana: I would rather not speak about individuals at all.
Lucija: You asked us about a defensive war, about individuals no.
Moderator: We can skip it, it is not a problem.
Ana: They have their lawyers, a whole team working for them, who are familiar with their affairs.
Lucija: We are just mere mortals.
Ana: I would rather not hurt any individuals, I do not want to talk about it (focus group with Sisak war veterans).

In some instances, participants readily acknowledged Croatian involvement in the Bosnian conflict. Survey results are indicative of this: when asked if Presidents Tuđman and Milošević agreed on a division of Bosnia in Karađorđevo, thereby implying some kind of illicit Croatian involvement, 34% answered that they did not know, 40% answered that they did believe it to some degree, whereas only 17.1% were neutral and 14.7% did not believe there was an agreement (Ipsos Puls 2012). Croatian involvement was presented in two perspectives: one negative

(Croatia, or the *HVO*, attacking their neighbours) and one positive (the Croatian army coming to save Bosnia). The negative perspective, expressed by a minority of participants among teachers and pensioners, focused on backroom deals or covert Croatian military operations in Bosnia:

> *Mladen:* It is a fact that [Tuđman] made a deal with Milošević to leave Posavina to Serbia, and for us to create Herceg-Bosnia. When you looked at meteorological maps on television, Croatia and Herceg-Bosnia were nearly the same colour. They already agreed that this would be a part of Croatia. You can see that was an agreement. And the Bosniaks are somewhere in the middle of it. This was ultimately a deal at the expense of the Bosniaks in Bosnia-Herzegovina (focus group with Zagreb pensioners).

The positive perspective, of Croatia saving Bosnia in some way, was particularly common with war veterans' groups and was tied to the idea that, following Operation Storm, the Croatian army continued into Bosnia to free the area around Bihać. In numerous instances, the siege of Bihać was referred to as "the next Srebrenica" and Croatia was viewed as preventing it from occurring (thereby further solidifying the narrative of self-defence, even outside of national borders):

> *Josip:* Military Operation Storm was a nice gesture for the international community. We returned our territories, but by returning our territories into the constitutional and legal framework of the Republic of Croatia, we also did something good for Bosnia and Herzegovina. We reached the defensive lines of Bihać, which was surrounded by Serbian forces. Then we chased them away, came to the defenders of Bihać, our and their generals shook hands and Croatia returned its army and *branitelji* to the territory of its state, and they stayed in their state. And then Bosnia became unburdened from a situation where Bihać could have maybe been in the same situation as Srebrenica.
>
> *Dalibor:* Not maybe, definitely (dyad with non-urban war veterans Slavonia)!

The two perspectives outlined above are not mutually exclusive. The interviewed war veterans' groups exclusively spoke of the positive one (if they spoke about it at all), while teachers (in particular) and pensioners (less so) often also highlighted the negative one. Teachers and pensioners often viewed the two as separate phases of Croatian involvement in the Bosnian conflict:

> *Dragan:* Croatia was definitely present there, even before the Tuđman-Izetbegović agreement. We were definitely on the cusp of international sanctions and there was pressure from the international public. Clearly the judgement by higher powers was that this involvement was not completely positive and friendly (interview with Zagreb teacher).

The role of Croatia in the conflict in Bosnia shows the contradictions created by the interaction of the war and justice narratives. Individuals' narratives on the topic often reached obstacles where they struggle to explain events or where they contradict themselves, especially when emotional and judicial narratives do not overlap. This was also evident in the 2001 parliamentary setting, where the Tuđman–Izetbegović agreement (agreed after Croatian involvement in Bosnia had already started) was used to justify Croatian forces operating outside of Croatia, much like it was used in focus groups. The importance of this lies not only in how the two narratives interact, but also how much debate there is surrounding the issue. The theme of Bosnia provides an opportunity to question the dominant war narrative in Croatia and, both on the level of elites and the everyday, there is evidence of this happening, of some form of debate occurring, but also of the war narrative for the most part making it difficult for the debate to intensify. The distancing from the conflict allowed participants a type of moral licensing, which enabled them not to have to confront this violent past (Sokolić 2017).

The elite and everyday narratives concerning Croatian involvement in Bosnia are correlated, but they prioritise different characteristics. Both broadly deny any negative Croatian involvement in a framework of nesting orientalism. The elite narrative is focused on the positive nature of Croatian involvement (Croatia the heroic saviour and benevolent paternal figure), while the everyday narrative emphasises the chaotic nature of the conflict (Bosnia as savage). The implication is that both construct Bosnia, its people and its conflict as the inferior "Other" (Sokolić 2017). Constructing Bosnia as savage serves as a "rhetorical screen" (Bakić-Hayden 1995: 929), which helps elites and individuals avoid confronting the realities of the conflict. The elite narrative of benevolent paternalism is an instrumentalised construct and a remnant of 1990s politics, which aimed to subsume parts of Bosnia within Croatia. The everyday narrative, on the other hand, reduces the "Other" through references to savagery, which helps construct European notions of Croatian self-identity, but which does not imply conquest (Sokolić 2017).

Praljak's Suicide as an Expressivist Moment

ICTY verdicts on Croatia's role in the Bosnian conflict contradict the dominant war narrative, but they do not seem to have had a significant effect on it. The narrative remains unchanged since the suicide of Praljak and any potential shift seems to have only fortified elite use of the most common tropes of the war narrative. This highlights how slow the process of transitional justice is, as well as how fragile it can be in the face of shocking moments. The effect is that the ICTY is still seen as biased and incompetent. Biased, because it is used as a vehicle for anti-Croatian politics. Incompetent, since it allowed the incident to occur and for the court to, once again, be hijacked by an indictee (Subotic 2017). The lesson for international war crimes trials is that key expressivist moments matter, since the interpretation of verdicts is prioritised among the societies they concern.

Media Reactions

Media opinion pieces and editorials on the topic of Praljak's verdict reinforced notions of ICTY political bias and incompetency, as well as the key tropes of the dominant war narrative. Deliberation did occur on some topics, which previously may not have taken place, but this was limited. Much like focus group results, this hints at the slow pace and limited effects of the transitional justice process in Croatia.

Media reporting across the spectrum of opinion agreed that the ICTY was an incompetent institution, which further primes the public for such attitudes. For example, Jutarnji List, a left-leaning daily newspaper, ran a story listing all individuals who died at the ICTY (Jutarnji List 2017). Both left- and right-leaning outlets discussed its political nature, but in a different manner. Right-leaning daily Večernji List wrote that the ICTY "was used for the modelling of political relations in the former

Yugoslavia" (Raspudić 2017); left-leaning daily Novi List saw the suicide as unsurprising, given the event itself was political (Mijića 2017). The cumulative effect is that this further erodes the legitimacy of the ICTY (partly through its own fault, since it did allow for such events to occur).

Reporting reinforced the dominant war narrative. Victimhood was a common trope, although there was disagreement over who was doing the victimisation. Was it the ICTY, the West, Serbia, Croatian politicians today, Croatian politicians from the past and so on. Victimisation was used as a mitigating circumstance to relativise crimes; for example, right-wing portal Dnevno.hr wrote that the "war between Bosniaks and Croats was the by-product of Serbian aggression on Bosnia and Herzegovina" (Holjevac 2017a). Crucially in this brief sentence, the aggression is stated as *on* Bosnia, rather than *within* Bosnia, reinforcing the notion of explicit Serbian aggression in an international conflict, rather than a civil war. Relativisation and nested orientalism were prevalent in reporting, and Jutarnji List asked "is it possible that in the anti-civilisational and nationalist ecstasy we want to surpass even Serbia?" (Pavić 2017). Right-wing outlets reinforced notions of continued struggle: Večernji List called Croatia the most idiotic country for winning the war, but losing the verdict (Raspudić 2017); Dnevno.hr called Praljak the last victim of the Homeland War (Holjevac 2017a) and predicted that Croats would disappear in Bosnia (Holjevac 2017b). This highlights the association with the nation-building project, within which the Croatian state, nation and people remain under threat. Questioning the war narrative or helping transitional justice authorities is seen as a threat to Croatia. For example, Večernji List, published an article that listed the politicians and generals who "testified against Croatia", implying that although individuals were on trial, these testimonies threatened the integrity of the state (Miljavac 2017).

A change in narrative was, however, present. Left-leaning media readily acknowledged negative Croatian involvement in Bosnia, just as some segments of participants did, but this now also spread to the right-leaning media. Večernji List wrote, "After nearly 20 years of silence in the Croatian public, today there is finally discussion about the Muslim-Croat war without reservations. No one questioned whether crimes happened on the Croat side and there were no stupid phrases such as 'our soldiers cannot commit war crimes'" (Raspudić 2017). This is both limited, yet significant. Limited, since the article continues by comparing this to the "much larger" number of crimes committed by Bosniaks against Croats and because this frame still constructs Croatian crimes as sporadic. Yet it is significant, because by acknowledging that war crimes did occur it primes the public to deliberate on the topic. It also illustrates that changes are occurring to the war narrative among a segment of the media that prioritises the defence of the narrative.

Narratives and their contestation are prioritised by all media outlets in different ways, roughly depending on if they are left or right leaning. Each in their own way, media outlets stress that the Praljak verdict is significant because of the narratives it promotes and the contestation among them. According to Jutarnji List, Croatia is politically and geographically divided into those "who believe Croatia was obviously an aggressor in Bosnia and Herzegovina, and others, who equally as strongly, believe that Croats were always and only victims" (Pavić 2017). In the media, the verdict is interpreted as the key point of contention in an ongoing and important struggle over the war narrative. On the left, this battle is openly recognised, "all important political actors were formed directly from wartime events, and all politics are war politics. Voting in elections is done on the basis of wartime brotherhood" (Mijića 2017), and calls to fight the mythologising of Praljak were present, "we should oppose such a narrative [of glorification] and the raising of a war criminal to the status of national hero and martyr" (Duhaček 2017). The left-wing press recognise the battle of narratives, while the right-wing media fight it. To the right, Praljak was Socrates who used his death by poison as a lesson; to the left, Praljak was likened to Nazi leaders who committed suicide, rather than face justice. The media frame is not directly about victims, legality or human rights norms; it is about "us writing our own history" (Tomičić 2017).

The work of war crimes tribunals, especially high-profile ones, is interpreted based on the narratives they promote. These expressivist effects were key to how the ICTY work was being received in Croatia. Even those outlets that were receptive to its work, focused on the implications judgements had on the war narrative. "Faced with the last and final injustice of the court, which will one day itself be judged, Praljak decided to interrupt the farce and turn it into tragedy. With this act he became a legend" (Lučić 2017). Praljak used the court as a stage, and, in the eyes of those who prioritise the war narrative, he won a key battle for Croatian nationhood, both by resisting the court and by reinforcing a specific vision of the war narrative. Whether the architects of the

ICTY wanted it to have distinct expressivist effects or not, these are central to how their work is received. Similar institutions need to be aware that, should they wish to have any resonance outside of their own courtroom, including with domestic legal practitioners whose work is often influenced by narratives of war, then they need to factor expressivist effects into account. The Praljak verdict, his trial, the trial of Prlić et al. and much of the work of the ICTY in Croatia will be remembered as theatrical. It is the "pornography of death" for a "ready public" (Mijića 2017); it is Shakespearean (Holjevac 2017b); it is a reality show (Duhaček 2017); and it is a tragedy (Lučić 2017).

Elite Reactions

Elites on the whole still support the dominant war narrative and use it for their own purposes, although opposition voices remain present. Again, this highlights the slow nature of transition, especially considering some of the actors and their arguments have not changed since initial debates on the topic in 2001. The incident has allowed for a deeper understanding of how elites interact with the war narrative. Countering it is perceived as a security threat and transgression is punished, or at least threatened. For example, Vesna Pusić and her party (now the Civic Liberal Alliance, or GLAS) did not attend the minute's silence for Praljak in the Croatian Parliament, which resulted in death threats for Pusić. Another member of her party, Beus Richembergh, also received death threats for declaring Praljak a convicted war criminal on Facebook (Milanović 2017). The HDZ stood behind the war narrative, but continued to use the same strategy Lamont (2010) noted during the tenure of Ivo Sanader: compliance with legal obligations and norms of the ICTY, while challenging those rulings before domestic audiences. Prime Minister Andrej Plenković rebuffed the ruling since it was "in contradiction with the historical truth and facts" and vowed that his government would use all possible legal mechanisms to fight the verdict (Milekić 2017). A few days later, he then softened his position by stating that Croatia always respected the verdict and only disagreed with small parts of it (ibid.).

Emblematic of the HDZ stance towards the ICTY is the speech Croatian President Kolinda Grabar-Kitarović gave to the United Nations Security Council shortly after the suicide. The speech encapsulated all of the contradictory key points of the war narrative and the HDZ stance: that the tribunal was good; that the tribunal was bad; that individuals committed crimes and the tribunal found them guilty; that Croatia had no collective guilt; that Croatia respected the tribunal, but rejected their last verdict; and that Croatia saved Bosnia. President Grabar-Kitarović begins the lengthy speech by reminding the council that Croatia helped establish the ICTY 25 years earlier and that it "met the expectations of the international community, that it played an important role in the battle against a culture of impunity and that it was a key instrument used to ensure responsibility for war crimes, crimes against humanity and genocide" (Grabar-Kitarović 2017). But, Grabar-Kitarović goes on to say, the court was too slow ("in too many cases, justice arrived too late or not at all"), and despite only dealing with individual responsibility, its political connotations "caused numerous legal and political consequences" (ibid.). This forms the basis of her and consecutive Croatian government critiques: that a distinction needs to be made between "individual responsibility and collective guilt" (ibid.). The implication is that no Croat was found guilty at the ICTY of committing crimes in Croatia (where they could be tied to the Croatian state), while Croats found guilty in Bosnia and Herzegovina were operating as individuals and were not sanctioned by the Croatian state. Conversely, Croatian governments were happy to urge the ICTY to convict other ethnicities on collective grounds.

On this basis, Grabar-Kitarović states that Croatia "rejects the interpretation of the recent ICTY verdict in the Prlić et al. case, that Croatia, the Croatian leadership at the time or the Croatian people (*narod*) are accused or guilty in the eyes of the ICTY" (ibid.). She also rejects their authority, "the tribunal does not have the authority to come to give verdicts on the responsibility of states and the verdicts of the tribunal in no way make conclusions about the responsibility of Croatia" (ibid.). Strictly speaking, this is true, since the ICTY only ever tried individuals, not states. This does not, however, mean that state leaders were not implicated; they were and many more would likely have been (potentially including Tuđman) if the court had acted faster. Their verdicts could have and sometimes did implicate and criminalise a state leadership, which in Croatia is often interpreted as the criminalisation of the Croatian struggle for independence (which it is not). Grabar-Kitarović's public rejection of the ICTY's authority is significant because it maintains the atmosphere of continued struggle. Croatia is constructed as continually besieged, this time by the West, and it is Grabar-Kitarović and her party that can protect Croatian independence, which is under threat. The verdict is interpreted, similar to that of Gotovina before, as a threat to the Croatian nation-building and state-building projects.

The speech then goes on to exhibit notions of paternal benevolence with regard to Croatia's role in Bosnia, typical of elite narratives. Grabar-Kitarović states that "Croatia was crucial in the saving of Bosnia and Herzegovina" and that "for years Croatia provided shelter to thousands of refugees from Bosnia and Herzegovina and treated more than ten thousand people in its hospitals [...] Simultaneously, Croats in Bosnia and Herzegovina were victims of war crimes committed against them by the Army of Bosnia and Herzegovina (*Armija BiH*), especially in Central Bosnia. These crimes are yet to be punished" (ibid.). The Bosnian conflict is constructed through reference to the war narrative: Croatia was an unprepared and barefooted victim of aggression, it continues to suffer, but it was still able to help its smaller neighbour Bosnia. In her conclusion, Grabar-Kitarović quotes Pope John Paul II, "there is no peace without justice, no justice without forgiveness", again highlighting the Catholic conception of forgiveness that forms a key part of Croat identity (ibid.).

The narrative sequence of the speech is illustrative of how the war narrative and judicial narratives interact. The sequence mirrors that of participants in the study, whose perception of the ICTY and understandings of law were influenced by the war narrative. The likely intended audience for this speech was not the Security Council, but the Croatian public at home, which will interpret it as Croatia wielding their influence in the world. President Grabar-Kitarović begins by stating that the ICTY is positive and necessary, implying that Croatia, as a member of the established European order, respects European values. But, the ICTY was also slow and political, which sets the foundation for her rejection of facets of the judicial narrative that did not comply with the war narrative. She then sets out her own folk theory of law. This theory is premised on the notion that trials of individuals cannot implicate a whole state or individuals not directly on trial, regardless of their role in any system of government. This theory is logically consistent, but it is not consistent with the findings of the ICTY that the Croatian leadership in Zagreb had a chain of command in Bosnia and took part in a joint criminal enterprise. In doing this, she is encouraging others to follow her legal logic and to reject that of the ICTY or other legal institutions, regardless of how sound they are. Her authority is derived from Croatia's role as the benevolent and paternal saviour of Bosnia, giving her added legitimacy at home. Later, her legitimacy is furthered through reference to Catholicism, thereby making it clear that she supports Croats. The notion of a continued struggle reminds the public that Croatia needs people in power who can best protect the state and nation, just as they did in the 1990s.

What does this speech say about the war narrative following the final trials of Croats at the ICTY? That the same tropes remain: Croatia was an innocent and unprepared victim of Serbian aggression; Croatia only acted in self-defence; Croatia saved Bosnia; Catholicism is a key identity marker; and the Croatian state remains under threat from numerous directions and must be defended. The one key difference is that the continued defence is now prioritised. Consequently, who provides this defence and who has the right to provide it becomes a key battleground in Croatian politics and society. The political scene becomes a fight over who has the right to defend Croatia and fight for its (continued) independence; those who win gain a form of social capital.

Opposition voices were present in Croatia. As discussed above, these were both in parliament and in the media. Most, however, only instrumentally rejected the war narrative. Other than some of the more outspoken individuals in Croatia on this topic (such as Pusić), most accepted some facets of ICTY rulings, as long as they did not contradict the dominant war narrative. This reflects the focus group results: some individuals were willing to accept that Croatia had some kind of negative role in Bosnia, but still did not believe Croatia committed aggression. Orsat Miljenić, a member of parliament from the Social Democratic Party (SDP) and former justice minister, reflected this exactly. He argued that Croatia's wartime policy towards Bosnia was bad, but not aggression; that the ICTY had not done a good job because it implicated the state, as opposed to individuals; and that there was no evidence that he saw that there was a joint criminal enterprise (Milekić and Dizdarević 2017). Therein lies the difficulty that transitional justice institutions face in attempting to instil human rights norms in a society: even those who do experience some kind of shift in opinion do not drastically change their world view. Some facets of the war narrative may change, but the narrative does not change wholesale. Instead, as narratives interact, many facets of the judicial narrative are rejected and those that are accepted are altered, to best fit in with the dominant and entrenched war narrative.

Conclusion

Praljak turned the ICTY into a stage for a tragedy of his own making. A relative unknown until the final verdict, he managed to cast himself as the lead character in a story of struggle between a powerful hegemon (the ICTY and the West) and an unarmed victim (a Croat general). His death spoke directly to the Croatian war narrative and, in the words of Subotic (2009, 2017), hijacked the process of transitional justice. The judicial narrative struggled to have any effect: the notion of joint criminal enterprise was barely discussed; Croatian involvement in Bosnia was acknowledged by some, who consequently received threats; and the victims' voices were silenced. The media reporting, regardless of political orientation, reinforced notions of ICTY incompetence and bias, feeding the atmosphere of cynicism in society. Their discussion focused on contestation over the war narrative, how Praljak will be remembered and how the war will be remembered. It did not discuss the crimes committed, the victims or the legal consequences of the verdict. Elites, especially the ruling HDZ, continued to present a contradictory strategy towards transitional justice: compliant for the international audience and defiant for the domestic audience. They did so by appealing to the tropes of the war narrative: victimhood, defence and paternal benevolence towards Bosnia. This narrative remains relatively unchanged since the 1990s. Both media and elites conceded that crimes did occur: but these were relativised within the war narrative.

Elite and everyday narratives generally overlap and feed off each other. These results, therefore, validate the results of the focus groups. Reactions to Praljak's suicide reflect how participants constructed their narratives of Croatian involvement in Bosnia. Participants broadly denied a negative Croatian role, since Croatia saved Bosnia and was viewed as superior in a framework of nesting orientalism. The key difference between elite and everyday narratives was in what characteristics within the framework were prioritised. Elites focused on benevolent paternalism, everyday participants on the barbarism of Bosnia; both reduce its status as the inferior "Other".

This chapter highlights that transitional justice processes are interpreted based on key moments. In this case, the judicial narrative presented by the ICTY has not had the desired effect of instilling human rights narratives among the public, media or political elites. It has had a small effect on certain segments, but generally the war narrative proved too strong to compete with. Judicial narratives regarding Bosnia were generally accepted only when they worked in concert with the war narrative. The Praljak suicide presents the starkest missed opportunity to deal with the legacy of war crimes committed by the Croatian state in Bosnia. The cases of Prlić et al.; Kordić and Čerkez; and Blaškić show a significant limitation of the ICTY and international war crimes trials. At best, they are legally sound, they leave behind an impressive evidence base, which clarifies the conflict, and they provide justice to victims. The case of Kordić and Čerkez achieved (at the very least) the first two, but did little to contribute to understandings of the Bosnian conflict in Croatia. This verdict had already ascertained that a chain of command existed between Zagreb and Croat forces in Bosnia. The crimes they were convicted for have been acknowledged by Croatian President Grabar-Kitarović, who in 2018 visited Ahmići to pay respect to the victims. This is a more positive outcome than that of Praljak, who has become a martyr for many and who managed to derail legal proceedings. This also makes it harder for Croatian political elites to acknowledge crimes, since they will be seen as opposing the Croatian war narrative.

This shows that expressivism matters. The trials of Kordić, Čerkez and Blaškić did not have an effect on society, while Praljak did. The ICTY is a vehicle for narrative contestation, which can struggle to control its expressivist message, be it positive or negative. This moves power away from the court. Its focus on its legal mission meant that it neglected, or was unaware of, its central role in the Croatian transitional justice process. It was not only the most visible instrument of regional transitional justice, it was also often the only consistently dependable institution that succeeded in fact-finding, documentation and prosecution. Local publics looked to it, although maybe not in the way the tribunal wanted to be looked at. The public, media and elites did not follow a process (e.g. the day-to-day proceedings of televised trials); instead, the tribunal caught their attention during key moments. "It had no room for mistakes" (Subotic 2017) and when these dramatic moments occurred, they defined the many years of work the tribunal had undertaken.

Notes

1. She has also served as First Deputy Prime Minister and Minister of Foreign and European Affairs (2012–2016) in a centre-left coalition under Prime Minister Zoran Milanović. In 2016, she left the Croatian People's Party, because they went into a coalition with the HDZ, to become an independent MP. She later joined the Civic Liberal Alliance (GLAS).
2. Vladimir Šeks and Ivo Sanader of the Croatian Democratic Union (HDZ) and Zdravko Tomac of the Social Democratic Party of Croatia (SDP). Ivo Sanader later became Prime Minister of Croatia. Tomac was always far more nationalistically oriented than most of his party and was aligned closely to HDZ policies during the 1990s. He was highly critical of the ICTY and formally left the party in 2003.

References

Bakić-Hayden, M. (1995). Nesting orientalism: The case of former Yugoslavia. *Slavic Review, 54,* 917–931.

Duhaček, G. (2017, November 29). Analiza [Analysis]. *Index.hr*. http://www.index.hr/vijesti/clanak/analiza-praljak-je-pomno-rezirao-svoju-smrt-zelio-je-da-ga-se-pamti-kao-mucenika-a-ne-zlocinca/1010642.aspx. Accessed 10 Apr 2018.

Gordy, E. (2014). *Guilt, responsibility, and denial: The past at stake in post-Milošević Serbia*. Philadelphia: University of Pennsylvania Press.

Grabar-Kitarović, K. (2017, December 6). *Kolinda Grabar-Kitarović speech to United Nations Security Council.* https://www.scribd.com/document/366499824/Kolinda-Izjava-pred-Vije%C4%87em-sigurnosti#from_embed. Accessed 10 Apr 2018.

Holjevac, M. (2017a, November 30). Praljak je žrtva pogrešnih politika, ne Tuđmanovih već onih nakon njega [Praljak is a victim of incorrect politics, not Tuđman's but those after it]. *Dnevno.hr*. http://www.dnevno.hr/vijesti/hrvatska/praljak-je-zrtva-pogresnih-politika-ne-tudmanovih-vec-onih-nakon-njega-1099650/. Accessed 10 Apr 2018.

Holjevac, M. (2017b, December 1). Praljak, posljednja žrtva Domovinskog rata [Praljak, the last victim of the Homeland War]. *Dnevno.hr*. http://www.dnevno.hr/vijesti/hrvatska/marcel-holjevac-praljak-posljednja-zrtva-domovinskog-rata-1100207/. Accessed 10 Apr 2018.

HRT. (2017, November 30). *Jandronković pročitao zajedničku izjavu: Presude na uvažavaju povijesne istine* [Jandroković reads a joint statement: The verdicts do not respect historical truths]. *HRT* Vijesti. Available at http://vijesti.hrt.hr/417952/jandrokovic-procitao-zajednicku-izjavu-presude-ne-uvazavaju-povijesne-istine. Accessed 10 Apr 2018, https://www.balkaninsight.com/en/article/zagreb-commemorates-praljak-by-rejecting-verdict-12-11-2017. Accessed 10 Apr 2018.

Ipsos Puls. (2012, January). *Izbori 2011* [Elections 2011].

Jutarnji List. (2017, November 29). Svi Haški osuđenici i osumnjičenici su umrli ili se ubili prije odsluženja kazne [All of The Hague convicts and suspects that died or were killed before serving their sentence]. *Jutarnji List.* https://www.jutarnji.hr/vijesti/hrvatska/svi-haski-osudenici-i-osumnjicenici-koji-su-umrli-ili-se-ubili-prije-odsluzenja-kazne-babic-i-dokmanovic-se-objesili-stojiljkovic-si-pucao-u-glavu/6797079/. Accessed 10 Apr 2018.

Lamont, C. K. (2010). *International criminal justice and the politics of compliance.* Farnham: Ashgate.

Lučić, I. (2017, December 3). Suci će se do smrti pitati – što ako smo osudili nevina čovjeka [The judge will ask themselves until they die—What if we convicted an innocent man]. *Večernji List.* https://www.vecernji.hr/vijesti/suci-smrt-osuda-nevin-ivo-lucic-1211617. Accessed 10 Apr 2018.

Mijića, B. (2017, December 4). Sokratova krivnja: Od Atenske škole do Haaga [Socrates' guilt: From the Athens school to The Hague]. *Novi List.* http://www.novilist.hr/Komentari/Kolumne/Komentar-Branka-Mijica/Sokratova-krivnja-Od-Atenske-skole-do-Haaga. Accessed 10 Apr 2018.

Milanović, V. (2017, November 30). Slobodan Praljak: War criminal or Croatian hero. *Al Jazeera.* https://www.aljazeera.com/news/2017/11/slobodan-praljak-war-criminal-croatian-hero-171130181546531.html. Accessed 10 Apr 2018.

Milekić, S. (2017, December 11). War criminal Praljak's death commemorated in Croatia. *Balkan insight.*

Milekić, S., & Dizdarević, E. (2017, November 29). Croatia PM: Bosnian croats' convictions were "moral injustice". *Balkan insight.* http://www.balkaninsight.com/en/article/croatia-rejects-party-of-bosnian-croats-verdict-11-29-2017. Accessed 10 Apr 2018.

Miljavac, P. (2017, December 2). Ne samo Mesić i V. Pusić, i neki generali u Haagu su svjedočili protiv Hrvatske [Not only Mesić and V. Pusić, some generals also testified against Croatia]. *Večernji List.* https://www.vecernji.hr/premium/generali-presuda-pavao-miljavac-stipe-mesic-slobodan-praljak-1211503. Accessed 10 Apr 2018.

Narodne Novine. (2006). *Deklaracija o Oluji NN* [Declaration on Operation Storm]. Available at http://narodne-novine.nn.hr/clanci/sluzbeni/127530.html.

Pavić, S. (2017, November 29). Za pravu istinu nigdje nije bilo sluha, a Praljak na to nije htio pristati [No one wanted to hear the real truth, and Praljak did not want to accept that]. *Jutarnji List.* https://www.jutarnji.hr/komentari/za-pravu-istinu-nigdje-nije-bilo-sluha-a-praljak-na-to-nije-htio-pristati-stvarna-prica-o-ratu-nije-zanimala-ni-zagreb-ni-sarajevo-ni-mostar-ni-haag/6797067/. Accessed 10 Apr 2018.

Raspudić, N. (2017, December 1). Hrvatska najidiotskija zemlja: Pobijedili u ratu, ostali bez entiteta i na kraju dobili osudu [Croatia is the most idiotic country: They won in war, were left without their entity and in the end received a verdict]. *Večernji List.* https://www.vecernji.hr/premium/slobodan-praljak-haaski-sud-nino-raspudic-herceg-bosna-1211195. Accessed 10 Apr 2018.

Sokolić, I. (2017). Denying the unknown: Everyday narratives about Croatian involvement in the 1992–1995 Bosnian conflict. *Südosteuropa, 65,* 632–653.

Steflja, I. (2017). The production of the war criminal cult: Radovan Karadžić and Vojislav Šešelj at The Hague. *Nationalities Papers, 46,* 52–68.

Subotic, J. (2009). *Hijacked justice: Dealing with the past in the Balkans.* Ithaca: Cornell University Press.

Subotic, J. (2017, November 30). In his final act, war criminal hijacks court. *Balkan insight.* http://www.balkaninsight.com/en/article/in-his-final-act-war-criminal-hijacks-court-11-30-2017. Accessed 10 Apr 2018.

Tomičić, L. (2017, December 3). Praljak – Tuđmanova žrtva i osuđeni ratni zločinac, a ne heroj [Praljak—Tuđman's victim and a convicted war criminal, not a hero]. *Novi List.* http://www.novilist.hr/Komentari/Kolumne/Ladovina-Ladislava-Tomicica/Praljak-Tudmanova-zrtva-i-osudeni-ratni-zlocinac-a-ne-heroj. Accessed 10 Apr 2018.

Večernji List. (2017, December 12). Odlikovanja RH nisu oduzeta ni Tihomiru Blaškiću, Dariju Kordiću... [The medals of the Republic of Croatia were also not taken from Tihomir Blaškić, Dario Kordić]. *Večernji List.* https://www.vecernji.hr/vijesti/tihomir-blaskic-dario-kordic-odlikovanja-1213585. Accessed 10 Apr 2018.

CHAPTER 9

Conclusion

The book analysed what effect the transitional justice process in Croatia has had on norms and narratives related to the 1991–1995 conflict. The results point to ambiguous effects. The process took place in an atmosphere of cynicism and distrust of institutions, which greatly affected how participants regarded transitional justice authorities and narratives presented from the top–down. Discussions on most topics across all target segments consistently shifted to how the environment in Croatia is corrupt and how politics in the state has ruined "everything". To some participants, the Croatian state was at fault, as much as Serbian aggression, for the dire situation that today's society is in. Justice narratives, as well as the hoped-for trickle-down effects of human rights norms, struggled to compete with personal and local everyday narratives, unless were in line with everyday expectations. This greatly affected how participants came to understand the world around them. A thorough and society-wide reckoning with past wrongdoings committed by Croatian forces or state authorities has not occurred, despite rulings at the ICTY and in domestic war crimes trials showing that they did happen. A significant normative and cultural change did not occur in society and it seems that, as Drumbl (2007) asserted, war crime trials preoccupied with retribution and deterrence (the primary aims of these courts) lack the capability to instigate such change in society.

In the eyes of participants, the nearly universal, predominant war narrative of self-defence and victimhood provided justification for certain

I. Sokolić, *International Courts and Mass Atrocity*,
Memory Politics and Transitional Justice,
https://doi.org/10.1007/978-3-319-90841-0_9

actions, including some that have been interpreted as war crimes by legal authorities. This narrative can be dangerous, since it creates a notion of "us, the victims" versus "them, the aggressors". Participants constructed a context for understanding the past from a variety of perspectives, but the war narrative was particularly influential due to its everyday nature and emotional appeal. In comparison, justice narratives are far removed from the everyday, they are seen as coming from institutions in The Hague or Zagreb. These institutions are often perceived as illegitimate, which can prevent trickle-down effects of transitional justice to occur. In extreme instances, the transitional justice process was interpreted as a continued aggression against Croatia. Some deliberation of the war narrative is, however, present and groups that deliberated on transitional justice issues did not see this enduring aggression. All groups, however, continued to interpret a range of events through the perspective of the Homeland War.

The war narrative is central to many other topics within the realm of transitional justice. Participants defined war crimes in relation to their understanding of Croatian defence. Consequently, they exhibited a certain tolerance for deviance in the context of crimes committed by Croats. Notions of an unorganised and unprepared Croatian defence were seen as mitigating circumstances to war crimes, which were often defined in relation to Serbian crimes committed as a part of planned aggression. Again, the elite and far-removed clashed with the local and everyday; transitional justice institutions in Croatia and the Netherlands struggled to instil a rule of law norm in the context of localised complexities and already present normative expectations. Respondents felt powerless in a system they felt was unresponsive, untrustworthy, corrupt and inefficient, which imposed justice on them from above and, often, afar.

Participants also based their legal reasoning on localised folk theories of law, which again allowed for an apologetic attitude towards certain crimes. This understanding of law was not legally consistent, but was instead consistent with the political and emotional narratives prevalent in respondents' views of the world. The effect of this is that the highly emotional war narrative plays a large role in shaping attitudes towards law. Moreover, factual inaccuracies often helped justify these narratives. This involved typical symbols of the war narrative, such as the *baka* with the rifle, which lowered Croatian war crimes to the level of ordinary crimes, if they were seen as crimes at all. These were seen as unexceptional crimes in war, as side effects of a horrible state of affairs, to be punished more leniently in comparison with exceptional Serb crimes, to be punished more harshly. The ICTY's and local courts' generally sound legal judgements and strict adherence to legal justice over political justice have not helped significantly develop understandings of law, but it has helped foster deliberation on these topics with certain groups of individuals. Localised narratives and normative processes may have undermined the trickle-down effects of rule of law norms, but that does not mean this will not change in the future, since the norms are at the very least being discussed.

The war narrative also defined how participants viewed Serbs, the key "Other" to Croat identity. The war narrative contributed greatly to the Orthodox Church being seen as aggressive and an obstacle to reconciliation, as opposed to the forgiving Catholic Church. Although a range of survey results and participants' comments pointed to openness towards the Serb minority and minorities in general, there was also consensus among participants and the wider public that Serbs should not be given equal language rights in Vukovar at the time. The issue of Cyrillic signs in Vukovar had two effects on participants, it reduced their trust in government institutions and made Croats feel threatened by a perceived Serb threat, to a lesser or greater extent. Moreover, individuals frequently use notions of collective guilt based on ethnicity to decide who is culpable for committed crimes. This can have serious implications during periods of higher tensions, when members of outgroups can become targets of violence.

All participants agreed that war veterans faced significant problems in Croatian society, but the exact nature and degree of these differed among participants. All target segments, however, agreed that war veterans' associations were politicised and often corrupt. Despite this, associations remain a useful ally to political parties that can use nationalist symbols to gain their allegiance and those of voters who agree with their plight (such as all groups in this study that did not deliberate on transitional justice). The link between Croatian economic transition and transitional justice highlights this potential. To many respondents, the two transitions were semantically linked and were referred to interchangeably. This allows political elites to divert attention from one by emphasising issues in the other, in other words by covering economic woes up (such as high unemployment or stinted economic growth) by portraying them as attacks on war veterans (lack of jobs for war veterans specifically) or on all of Croatia (Cyrillic signs in Vukovar). This highlights how a period of change can be welcomed and how it can be remembered.

Croatian involvement in the Bosnian conflict and the verdict, as well as suicide, of Slobodan Praljak verify these findings and highlight the importance of the ICTY's expressivist effects. These events could have led to a reappraisal of certain facets of the war narrative, but this did not occur. Croatia is instead considered a saviour of Bosnia, and the verdict in the Prlić et al. case has not highlighted the crimes committed by Croat forces in Bosnia, nor has it helped the spread of the human rights norms. Instead, it highlights how the expressivist messages of international criminal courts can be difficult to control.

In so many facets, the war narrative enjoyed universal agreement among study participants and nearly universal agreement with the Croatian public, meaning the trickle-down effects of norms and justice cascades do not occur, as the justice narrative is wholly rejected. In other instances, with some groups and target segments, the complex interaction between two, or more, narratives produced a deliberation on topics relevant to transitional justice. This does not mean that norms associated with the process will take hold in society, but it does at the very least lead to a discursive space marked by numerous narrative options, rather than a monopoly. In the case of Croatia, as with many other case studies around the world, norm advocates were present and influential in society. These norm advocates, however, did not promote human rights but instead primarily promoted the war narrative and, often, the more extreme elements of it.

This analysis provides a further case study for how pressure for norm change comes from a variety of sources and that this pressure can be for or against human rights norms. The spiral model of norm change (Risse et al. 1999), which assumes that pressure on human rights norm violating governments will come from below, through domestic norm believers and transnational human rights networks, is correct in the case of Croatia, since these actors did exist and exerted pressure. It is, however, debatable how much influence they ever had and if they could ever have hoped to achieve significant results in the face of a grouping like the war veterans, who laid the foundation of their arguments in the powerful war narrative. The central role of emotion in periods of drastic change, or entrenched transition as in Croatia, has been overlooked in research on post-socialist societies (Schäuble 2014: 15). The case of Croatia shows how pressure from below can hamper the spread of human rights norms, especially when combined with dominant and emotional everyday narratives.

The following section of the chapter provides two comparative analyses based on a deliberative understanding of transitional justice: first, of the Croatian case in comparison with those of Serbia and Bosnia; second, of the Homeland War to the Second World War and Yugoslav periods. The chapter then turns to lessons learned from the Croatian case study, concerning victims, perpetrators and alternative solutions. Finally, the chapter and book conclude with a look at the participants in this study, how the memory of conflict continues to affect them and how they construct the world around them.

Was Transitional Justice Successful? A Regional Comparison

It is highly debatable if the process of transitional justice can be reduced to a binary result of success or failure. It is equally debatable if causality can ever be ascertained in such a complex process, when its beginning and end remain hard to pinpoint and its realms of influence unknown. Despite the numerous instances of transitional justice across the globe, few cases are of any comparative use due to their intrinsic uniqueness. Even the countries of the former Yugoslavia provide little in the sense of parallels to be drawn.

Small-N comparative analysis is made difficult due to the highly divergent contexts of transition in each of these states. In other words, the independent variables influencing the outcome of the transitional justice process are numerous and vary significantly in each case. These include, but are not limited to: exposure to conflict; conflict outcome; nature of conflict; current ethnic division in society; type of transition; EU integration process; atrocities committed; and the dominant war narrative of the largest ethnic group. Figure 9.1 provides an illustration and summary of these variables.[1] The table is only illustrative, since many of these assumptions are far from agreed upon by the scholarship and hold nuances that a single table cannot encompass. This further highlights the complex, unique and contingent nature of the transitional justice process, in the region as well as globally. The table also omits a number of other possible variables, such as the memory of the Second World War, the memory of the Yugoslav period, the nature of the conflict (civil war,

	Croatia	Serbia	Bosnia and Herzegovina	Kosovo	Slovenia
Exposure to conflict	Domestic and international	International	Domestic	Domestic	Domestic
Conflict outcome	Perceived winner	Perceived loser	Frozen due to international intervention	Perceived winner following international intervention	Perceived winner
Length of conflict (approximately)	Five years, focused on two intense periods.	Five years, then two years.	Four years, almost constant	Two years	10 days
Current ethnic division	One large minority with special rights.	Predominantly mono-ethnic	Multi-ethnic; three minorities with divided powers.	Multi-ethnic on paper; in practice one large minority	Mono-ethnic
Type of transition	To competitive authoritarianism, then liberal democracy through elections	To competitive authoritarianism, then liberal democracy through civil unrest	To liberal democracy through international intervention	To liberal democracy through international intervention. Not fully recognised as a state.	To liberal democracy through elections.
EU integration process	Joined in 2013	Negotiations opened	Candidate country	Stabilisation and Association Agreement	Joined in 2004
Atrocities committed?	Yes	Yes	Yes	Yes	No
Dominant war narrative (of major ethnic group)	Victimisation; self-defence; victory; anti-Serb	Victimisation; defeat; anti-West; anti-Muslim	Victimisation; self-defence; all sides opposed to each other	Victimisation; self-defence; victory; anti-Serb	Victimisation; self-defence; victory

Fig. 9.1 Overview of independent variables in former Yugoslav states

international conflict or a hybrid), the type of government, state of the economy, levels of corruption and so on. The most valid comparison is that between Croatia, Serbia and Bosnia, whose conflicts are intrinsically connected (if not one and the same) and were adjudicated at the ICTY.

The outcome to be analysed in transitional justice is equally ambiguous. If success cannot be ascertained, then what dependable variable is more appropriate? The process itself was very different in each country. For example, it is debatable if the post-conflict transitional justice process in Slovenia is comparable to that of the other states, whose conflicts were so much more. In this book's framework of deliberative justice, the most appropriate dependable variable is discursive engagement through public deliberation. To facilitate comparison, this is defined broadly, as the opening of space for the deliberation and contestation of narratives related to the most recent conflicts. If transitional justice has had an effect in Croatia, Serbia or Bosnia, then it will have opened up this discursive space. This comparison highlights the "promise and the limitation of international law in challenging environments" (Nettelfield 2010: 288).

Each case shows that obstacles to transitional justice were significant, that the aims of the process were not wholly met, but that they achieved something (potentially significant).

In Croatia, as previous chapters have argued, judicial narratives presented by transitional justice institutions struggled to compete with the dominant war narrative of victimhood and self-defence. These narratives sometimes worked in concert with each other, but often they clashed and the dominant war narrative was not questioned. This affects understandings of law, attitudes towards the Serb minority, the position of war veterans and views on the conflict in Bosnia. The transitional justice process fostered some deliberation among certain segments of society, but this was limited.

In Serbia, there is a pervasive narrative of denial and the ICTY seems to have had limited impact on political elites, the rule of law, civil society or the public (McMahon and Forsythe 2008). Much like in Croatia, the local political situation made it difficult for the transitional justice process to have an effect (Ostojić 2014). The publication of facts and well-run trials, both domestically and internationally, did not effectively promote the questioning of Serbia's role in the 1990s conflicts since it lacked an open dialogue with the people it aimed to engage (Gordy 2014: 184). The Serbian case also highlights the importance of expressivist moments, which can come to define the whole process. Gordy (2014) argues the single largest opportunity was the "Scorpions" video that showed Serb paramilitaries executing Bosnian Muslim prisoners. The effect, however, was limited, "Briefly, a window was opened. While it was open, the debate shifted. Following sustained engagement by media and political parties, it was closed" (Gordy 2014: 223). This and other moments could have stirred significant deliberation, but for a variety of reasons, did not.

The ICTY did not completely erode the narrative of denial, but it did create momentary shifts in the debate that opened up a limited discursive space. In Serbia, this created a process of pluralisation, which is still ongoing (Rangelov 2014: 180). It created sites where the tensions between nationalism and the rule of law can become expressed and negotiated, even if they are often rejected. This led to increased domestic legal institutional capacity, increased involvement of non-state actors in transitional justice and increased opportunities for discursive engagement for liberal segments of society (ibid.: 180–184). This is significant in the Serbian context of nationalism and ethnic homogenisation. Many of the goals of transitional justice in Serbia were not met, but similar to Croatia, a space was opened for the deliberation and contestation of narratives. This also does not take into account that without the ICTY in Serbia, progress would have been far more limited (Klarin 2009).

The Bosnian context is more complex than that of Serbia and Croatia due to the post-Dayton division of the state, which entails three distinct ethnic narratives. Each sees itself as the victim of the other two. Transitional justice, and especially the ICTY, often created collective divisions between the citizens of Bosnia along these lines (Nettelfield 2010: 290). These were often pronounced during key verdicts. As in Croatia and Serbia, this was due to localised complexities. In this case, it was the charged political environment created by the Dayton Peace Agreement (ibid.: 292). International criminal law had a role to play in post-conflict Bosnia, but this was often secondary next to more pressing post-conflict needs (ibid.). When approached through the expressivist and deliberative lens, however, an effect is apparent. Institutional capacity was increased by the transitional justice process, for example by helping victims' associations organise into networks and by helping civil society work across entities, and the Bosnian government did begin to discuss crimes that happened under its leadership (ibid.). A similar pattern, therefore, is evident in Bosnia: the transitional justice process struggled in the face of multifaceted obstacles, in this instance both institutional and cultural, but it did foster opportunities for deliberation in society.

This brief comparative analysis highlights how transitional justice—in Croatia, the former Yugoslav states and further afield—is a complex process in which expressivist elements are key. In Croatia, Serbia and Bosnia, it was the expressivist effects that helped create opportunities for deliberation and contestation of narratives. In each case, key expressivist moments were essential to how the process was to be adjudged and many of these were missed opportunities for change. This was due to local narratives, often of victimisation, that were too strong for judicial narratives to overcome. In all cases, the transitional justice process was "hijacked" (Subotic 2009) and, in hindsight, local complexities mattered more than initially thought. A comparative perspective makes the ICTY's limitations clear, but the conclusions are not exclusively negative: the transitional justice process has made a plurality of narratives possible and has fostered space for deliberation in each case. Moreover, it is impossible to ignore the precedents set by the ICTY (such as Croatian aggression in Bosnia) and the fact that no other institution was likely to undertake this difficult task. The ICTY has certainly left behind a void since its closure, which is now allowing issues of justice to be overlooked more than before.

Was the process more successful in one case over any other? This is difficult to say, since each context is so unique and the criteria by which to judge the outcome are not agreed upon. Bosnia and Serbia had a much more difficult beginning to their processes than Croatia, which was spurred on by the desire to join the EU and NATO. Perhaps Croatia's trajectory has therefore, especially between 2000 and 2013, been more stable and the contributions of transitional justice clearer. External involvement in the transitional justice process has received considerable criticism, but it is proving far more complex than previously thought. In the Croatian case, it may have been necessary to overcome domestic elite and everyday resistance to the transitional justice process. What all cases in unison highlight are the possibilities, but also the limitations, of post-conflict transitional justice in these former Yugoslav states.

Due to the difficulty in conducting regional comparisons, one comparison that may be of more use with regard to a deliberative interpretation of transitional justice is Croatia's first such process, dealing with crimes committed during the Second World War and during the Yugoslav regime. The legacy of both the Ustasha and the Yugoslav regimes remains in many ways misunderstood. The communist past, for example, was almost wholly ignored and not systematically addressed, as opposed to many other Eastern European countries which did tackle this period of their histories to varying degrees (Subotic 2015: 204). Such a process was difficult under the Yugoslav circumstances of the 1990s, which were marked by violent conflict and nationalism. The consequence of this was that human rights abuses from the communist period were presented as attacks by one ethnicity against another, depending on who was asked (Subotic 2015: 190). Communist crimes were never analysed in a political vacuum and were used for the purposes of nationalistic mobilisation (Subotic 2015: 190). In other words, transitional justice was politicised from the outset and serious examination of this period is yet to happen (Subotic 2015: 205). As Subotic (2015: 205) warns, "if there is one lesson to be learned from the Yugoslav experience, it is for the transitional justice scholars and practitioners not to give up this historical ground so easily to others, but to insist on a careful and systematic evaluation of the communist past".

Similarly, a lack of systematic studies of Second World War, Ustasha and Partisan crimes has led to highly diverging understandings of this period of Croatian history. These different memories and associated commemorations have polarised Croatian society and instigated political, media and cultural debates (Pavlaković 2008). More recent events, such as the debate surrounding the shouting of "*Za dom, spremni*" at football matches, exemplify how a lack of understanding of the past can lead to dangerous present-day interpretations. Chief among these incidents was the shouting of the salute by a Croatian national team football player, Josip Šimunić, to a crowd of 25,000 spectators in Zagreb in November 2013. The Australian-born player highlighted his lack of understanding of the past himself in numerous subsequent interviews. In a post-match interview, he said he "associates home with love, warmth and positive struggle – everything that we showed on the pitch to win our place in the World Cup... Some people have to learn history" (Bieber 2013). Later, at his Court of Arbitration for Sport (CAS) trial, he continued to defend his views and claimed that he considered the salute to be patriotic and that he did not understand whom he actually insulted (Novi List 2014).

More importantly, as Brentin (2016: 9) points out, while much media attention was directed at the incident, it focused on Šimunić himself and few outlets discussed the significance of the player "performing" in front of a "receptive" audience that had already been chanting the salute throughout the game. Accounts were centred on his individual stupidity, rather than the societal problem, much like in reporting on transitional justice issues that generally orientated towards reporting on incidents rather than broader analysis.[2] While most media outlets condemned the incident, social media reactions were far more ambiguous. Comments to many articles and on Facebook pages of newspapers often contradicted the outlets criticisms of the event based on different interpretations of the "true" meaning of the salute (Brentin 2016: 9). These incidents have alarmed commentators and have highlighted how intense the interaction between different interpretations of the past within Croatian society can be. Most worryingly, they have highlighted how Ustasha symbols, which connote a specific interpretation of the past, have become normal in mainstream Croatian sport, culture and politics (Brentin 2016: 11). Narratives from the Homeland War have increasingly been applied to the Second World War, which aim to represent the NDH regime in a more positive light (Blanuša 2017). This forms a part of a continued nation-building effort for a state that is defined by ethnicity and narratives of armed conflict.

These examples show how easily memory can be used for nationalist mobilisation, especially when the discursive space is dominated or monopolised by nationalist elements. In this sense, deliberation of issues leads to a discussion about the past and does not allow it to be easily hijacked for other purposes. This also gives a good reason for establishing a tribunal outside of the former Yugoslavia, since it forces at least some part of the process of reckoning to be undertaken, although this does not mean that the target society will mechanically deliberate on it. Respondents in the Zadar pensioners group, overtly sympathetic to Pavelić and potentially the *NDH* regime, directly addressed this issue. They felt that an institution such as the ICTY would have left a better legacy of that period through its ability to produce documentation, although this does not mean they would have necessarily been happy with such an institution's ultimate verdict (the participants seemed to think they would absolve Pavelić). The ICTY provided a set of "reference points" that focused public debate on the interpretation of facts, rather than the establishment of them (Rangelov 2014: 48). The inherent uncertainty lies in who will engage with the trial and how, but this is also the significance of the process, since "indeterminacy is seen here as pregnant with opportunity" (Rangelov 2014: 48).

Moreover, for a nation to thrive without significant internal conflict or inconsistency, it must accept its own existence through time and, thereby, acknowledge acts committed in its past that still burden the contemporary community (Maier 1988: 14). Because many Croatians (adopting Maier's and Habermas' argument regarding Germans) had grown up in a psychological and institutional framework that had once descended into violence, it is possible that all Croatians are still potential perpetrators and the situation could happen again. Although this is quite an abstract concept, it does highlight the need to interpret and debate the past, but to also achieve a balance so as not to become obsessed and burdened by it.

It remains difficult to compare progress in any instance of transitional justice to another. In the case of Croatia, two violent periods of history have previously been ignored or hijacked for the purposes of nationalist mobilisation. If the most recent instance of transitional justice, from the 1991–1995 conflict, is compared to the previous two, then there may be reason to be optimistic. Although the Croatian public continue to interpret events in the past through the prism of the Homeland War, this most recent conflict also features deliberation in certain segments of society. By removing a part of the transitional justice process from the region, the ICTY at a minimum attempted to ascertain what occurred in the region, giving publics the chance to focus on interpretation. Although this did not guarantee a debate about the past in the region, it did at least provide some basis for it. It also helped develop local judiciary capacity, which may have held more potential to initiate deliberation. A plurality of views is present on facets of the Homeland War, and among participants in this study, these views were not polarising. The one group that ended in an argument ultimately disagreed over issues pertaining to the Second World War and the Yugoslav regime, rather than the most recent conflict, which highlights the unresolved nature of the former two compared to the latter. While it may not be possible to adjudge transitional justice an outright success, it can be said that it has achieved much more than has previously occurred in Croatian society and possibly more than many may have expected at the outset.

Rangelov (2014) effectively uses the deliberative character of legal processes to create a framework for analysis for three former Yugoslav countries: Croatia, Serbia and Slovenia. This book further supports his case study of Croatia by providing a broader picture of where deliberation occurred within the realm of transitional justice. Is this a comparatively useful framework for future studies? The outcome of these two studies would say that it is, but only in combination with other forms of analysis that can help overcome the framework's limitations.

What this approach to transitional justice does show is that something is occurring in society, whereas so many other studies have shown little to no effect (Hafner-Burton and Ron 2007; Hafner-Burton and Tsutsui 2007; Horne 2015; Lynch and Marchesi 2015; Thoms et al. 2010). This may be exactly because what the process can help incite is a discussion about the past. The approach used in this book shows that this is happening in Croatian society by highlighting the nature and extent of the nuanced interaction between various narratives. This also shows how such processes are not mechanical, but fluid and highly complex. Unlike in previous instances of potential transitional justice in Croatia, which could have dealt with the legacies of Second World War or communist crimes but did not, the legacy of the Homeland War is deliberated upon by certain segments of society and has, for the most part, not been appropriated for the purposes of political goals. This is based on the assumption that deliberation on these issues will make it harder for nationalism and ethnic conflict to grow. A return to conflict is, however, still possible and unresolved issues from the past, for example the legacy of Ustasha and Partisan crimes in Croatia, can still come to define modern-day politics.

Finally, a reasonable timeframe for analysis of transitional justice remains debatable. Over 20 years have passed since the conflict ended, meaning we are no longer only witnessing short-term effects. It is, however, unclear when the "transition" part of "transitional justice" ends and when we can stop considering Croatian society as undergoing the process of transitional justice. Given that Croatian society is currently still struggling to interpret crimes committed in the 1940s, it is not unreasonable to assume that the legacy of the Homeland War will be long-lasting. Frameworks for analysis need to take into account that the effects of transitional justice can only become apparent in the long term (Stover and Weinsten 2004). This potentially highlights the transformative justice scholarship as the next step in the study of the process. It conceptualises the goals of transitional justice as long term and takes into account the contexts that can influence public needs and expectations (Lambourne 2009; Sharp 2013). Expectations may need to be restrained, especially in the context of domestic governments acquiescing to transitional justice institutions (McAuliffe 2017). Arguably, however, the real litmus test for transitional justice is whether a return to violence eventually happens.

Lessons for the Future

What could have been done differently in Croatia? This is a dangerously open-ended question that points more towards numerous incremental changes in the realm of practicality, rather than legal process. At the very least, the Croatian case provides a number of lessons for transitional justice.

Victims

Participants in the study highlighted the plight of victims of the conflict. For many, not only in the veterans' and victims' groups, these were highly emotional and personal matters. The emotional nature of these topics makes them easy to appropriate for political purposes and resolving them could limit the space that such opportunists act in. Specifically, focus groups and interviews highlighted three areas in which the status of victims could be improved. First and foremost is the issue of missing persons. This was raised in all groups, including those that were still searching for relatives and those who were relatively far removed from the conflict. This remains an issue in Bosnia, Kosovo and Serbia as much as, if not more, than in Croatia. It is conceivable to conduct a more systematic search for graves, and it is possible that records of graves exist with the respective militaries. At the very least, such a practical move would remove much emotion from these debates. Related to this is the notion that the exact number of deceased could be ascertained, thereby lessening the amount of dispute over numbers.

Secondly, victims who survived the conflict but continue to suffer from the effects of it could be given more rights, assistance and support. For example, laws addressing sexual violence during the conflict have been slow to develop. The Croatian parliament only adopted the Law on the Rights of Victim of Sexual Violence during the Armed Aggression against the Republic of Croatia in the Homeland War in 2015 (Narodne Novine 2015). This law provides extensive rights, assistance and support for victims of wartime sexual violence (Clarke 2016). Moreover, the government is building four veterans' centres in Daruvar, Petrinja, Sinj and Šibenik as a part of a 20-year project to help war veterans and victims better integrate into society (Clarke 2016: 143). The mere presence of the law and the centres is, however, not enough to help victims receive appropriate assistance and support. Moreover, psychological assistance in rural areas, in particular, remains limited (Schäuble 2014: 201). At this early stage, it is also imperative and practically possible to publicise these developments and new rights widely (Clarke 2016: 143). This highly pragmatic process also opens up an opportunity for public deliberation on the issue of wartime sexual violence, which can help address the social norms that made it socially acceptable to ignore for this long (Clarke 2016; Duggan et al. 2008).

Thirdly, a large number of individuals remain displaced regionally and globally. The implementation and enforcement of laws facilitating their return are lax, especially given the still present tensions in the region's societies. Nevertheless, more supervision from authorities could help ensure that the laws are being properly prescribed.

Perpetrators and Their Legacy

Despite the imperfect record of both international and domestic legal efforts at finding and trying perpetrators at all levels across the region, certain parts of society do want to find out who the perpetrators of the violence were, what their current whereabouts are and what their motivations were. Following the acquittals of Gotovina and Markač (and hence the legal clearing of their names), Croatian President at the time, Ivo Josipović, stressed the need to find the real perpetrators of the crimes that the former generals were accused of (Jović and Romić 2012). Although some may disagree with such efforts, they do so with limited legitimacy. Even those who only wish to see perpetrators from the opposing side tried can offer few legitimate arguments as to why all perpetrators should not be tried, although as the analysis has shown, who constitutes a perpetrator differs greatly between one's own and the opposing side. All participants expressed the more general desire, likely also present in the general public, to identify the key causes of the violence and to try and punish individuals responsible for it. One of the enduring questions that hangs over everyone's heads is "how did it come to this?"

For some, the violence from the conflict has not stopped. Much of Croatia, as well as Bosnia and Kosovo, remains mined. Croatian demining efforts are extensive but leftover devices continue to claim lives and hamper efforts at rebuilding infrastructure. More could be done regionally to deal with this problem and to clamp down on what is in parts a highly corrupt industry (UNDP 2015).[3]

What Other Options Existed?

Since attitudes and decisions on topics of transitional justice are so personal and emotional, it is debatable if trials could have ever provided an effective remedy. Maybe Snyder and Vinjamuri (2003), Christie (2001) and many others are correct in concluding that although under some uncommon and particular circumstances trials can help with this process, these are so rare that it is difficult to draw any effective parallels between trials and reconciliation. Again, Bass' (2000: 304) pessimistic view of international criminal tribunals as the "least awful alternative" sounds plausible. The elements of justice and fact-finding discussed above hold some pragmatic, although possibly still idealistic, alternatives. What the results of this book show is that if the transitional justice process is to successfully engage with personal and emotional problems, then the everyday elements of the process also need to be taken into account.

Such, more ambitious ventures, may be better suited to projects outside of the courtroom.

Truth commissions and fact-finding efforts are one such possibility. The archives they build can be understood not as propagators of certain versions of the truth (although they often are, in poorly run efforts), but as spaces where the past can be debated, interpreted and reinterpreted by various actors (Jones and Oliveira 2016). This facet of archives aids deliberation on the past and the entrenchment of democracy (Jones and Oliveira 2016). Civil society may be better positioned to cater to these types of projects than any court ever could.

The ICTY does have elements of this in its work, since the ICTY Court Records, or archives, will be one of its key legacies. They provide a repository of all of its investigative work, but the question remains what to do with them upon completion of the Tribunal's mandate. As much as there may have been a benefit to holding the Tribunal outside of the region, likewise there may be a benefit to keeping the archive at a distance. This may, however, lead to the archives suffering from the same lack of legitimacy as the ICTY. If the archives were to be moved to the region, then would they be kept in multiple locations? What is the symbolism of this? Is it at all practical? What location and form of archive will lead to deliberation of the past and a more thorough understanding of it, so as to avoid a return to violent nationalism in the region? These are the difficult questions that the transitional justice process in the former Yugoslavia will face in the near future and which may define how the work of the ICTY will be remembered. Arguably, this will be its greatest legacy.

Going forward, it may also be beneficial for institutions involved in the transitional justice process to focus less on merely providing more information to publics in the region, but to also better understand why they are making the choices and under what circumstances. Inundating publics with information and blaming them for not accessing the readily available data or pointing out inherent contradictions in attitudes may not help resolve any of the key obstacles that the legacy of conflict has created. Instead, it may be more important to better understand what feels "right" for individuals, in that circumstance and at that time, when they make decisions that may be discriminatory towards others. The focus is, therefore, not on information but on resolving psychological blockages.

Memories of War

What this book showed was how a small number of individuals constructed their memory and understanding of the Homeland War, as well as how this affects their lives today. The study would not have been possible without their honesty and willingness to relive, often painful and traumatic, memories. The issues discussed were in the realms of politics, law and culture, but to all participants they were highly emotional. Many experienced the war at close range in a shockingly personal way. A Zadar war veteran openly spoke about how she lost four brothers and her husband. A woman in Banovina had to hide in her basement as a child, while her parents were killed nearby by Serb paramilitaries. Some had to flee their homes, never to return. Others were fortunate enough not to have experienced extreme personal loss, but fought on the various front lines of the war. They were the rudimentary defence that has come to define the Croatian war narrative. A Sisak war veteran went to war "in sneakers with a kinder egg [hand grenade] on me, for protection. While they shot at us with tanks and planes" (focus group with Sisak war veterans).

Teachers in this study were, for the most part, too young to have experienced the war as directly as the war veterans and many of the pensioners. Instead, they witnessed it from bomb shelters or heard about it on television and radio, as well as from friends and relatives involved in the fighting. This target segment still shared the trauma of the other target segments; they still saw the same threat to their existence:

> *Lena*: I know what it looked like in the summer of 1991. Your colleagues up until yesterday just disappeared over night. A girl who I went to musical school with for four years, not a word, she just left. And at night in August, all of a sudden the shelling starts. They started falling all over the city. She knew something, I did not know it. So then we can ask, what are facts and what did you experience yourself and what was passed on in the family? That is something that I will also say to my own children (interview with Zagreb teacher).

All of the participants shared a common trauma, although at different levels. They spoke about it in a similar, local and personal, fashion. As the above teacher highlighted, this trauma and the strength of the narratives participants used to explain it to themselves continue to affect the way in which participants view the world around them. Some are still reliving the war on a daily basis; others only see it in relatively specific topics. After all, I was asking these individuals questions about the war, be it directly or indirectly, so it is not surprising they frequently brought it up. What was more obvious was how in certain ways the communities where participants lived remained plagued by the legacy of the war.

War veterans' and victims' groups in all locations were still searching for the bodies of their loved ones. More than once they said they would give anything to be able to find a grave to light a candle at. Groups felt this was the worst fate of all, to not know where your loved ones were buried:

> *Jasna*: My brother died in the war as a soldier, but my aunt used to tell my mother "Be quiet, you are lucky because you have somewhere to light a candle".
> Marijana agrees
> *Jasna*: I wander around everywhere and nowhere can I find such peace.
> Marijana and Lara agree
> *Lara*: It is very ugly to say this, but I was happy when I found my parents' grave.
> *Marijana*: A person finds some kind of peace. Now their birthdays come and go, Christmas, Easter, and I have no cross to light a candle at.
> *Lara*: This eternal unrest.
> *Blanka*: I will just add that when I moved my husband's bones to the family grave, a relative of mine said I looked joyful.
> *Lara*: Yes, because you found peace.
> *Blanka*: And I replied, "You cannot understand the relief I feel that my husband now rests in his home" (focus group with non-urban war veterans Banovina).

This same group also felt their old neighbours, now back, were all potential perpetrators, at worst, and witnesses at best. Those who fought in the war relived the war in a different way, through PTSD. Many individuals sought treatment for this, war veterans' groups acted as a therapeutic outlet for individuals, but some were not aware of how much the war still haunted them. One individual broke down in tears in the middle of a discussion; another had to return to a rehabilitation centre following their participation. For many participants, the war was still a heavy burden on their lives. To others it was so to a lesser degree, but they continued to view the world around them with suspicion and continued to see a divided society. War veterans in Slavonia asked the researcher if he held a Croatian passport before they could hold the agreed dyad, pensioners in Zagreb stormed out of the group following an argument over interpretations of what Yugoslavia was.

All participants also shared, to varying degrees, a notion that hope had turned to despair. That Croatia suffered and fought to the death for its independence, only for that to later be corrupted. They distrusted institutions meant to protect them, their Serb neighbours, the Serbian state, the Serbian Orthodox Church and most sources of information available to them. Their memories were not only laced with emotion, they were defined by it. So much so that they reflected on the worlds of politics, law and culture through emotion. To these individuals, the lasting legacy of the Homeland War was distrust and disappointment with the world around them, within which they felt abandoned by the very state they fought to create.

These results paint a relatively depressing picture of stereotypes in Croatia and the prevalence of a certain version of the war narrative. They also highlight how difficult it is to promote alternative narratives when mechanisms to achieve this are limited, in a society plagued by institutional distrust. The ingrained attitudes about "communists", people who hate Croatia and the pervasiveness of conspiracy theories are alarming. Domestic politics is run by a relatively liberal elite that seems to be out of touch with the majority of citizens. There is, however, some hope. It lies partly in the notion that the Homeland War is at least being deliberated on more than prior periods of conflict and transition in Croatian history. In particular, it lies with younger generations and more educated segments of society, who show more positive attitudes and openness towards transitional justice.

Notes

1. The table includes Slovenia since it is Croatia's neighbour, experienced the outbreak of violence at a similar time to Croatia and has joined the EU. Kosovo is included since crimes there also featured at the ICTY.
2. This was not, however, universal. Boris Dežulović of *Novi List* stressed that this was a societal problem and that the salute had become normal among Croatian football fans.
3. For more up to date information, see http://www.mineactionreview.org/country/bosnia-and-herzegovina/anti-personnel-mines.

References

Bass, G. J. (2000). *Stay the hand of vengeance: The politics of war crimes tribunals*. Princeton: Princeton University Press.

Bieber, F. (2013, November 21). Ready for the homeland? Simunic and a bit of normal fascism. *Balkan Insight*. Available at http://www.balkaninsight.com/en/blog/ready-for-the-homeland-simunic-and-a-bit-of-normal-fascism. Accessed 3 May 2016.

Blanuša, B. (2017). Trauma and taboo: Forbidden political questions in Croatia. *Politička Misao, 54*, 170–196.

Brentin, D. (2016). Ready for the homeland? Ritual, remembrance, and political extremism in Croatian football. *Nationalities Papers (web)*. Available at http://dx.doi.org/10.1080/00905992.2015.1136996.

Christie, N. (2001). Answers to atrocities: Restorative justice as an answer to extreme situations. In E. A. Fattah & S. Parmentier (Eds.), *Victim policies and criminal justice on the road to restorative justice* (pp. 379–387). Leuven: Leuven University Press.

Clarke, J. N. (2016). In from the margins: Survivors of wartime sexual violence in Croatia and an early analysis of the new law. *Journal of Human Rights Practice, 8*, 128–147.

Drumbl, M. A. (2007). *Atrocity, punishment and international law*. Cambridge: Cambridge University Press.

Duggan, C., Bailey, C., & Guillerot, J. (2008). Reparations for sexual and reproductive violence: Prospects for achieving gender justice in Guatemala and Peru. *The International Journal of Transitional Justice, 2*, 192–213.

Gordy, E. (2014). *Guilt, responsibility, and denial: The past at stake in post-Milošević Serbia*. Philadelphia: University of Pennsylvania Press.

Hafner-Burton, E., & Ron, J. (2007). Human rights institutions: Rhetoric and efficacy. *Journal of Peace Research, 44*, 379–384.

Hafner-Burton, E., & Tsutsui, K. (2007). Justice lost! The failure of international human rights law to matter where needed most. *Journal of Peace Research, 44*, 407–425.

Horne, C. M. (2015). The timing of transitional justice measures. In N. Nedelsky & L. Stan (Eds.), *Post-communist transitional justice: Lessons from twenty-five years of experience* (pp. 123–147). New York: Cambridge University Press.

Jones, B., & Oliveira, I. (2016). Truth Commission Archives as 'New Democratic Spaces'. *Journal of Human Rights Practice, 8*, 6–24.

Jović, I., & Romić. T. (2012, November 16). Milanović i Josipovič generalima: Stoički ste podnijeli žrtvu, hvala! [Milanović and Josipovič to the generals: You took the sacrifice stoically, thank you!] *Večernji List*. Available at http://www.vecernji.hr/hrvatska/milanovic-i-josipovic-generalima-stoicki-ste-podnijeli-zrtvu-hvala-475959. Accessed 3 May 2016.

Klarin, M. (2009). The impact of the ICTY trials on public opinion in the former Yugoslavia. *Journal of International Criminal Justice, 7*, 89–96.

Lambourne, W. (2009). Transitional justice and peacebuilding after mass violence. *International Journal of Transitional Justice, 3*, 28–48.

Lynch, M., & Marchesi, B. (2015). The adoption and impact of transitional justice. In N. Nedelsky & L. Stan (Eds.), *Post-communist transitional justice: Lessons from twenty-five years of experience* (pp. 73–98). New York: Cambridge University Press.

Maier, C. S. (1988). *The unmasterable past: History, holocaust, and German national identity*. London: Harvard University Press.

McAuliffe, P. (2017). *Transformative transitional justice and the malleability of post-conflict states*. Cheltenham: Edward Elgar.

McMahon, P. C., & Forsythe, D. P. (2008). The ICTY's impact on Serbia: Judicial romanticism meets network politics. *Human Rights Quarterly, 30*, 412–435.

Narodne Novine. (2015). *Zakon o pravima žrtava seksualnog nasilja za vrijeme oružane agresije na Republiku Hrvatsku u Domovinskom ratu* [Law on the rights of victims of sexual violence during the armed aggression against the Republic of Croatia in the Homeland War]. Available at http://narodne-novine.nn.hr/clanci/sluzbeni/2015_06_64_1221.html.

Nettelfield, L. J. (2010). *Courting democracy in Bosnia and Herzegovina: The Hague tribunal's impact in a postwar state*. Cambridge: Cambridge University Press.

Novi List. (2014, May 12). *Arbitražni sud odbio Šimuniča: Nedvosmisleno je koristio ustaški uzvik* [The court of arbitration has rejected Šimunič: He undoubtedly used an ustasha salute]. Available at http://www.novilist.hr/Sport/Nogomet/Arbitrazni-sud-odbio-Simunica-Nedvosmisleno-je-koristio-ustaski-uzvik. Accessed 2 May 2016.

Ostojić, M. (2014). *Between justice and stability: The politics of war crimes prosecutions in post-Milošević Serbia*. Farnham: Ashgate.

Pavlaković, V. (2008). *Red stars, black shirts: Symbols, commemorations, and contested histories of World War Two in Croatia*. Seattle: The National Council for Euroasian and East European Research.

Pavlaković, V. (2014). Fulfilling the thousand-year-old dream: Strategies of symbolic nation-building in Croatia. In P. Kolstø (Ed.), *Strategies of symbolic nation-building in south eastern Europe* (pp. 19–50). Farnham: Ashgate.

Rangelov, I. (2014). *Nationalism and the rule of law: Lessons from the Balkans and beyond*. Cambridge: Cambridge University Press.

Risse, T., Ropp, S. C., & Sikkink, K. (1999). *The power of human rights: International norms and domestic change*. Cambridge: Cambridge University Press.

Schäuble, M. (2014). *Narrating victimhood: Gender, religion and the making of place in post-war Croatia*. Oxford: Barghahn.

Sharp, D. (2013). Interrogating the peripheries: The preoccupations of fourth generation transitional justice. *Harvard Human Rights Journal, 26,* 517–526.
Snyder, J. L., & Vinjamuri, L. (2003). Trials and errors: Principle and pragmatism in strategies of international justice. *International Security, 28,* 5–44.
Stover, E., & Weinsten, H. M. (2004). *My neighbor, my enemy: Justice and community in the aftermath of mass atrocity.* Cambridge: Cambridge University Press.
Subotic, J. (2009). *Hijacked justice: Dealing with the past in the Balkans.* Ithaca: Cornell University Press.
Subotic, J. (2015). The mythologizing of communist violence. In L. Stan & N. Nedelsky (Eds.), *Post-communist transitional justice: Lessons from twenty-five years of experience* (pp. 188–210). New York: Cambridge University Press.
Thoms, O., Ron, J., & Paris, R. (2010). State-level effects of transitional justice: What do we know? *The International Journal of Transitional Justice, 4,* 329–354.
United Nations Development Programme (UNDP). (2015, May 13). *Draft mine action governance and management assessment for BiH.*

Index

I. Sokolić, *International Courts and Mass Atrocity*, Memory Politics and Transitional Justice, https://doi.org/10.1007/978-3-319-90841-0

CPSIA information can be obtained
at www.ICGtesting.com
Printed in the USA
LVHW061008051119
636392LV00004B/120/P